Annie's Favorite Christmas Projects

Dear Friends,

Even though I have the most wonderful memories of the Christmas mornings of my childhood, I find that I enjoy the Christmas holiday more and more with each passing year!

I'm not referring to the overtly commercial season with its many advertisements and myriad distractions. I'm not even speaking of the sights, sounds and smells traditionally associated with the holiday. Rather I'm talking about the time of year when we can share with our friends, families and loved ones the joy and affection that we feel for each and every one of them.

The spirit of Christmas is truly the essence of giving, not only in the tantalizing form of fresh-baked goodies or the excitement of beautifully wrapped boxes under the tree, but in the warm simplicity of gifts handmade and offered with love from a generous heart and open arms.

That's the reason I filled this book full to overflowing (much like Santa's sleigh) with toys and tree trims, snowflakes and sweaters, afghans and angels. I assembled a winter wonderland with you in mind—this one-of-a-kind collection was chosen especially for the joy of making and of giving!

Choose your own favorites from the eight project-packed chapters inside. They offer designs for elegant ornaments and winter warmers, frosty fashions and angelic attractions, skirts, stockings and more! You'll find Santa's workshop, holiday home projects, a flurry of snowflake patterns, helpful hints and much, much more. With this volume in your crochet library, you'll never be at a loss for Christmas crochet again!

Open your heart and your home this holiday season to those you love most, as well as to those who may not have the blessings that have been bestowed upon you. When you do, it's guaranteed to make this holiday season the most satisfying one of your life!

Happy Holiday Crocheting,

Annie

Editorial Director
Andy Ashley

Production Director
Ange Van Arman

Editorial
Senior Editor
Jennifer McClain

Editor
Ann White

Editorial Staff
Shirley Brown, Liz Field, Donna Jones,
Nina Marsh, Donna Scott

Photography
Scott Campbell, Tammy Coquat-Payne
Martha Coquat

Book Design & Production
Coy A. Lothrop

Production Manager
Vicki Staggs

Color Specialist
Betty Radla

Production Coordinator
Glenda Chamberlain

Product Presentation
Design Coordinator
Sandy Kennebeck

Inhouse Designer
Mickie Akins

Design Copy
Linda Moll Smith

Library of Congress Cataloging-in-Publication Data
ISBN: 0-9655269-4-1
First Printing: 1998
Library of Congress Catalog Card Number: 98-72352
Published and Distributed by
Annie's Attic, LLC, Big Sandy, Texas 75755
Printed in the United States of America.

Table of Contents

Angelic Attractions

Hark the Herald Angels Sing!

Hark! the herald angels sing,
"Glory to the new born King!
Peace on earth, and mercy mild,
God and sinners reconciled."
Joyful, all ye nations rise,
Join the triumph of the skies,
With th'angelic host proclaim,
"Christ is born in Bethlehem."
Hark! the herald angels sing,
"Glory to the new born King!"

Elegant Angels

Designed by Wilma Bonner

Basic Instructions

(Use with instructions for each Angel.)

MATERIALS FOR ONE:

❑ Size 10 crochet cotton thread:
    700 yds. white for Membrance
    900 yds. white for Edith
    20 yds. pink *(for Membrance)*
    20 yds. green *(for Membrance)*
❑ Four 6mm white pearl beads *(for Membrance)*
❑ 30" piece of ½" white polyester cable cord
❑ 2 yds. of ⅛" satin ribbon
❑ Artificial flowers with leaves
❑ Additional trims as desired
❑ Polyester fiberfill
❑ Small paint brush
❑ White latex paint
❑ Transparent tape
❑ Fabric stiffener
❑ Stiff brush
❑ Plastic food wrap
❑ 22" x 28" sheet of poster board
❑ 2" x 5" x 10" Styrofoam® block
❑ 16" piece of heavy cardboard
❑ Rustproof straight pins
❑ 1½" flat-bottom wooden ball knob
❑ Hot glue gun and glue sticks
❑ No. 6 steel hook or hook needed to obtain gauge

GAUGE: 9 dc = 1"; 3 dc rows = 1".

BASIC STITCHES: Ch, sl st, sc, hdc, dc, tr.

SPECIAL STITCHES: For **V st**, (dc, ch 2, dc) in next ch sp or in next st.
For **shell,** (2 dc, ch 2, 2 dc) in next ch sp.
For **picot,** (sc, ch 3, sc) in next st or ch sp.

PREPARATION

1: Paint wooden knob with paint brush and white paint. Let dry.
2: To make **cone** for Skirt form, draw a circle 21½" for Membrance and 22" for Edith on poster board, then draw a line through the center to form a half circle. Cut the half circle from poster board *(see illustration)*; roll the curved edge and tape edges together to secure. Cut ½" from the top. Cover cone with plastic food wrap.
3: For **Bodice form,** trim the top edges of the 2" x 5" x 10" piece of Styrofoam according to illustration. Cover with plastic food wrap.

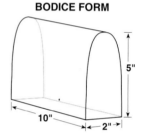

Half circle cut from poster board.

Cut ½" from top.

CONE HEIGHT

BOTTOM DIAMETER

BODICE FORM

5"

10"

2"

STIFFENING

1: Cover ironing board *(or a large piece of cardboard)* with plastic wrap. Stuff Head with polyester fiberfill. Saturate Bodice, one Wing and Skirt with undiluted fabric stiffener, keeping Head as dry as possible.
2: Lay Wing on ironing board and shape, pin in place with rustproof straight pins.
3: Place Bodice over Bodice form *(take care to keep Head upright),* shape and pin edges in place with rust-proof straight pins.
4: Stretch Skirt over cone, shape and pin bottom edges to cardboard or ironing board with rust-proof straight pins *(on Edith, bottom will spread out over ironing board).*
5: For **Arms,** cut a 15" length of cable cord for 15"-tall Angel or cut a 17" length of cable cord for 16½"-tall Angel; wrap ends with transparent tape, saturate cord with fabric stiffener and shape on plastic covered ironing board *(see illustration).*
6: Let all pieces dry. When thoroughly dry, remove pins and forms and brush off excess stiffener with a stiff brush.
7: Trace outline of stiffened Wing on paper, place paper between plastic wrap and ironing board.
8: Saturate second Wing with undiluted fabric stiffener, place on ironing board over plastic wrap and

continued on page 8

Elegant Angels

continued from page 6

outline, shape to match outline and pin in place. Let dry. Remove pins and brush same as first Wing.

HAIR

1: Wrap crochet thread 80–100 times around 16" piece of heavy cardboard, cut from cardboard along one edge, fold thread strands in half and wrap a piece of transparent tape around strands at fold.

2: Repeat step 1 forming a second section of Hair.

3: Glue taped center of one section of Hair to center back of Head allowing the ends of the strands to fall to the front and to the back; glue the center of the second section of Hair across the first section allowing the ends of the strands to fall to the sides.

4: Measure a piece of cable cord to fit loosely around the Head over the Hair, beginning at back of neck, going just above forehead and ending at back of neck *(see illustration)*; secure both ends of cable cord with transparent tape and cut. Glue ends to back of neck.

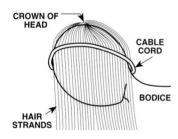

5: Hold Head and Bodice with face down and with Hair strands falling over the face; distribute strands evenly around the Head under the cable cord. If needed, gently brush strands to separate.

6: To secure, place a drop of glue under the Hair at forehead and on each side, being sure glue catches Hair and cable cord. Let glue dry.

7: Make a loose ponytail by gently pulling Hair strands back to crown of Head covering cable cord, tie with a separate strand of crochet thread.

8: For each curl, use your crochet hook to separate a section of Hair and trim to desired length. Dampen the section with fabric stiffener, wrap around handle end of the hook, slide curl off hook and glue in place on Head; secure with rustproof straight pins until glue dries. Repeat until all strands have been used. Let dry and remove straight pins.

ASSEMBLY

1: Glue flat side of painted knob to top of Skirt.

2: Glue center of Arms over top of knob with hands together at front of Skirt.

3: Glue Bodice centered over Arms and knob.

4: Glue Wings to back of Bodice.

5: Tie ribbon in a multi-loop bow. Glue flower and bow to hands. Add additional trims as desired.

Membrance

FINISHED SIZE: Approximately 15" tall.

NOTE: Use white crochet cotton unless otherwise stated.

HEAD

Rnd 1: Ch 5, sl st in first ch to form ring, ch 1, 10 sc in ring, join with sl st in first sc. *(10 sc made)*

Rnd 2: (Ch 2, hdc) in first st, 2 hdc in each st around, join with sl st in top of ch-2. *(Ch-2 counts as first hdc—20 hdc made.)*

Rnd 3: Ch 1, sc in first st, 2 sc in next st, (sc in next st, 2 sc in next st) around, join. *(30 sc)*

Rnd 4: Ch 2, 2 hdc in next st, (hdc in next st, 2 hdc in next st) around, join. *(45 hdc)*

Rnds 5–6: Ch 2, hdc in each st around, join.

Rnds 7–8: Ch 1, sc in each st around, join.

Rnd 9: Ch 2, hdc in each st around, join.

Rnd 10: Ch 1, sc in each st around, join.

Rnds 11–12: Repeat rnds 9 and 10.

Rnd 13: Ch 1, sc in first 4 sts, skip next st, (sc in next 4 sts, skip next st) around, join. *(36)*

Rnd 14: Ch 2, hdc in each st around, join.

Rnd 15: Ch 2, hdc in next 4 sts, skip next st, (hdc in next 5 sts, skip next st) around, join. *(30 hdc)*

Rnd 16: Ch 1, sc in each st around, join.

Rnd 17: Ch 2, hdc in next 3 sts, skip next st, (hdc in next 4 sts, skip next st) around, join. *(24 hdc)*

Rnd 18: Ch 1, sc in first st, skip next st, (sc in next st, skip next st) around, join. *(12 sc)*

Rnds 19–20: For **Neck,** ch 1, sc in each st around, join. **Do not** fasten off.

BODICE

Rnds 1–2: (Ch 3, dc) in first st, 2 dc in each dc around, join with sl st in top of ch-3. *(24, 48 dc made)*

Rnd 3: Ch 3, 2 dc in next dc, (dc in next dc, 2 dc in next dc) around, join. *(72)*

Rnd 4: Ch 3, dc in next 10 dc, ch 1, skip next dc, (dc in next 11 dc, ch 1, skip next dc) around, join. *(66 dc, 6 ch sps)*

Rnd 5: Sl st in next dc, ch 3, dc in next 8 dc, ch 1, skip next dc, **V st** *(see Special Stitches on page 6)* in next ch sp, ch 1, skip next dc, (dc in next 9 dc, ch 1, skip next dc, V st, ch 1, skip next dc) around, join. *(54 dc, 6 V sts)*

Rnd 6: Sl st in next dc, ch 3, dc in next 6 dc, ch 1, skip next dc, V st in first dc of next V st, V st in last dc of same V st, ch 1, skip next dc, (dc in next 7 dc, ch 1, skip next dc, V st in first dc of next V st, V st in last dc of same V st, ch 1, skip next dc) around, join. *(42 dc, 12 V sts)*

Rnd 7: Sl st in next dc, ch 3, dc in next 4 dc, ch 2, skip next dc, (V st in first dc of next V st) 2 times, V st in last dc of same V st, ch 2, skip next dc, *dc in next 5 dc, ch 2, skip next dc, (V st in first dc of next V st) 2 times, V st in last dc of same V st, ch 2, skip next dc; repeat from * around, join. *(30 dc, 18 V sts)*

Rnd 8: Sl st in next dc, ch 3, dc in next 2 dc, ch 2, skip next dc, (V st in first dc of next V st) 3 times, V st in last dc of same V st, ch 2, skip next st, *dc in next 3 dc, ch 2, skip next dc, (V st in first dc of next V st) 3 times, V st in last dc of same V st, ch 2, skip next dc; repeat from * around, join. *(18 dc, 24 V sts)*

Rnd 9: Ch 2, dc next 2 dc tog *(ch-2 and dc-2-tog counts as dc-3-tog)*, ch 2, (V st in first dc of next V st) 4 times, V st in last dc of same V st, ch 2, *dc next 3 dc tog, ch 2, (V st in first dc of next V st) 4 times, V st in last dc of same V st, ch 2; repeat from * around, skip ch-2, join with sl st in top of next dc-2-tog. *(6 dc-3-tog, 30 V sts)*

Rnd 10: (Ch 5, dc) in first st *(counts as first V st)*, (V st in first dc of next V st) 5 times, V st in last dc of same V st, *V st in next dc-3-tog, (V st in first dc of next V st) 5 times, V st in last dc of same V st; repeat from * around, join with sl st in third ch of ch-5. *(42 V sts)*

Rnd 11: (Ch 5, dc) in first st, (V st in first dc of next V st) around, join with sl st in third ch of ch-5.

Rnd 12: Ch 1, sc in first st, ch 5, sc in next dc, (sc in next dc, ch 5, sc in next dc) around, join.

Rnd 13: (7 sc in next ch sp, sl st in next 2 sc) around. Fasten off.

SKIRT

Rnd 1: Ch 12, sl st in first ch to form ring, ch 3, 10 dc in ring, ch 1, (11 dc in ring, ch 1) 3 times, join with sl st in top of ch-3. *(44 dc, 4 ch sps)*

Rnd 2: (Ch 3, dc) in first st, dc in next 9 dc, 2 dc in next dc, ch 1, (2 dc in next dc, dc in next 9 dc, 2 dc in next dc, ch 1) 3 times, join. *(52 dc)*

Rnd 3: (Ch 3, dc) in first dc, dc in next 11 dc, 2 dc in next dc, ch 2, (2 dc in next dc, dc in next 11 dc, 2 dc in next dc, ch 2) 3 times, join. *(60 dc)*

Rnd 4: Ch 3, dc in next 14 dc, ch 3, (dc in next 15 dc, ch 3) 3 times, join.

Rnd 5: Ch 3, dc in next 14 dc, ch 1, V st in second ch of next ch-3 sp, ch 1, (dc in next 15 dc, ch 1, V st in second ch of next ch-3 sp, ch 1) 3 times, join. *(60 dc, 4 V sts)*

Rnd 6: Ch 3, dc in next 14 dc, ch 1, **shell** *(see Special Stitches on page 6)* in next V st, ch 1, (dc in next 15 dc, ch 1, shell in next V st, ch 1) 3 times, join.

NOTE: Work in ch sps of shells and skip all other ch sps unless otherwise stated.

Rnd 7: Ch 3, dc in next 14 dc, ch 1, shell in next shell, ch 1, (dc in next 15 dc, ch 1, shell in next shell, ch 1) 3 times, join.

Rnd 8: Ch 3, dc in next 14 dc, ch 1, (3 dc, ch 2, 3 dc) in next ch-2 sp *(at center of shell)*, ch 1, *dc in next 15 dc, ch 1, (3 dc, ch 2, 3 dc) in next ch-2 sp, ch 1; repeat from * 2 more times, join.

Rnd 9: Sl st in next dc, ch 3, dc in next 12 dc, *[ch 1, skip last dc of group, (3 dc, ch 2, 3 dc) in next ch-2 sp, ch 1, skip first dc of next dc group], dc in next 13 dc; repeat from * 2 more times; repeat between [ ], join. *(76 dc)*

Rnd 10: Sl st in next dc, ch 3, dc in next 10 dc, *[ch 2, skip last dc of group, V st in next dc, skip next 2 dc, V st in next ch sp, skip next 2 dc, V st in next dc, ch 2, skip first dc of next dc group], dc in next 11 dc; repeat from * 2 more times; repeat between [ ], join. *(44 dc, 12 V sts)*

Rnds 11–13: Sl st in next dc, ch 3, *dc in each dc across to last dc of group, ch 3, skip last dc of

group; working across next V st group, (V st in first dc of next V st) across with V st in last dc of last V st in group, ch 3, skip first dc of next dc group; repeat from * around, join. *(36 dc, 28 dc, 20 dc)*

Rnd 14: Ch 2 *(not counted as a st)* dc next 4 dc tog, ch 3, (V st in first dc of next V st) 7 times, V st in last dc of last V st in group, ch 3, *dc next 5 dc tog, ch 3, (V st in first dc of next V st) 7 times, V st in last dc of last V st in group, ch 3; repeat from * around, skip ch-2, join with sl st in top of dc-4-tog.

Rnd 15: (Ch 5, dc) in first st, (V st in first dc of next V st) 8 times, V st in last dc of same V st, *V st in next dc-5-tog, (V st in first dc of next V st) 8 times, V st in last dc of same V st; repeat from * around, join with sl st in third ch of ch-5.

Rnds 16–28: (Ch 5, dc) in first st, (V st in first dc of next V st) around, join.

Rnd 29: Ch 1, sc in first st, ch 5, skip next ch sp, sc in next dc, (sc in next dc, ch 5, skip next ch sp, sc in next dc) around, join.

Rnd 30: (7 sc in next ch sp, sl st in next 2 sc) around. Fasten off.

Flower (make 4)

Rnd 1: With pink, ch 4, sl st in first ch to form ring, ch 6, (dc in ring, ch 3) 5 times, join with sl st in third ch of ch-6. *(6 dc, 6 ch sps)*

Rnd 2: Ch 1, sc in first st, 3 tr around side of same st on rnd 2 *(see illustration)*, ch 3, (sc in next dc, 3 tr around side of same dc, ch 3) around, join. Fasten off.

Leaf (make 8)

Row 1: With green, ch 10, sc in second ch from hook sc in next 7 chs, 2 sc in last ch; continuing on opposite side of ch, sc in next 8 chs, turn. *(18 sc made)*

Row 2: Ch 1, sc in first st, (hdc in next 2 sts, dc in next st, 2 tr in next st, dc in next st, hdc in next 2 sts, sc in next st), sc in next st; repeat between ( ). Fasten off.

WING (make 2)

Row 1: Ch 4, 14 dc in fourth ch from hook, turn. *(15 dc made)*

Rows 2–3: Ch 4, dc in next st, (ch 1, dc in next dc) across, turn.

Rows 4–5: Ch 5, dc in next st, (ch 2, dc in next st) across, turn.

Row 6: (Ch 4, dc) in first st, (dc, ch 1, dc) in each st across, turn. *(30 dc)*

Rows 7–8: (Ch 4, dc) in first st, *skip next st, (dc, ch 1, dc) in next st; repeat from * across with (dc, ch 1, dc) in last st, turn. *(32 dc, 34 dc)*

Rows 9–13: (Ch 5, dc) in first st, *skip next st, (dc, ch 2, dc) in next st; repeat from * across with (dc, ch 2, dc) in last st, turn. *(At end of row 13, 44 dc.)*

Row 14: Ch 1, sc in first st, ch 5, skip next ch sp, sc in next st, (sc in next st, ch 5, skip next ch sp, sc in next st) across, turn.

Row 15: Sl st in first st, 7 sc in next ch sp, (sl st in next 2 sts, 7 sc in next ch sp) across with sl st in last st. Fasten off.

continued on page 10

Elegant Angels

continued from page 9

FINISHING & ASSEMBLY
1: Follow Preparation and Stiffening instructions in Basic Instructions on page 6.

2: Saturate Flowers and Leaves with fabric stiffener, shape on plastic covered surface.

3: When Skirt and Flowers are dry, glue Flowers over rnds 17–20 on Skirt just below each dc-5-tog.

4: Glue one pearl bead to center of each Flower.

5: Glue two Leaves just below each Flower on Skirt *(see photo)*.

6: Work remaining Hair and Assembly instructions in Basic Instructions on page 8 to complete Angel.

Edith

FINISHED SIZE: Approximately 16½" tall.

HEAD
Rnd 1: Ch 5, sl st in first ch to form ring, ch 1, 10 sc in ring, join with sl st in first sc. *(10 sc made)*

Rnd 2: (Ch 2, hdc) in first st, 2 hdc in each st around, join with sl st in top of ch-2. *(20 hdc)*

Rnd 3: Ch 1, sc in first st, 2 sc in next st, (sc in next st, 2 sc in next st) around, join. *(30 sc)*

Rnd 4: Ch 2, 2 hdc in next st, (hdc in next st, 2 hdc in next st) around, join. *(45 hdc)*

Rnd 5: Ch 2, hdc in each st around, join.

Rnd 6: Ch 1, sc in first 4 sts, 2 sc in next st, (sc in next 4 sts, 2 sc in next st) around, join. *(54 sc)*

Rnds 7–11: Ch 2, hdc in each st around, join.

Rnd 12: Ch 1, sc in each st around, join.

Rnd 13: Ch 1, sc in first 5 sts, skip next st, (sc in next 5 sts, skip next st) around, join. *(45)*

Rnd 14: Ch 2, hdc in each st around, join.

Rnd 15: Ch 1, sc in first 4 sts, skip next st, (sc in next 4 sts, skip next st) around, join. *(36 sc)*

Rnd 16: Ch 2, hdc in next 4 sts, skip next st, (hdc in next 5 sts, skip next st) around, join. *(30 hdc)*

Rnd 17: Ch 1, sc in each st around, join.

Rnd 18: Ch 2, hdc in next 3 sts, skip next st, (hdc in next 4 sts, skip next st) around, join. *(12)*

Rnd 19: Ch 2, skip next st, (hdc in next st, skip next st) around, join. *(12)*

Rnds 20–21: Ch 1, sc in each st around, join. **Do not fasten off.**

BODICE
Rnd 1: (Ch 3, dc) in first st, 2 dc in each st around, join with sl st in top of ch-3. *(24 dc made)*

Rnd 2: Ch 3, dc in next 2 dc, ch 6, dc in next 3 dc, ch 1, (dc in next 3 dc, ch 6, dc in next 3 dc, ch 1) 3 times, join. *(24 dc, 8 ch sps)*

Rnd 3: Ch 3, dc in next 2 dc, 13 dc in next ch-6 sp, dc in next 3 dc, ch 2, (dc in next 3 dc, 13 dc in next ch-6 sp, dc in next 3 dc, ch 2) around, join.

Rnd 4: Ch 3, dc in next 2 dc, ch 1, skip next dc, sc in next 11 dc, ch 1, skip next dc, dc in next 3 dc, ch 2, (dc in next 3 dc, ch 1, skip next dc, sc in next 11

dc, ch 1, skip next dc, dc in next 3 dc, ch 2) around, join.

Rnd 5: Ch 3, dc in next 2 dc, ch 2, skip next sc, sc in next 9 sc, ch 2, skip next sc, dc in next 3 dc, ch 1, (dc, ch 2, dc) in next ch sp, ch 1, *dc in next 3 dc, ch 2, skip next sc, sc in next 9 sc, ch 2, skip next sc, dc in next 3 dc, ch 1, (dc, ch 2, dc) in next ch sp, ch 1; repeat from * around, join.

Rnd 6: Ch 3, dc in next 2 dc, *(ch 3, skip next sc, sc in next 7 sc, ch 3, skip next sc, dc in next 3 dc, ch 2, dc in next dc, ch 2, **shell** *(see Special Stitches on page 6)* in next ch sp, ch 2, dc in next dc, ch 2), dc in next 3 dc; repeat from * 2 more times; repeat between ( ), join.

NOTE: Work in ch sps of shells and V sts and skip all other ch sps unless otherwise stated.

Rnd 7: Ch 3, dc in next 2 dc, *[ch 3, skip next sc, sc in next 5 sc, ch 3, skip next sc, dc in next 3 dc; for **lattice pattern, (ch 2, dc in next dc) across to first dc of next shell, ch 2, dc in next dc, ch 2, skip next dc, shell, ch 2, skip next dc, dc in last dc of shell, ch 2, (dc in next dc, ch 2)** across to next 3-dc group], dc in next 3 dc; repeat from * 2 more times; repeat between [ ], join.

Rnd 8: Ch 3, dc in next 2 dc, *(ch 3, skip next sc, sc in next 3 sc, ch 3, skip next sc, dc in next 3 dc, work lattice pattern across to next 3-dc group), dc in next 3 dc; repeat from * 2 more times; repeat between ( ), join.

Rnd 9: Ch 3, dc in next 2 dc, *(ch 3, skip next sc, sc in next sc, ch 3, skip next sc, dc in next 3 dc, work lattice pattern across to next 3-dc group), dc in next 3 dc; repeat from * 2 more times; repeat between ( ), join.

Rnd 10: Ch 3, dc in next 2 dc, *(skip next sc, dc in next 3 dc, work lattice pattern across to next 3-dc group), dc in next 3 dc; repeat from * 2 more times; repeat between ( ), join.

Rnd 11: Ch 2 *(not counted as a st)*, dc next 5 dc tog, work lattice pattern across to next 3-dc group, *dc next 6 dc tog, work lattice pattern across to next 3-dc group; repeat from * around, join with sl st in first dc-5-tog.

Rnd 12: Ch 1, skip first st, *(2 sc in next ch sp, picot in next dc) 7 times, skip next dc of shell, picot in ch sp of shell, skip next dc of shell, (picot in next dc, 2 sc in next ch sp) 7 times, picot in next dc-6-tog; repeat from * around with last picot in skipped dc-5-tog, join. Fasten off.

SKIRT
Rnd 1: Ch 8, sl st in first ch to form ring, ch 3, 2 dc in ring, ch 3, (3 dc in ring, ch 3) 3 times, join with sl st in top of ch-3. *(12 dc, 4 ch sps)*

Rnd 2: (Ch 3, dc) in first st, *[dc in next dc, 2 dc in next dc, ch 1, (dc, ch 1, dc) in second ch of ch-3, ch 1], 2 dc in next dc; repeat from * 2 more times; repeat between [ ], join. *(28 dc, 12 ch sps)*

Rnds 3–7: (Ch 3, dc) in first st, *[dc in each dc across to last dc of group, 2 dc in next dc, ch 1, skip next ch sp, shell in next ch sp, ch 1], 2 dc in next dc; repeat from * 2 more times; repeat between [ ], join.

Rnd 8: Ch 3, dc in next 4 dc, *[ch 3, skip next 2 dc; for **large V st (lg V st), (dc, ch 3, dc)** in next dc, ch 3, skip next 2 dc, dc in next 5 dc, ch 1, shell, ch 1], dc in next 5 dc; repeat from * 2 more times; repeat between [ ], join. *(40 dc, 4 lg V sts, 4 shells, 16 ch sps)*

Rnd 9: Ch 3, dc in next 4 dc, *(5 dc in next ch sp, 7 dc in next V st, 5 dc in next ch sp, dc in next 5 dc, ch 1, shell, ch 1), dc in next 5 dc; repeat from * 2 more times; repeat between ( ), join. *(108 dc, 4 shells, 8 ch sps)*

Rnd 10: Ch 3, dc in next 4 dc, *(ch 5, skip next 8 dc, lg V st in next dc, ch 5, skip next 8 dc, dc in next 5 dc, ch 1, shell, ch 1), dc in next 5 dc; repeat from * 2 more times; repeat between ( ), join. *(40 dc, 4 lg V sts, 4 shells, 16 ch sps)*

Rnd 11: Ch 3, dc in next 4 dc, *(7 dc in each of next 3 ch sps, dc in next 5 dc, ch 1, shell, ch 1), dc in next 5 dc; repeat from * 2 more times; repeat between ( ), join. *(124 dc, 4 shells, 8 ch sps)*

Rnd 12: Ch 3, dc in next 4 dc, *(ch 5, skip next 10 dc, lg V st in next dc, ch 5, skip next 10 dc, dc in next 5 dc, ch 1, shell, ch 1), dc in next 5 dc; repeat from * 2 more times; repeat between ( ), join. *(40 dc, 4 lg V sts, 4 shells, 16 ch sps)*

Rnds 13–21: Repeat rnds 12 and 13 alternately, ending with rnd 12.

Rnd 22: Ch 3, dc in next 4 dc, *(ch 1, skip next dc, sc in next 19 dc, ch 1, skip next dc, dc in next 5 dc, ch 2, dc in first dc of shell, ch 2, shell, ch 2, skip next dc, dc in last dc of shell, ch 2), dc in next 5 dc; repeat from * 2 more times; repeat between ( ), join. *(48 dc, 76 sc, 4 shells)*

Rnds 23–26: Ch 3, dc in next 4 dc, *(ch 2, skip next sc, sc in each sc across to last sc of group, ch 2, skip next sc, dc in next 5 dc, work lattice pattern —*see rnd 7 of Bodice*—across to next 5-dc group), dc in next 5 dc; repeat from * 2 more times; repeat between ( ), join.

Rnds 27–30: Ch 3, dc in next 4 dc, *(ch 3, skip next sc, sc in each sc across to last sc of group, ch 3, skip next sc, dc in next 5 dc, work lattice pattern across to next 5-dc group), dc in next 5 dc; repeat from * 2 more times; repeat between ( ), join.

Rnd 31: Ch 3, dc in next 4 dc, *(ch 3, skip next sc, sc in next sc, ch 3, skip next sc, dc in next 5 dc; changing ch-2 to ch-3 for all ch sps on each side of shell, work lattice pattern across to next 5-dc group), dc in next 5 dc; repeat from * 2 more times; repeat between ( ), join.

Rnd 32: Ch 2, dc next 4 dc tog, *(ch 1, skip next sc, dc next 5 dc tog, ch 1, 3 sc in each ch sp and sc in each dc across to next shell, sc in next 2 dc of shell, 2 sc in next ch sp, sc in next 2 dc, 3 sc in each ch sp and sc in each dc across to next 5-dc group, ch 1), dc next 5 dc tog; repeat from * 2 more times; repeat between ( ), skip ch-2, join with sl st in top of dc-4-tog.

Rnd 33: Ch 1; skipping each dc-5-tog, *picot in next ch-1 sp, sc in next ch-1 sp, (sc in next 3 sc, picot in next sc) 11 times, sc in next 4 sc, picot in next sc, (sc in next 3 sc, picot in next sc) 10 times, sc in next 3 sc, sc in next ch-1 sp; repeat from * around, join. Fasten off.

WING (make 2)

Row 1: Ch 21, dc in seventh ch from hook, (ch 2, skip next ch, dc in next ch) 2 times, ch 2, skip next ch, shell in next ch, (ch 2, skip next ch, dc in next ch) 4 times, turn. *(8 dc, 1 shell)*

Rows 2–18: Ch 5, (dc in next dc, ch 2) across to shell, dc in first dc of shell, ch 2, shell in shell, ch 2, dc in last dc of shell, (ch 2, dc in next dc) across with last dc in third ch of ch-5, turn. *(At end of row 18, 42 dc, 1 shell.)*

Row 19: Ch 1, picot in first dc, 2 sc in next ch sp, (picot in next dc, 2 sc in next ch sp) across to shell, picot in first dc of shell, sc in next dc, picot in next ch sp, sc in next dc, picot in last dc of shell, (2 sc in next ch sp, picot in next dc) across. Fasten off.

FINISHING & ASSEMBLY

Follow Basic Instructions on page 6 to complete Angel. ❄

A Christmas Without Music

One of the most beloved Christmas carols of all time, *Silent Night*, was written in 1818 by an Austrian priest, Joseph Mohr, and set to music by composer Franz Gruber.

It is said that Joseph was told a few days before Christmas that the church organ in the parish of Oberndorf was broken and could not be repaired in time for Christmas Eve services. He was saddened by this and could not bear to think of Christmas without music. On Christmas Eve, he sat down and wrote three stanzas, then gave the poem to Franz Gruber. He requested that it be set to music for soloists, chorus and guitar. That same evening Franz brought the simple composition to Joseph and still later that night, the people in the little Austrian church sang *Stille Nacht* for the first time.

4: Starting and ending at front, weave 18" ribbon through beading rnd on Body. Insert potpourri ball into Body. Insert end of stick through top of potpourri ball. Pull ribbon tightly and tie end in bow. Glue rose to Body below bow.

5: For each Arm, weave 10" ribbon through beading rnd, pull to tighten and tie ends in bow. Tack each Arm slightly toward the front over rnds 10–11 of Body just below neckline with matching yarn and tapestry needle. Glue one wooden bead to end of each Arm for hand.

6: Glue Halo to back of Head.

7: Tack center of Wings (with smaller sections at bottom) to back of Body below neck ruffle.

8: Glue five pearls ¼" apart down fp sts below bow as shown in photo. ✳

History of the Holiday

The word Christmas comes from the Old English term *"Cristes maesse,"* meaning *"Christ's mass,"* the name for the worship festival service held on December 25 to commemorate the birth of Jesus Christ. While it is accepted that Jesus was born in the small town of Bethlehem, there is no certain information regarding the date of his birth—not even of the year! One of the main reasons for this uncertainty is that the stories of his birth, which were recorded in the New Testament books of Matthew and Luke, were written several decades after the actual events.

The Christian church itself paid little attention to the celebration of Jesus' birth for several centuries. In that time, Easter, the day of his resurrection, was considered to be the major Christian festival. Only as the church gradually developed a calendar to commemorate the major events of Christ's life, did it move to celebrate his birth.

Because there was no knowledge about the actual date of Jesus' birth, a day had to be selected. While the Eastern Orthodox church within the Roman Catholic church chose January 6 to mark the celebration, the Western church chose December 25. An ancient Roman almanac shows that Christmas was celebrated on December 25 in Rome as early as AD 336.

In the late 4th century, the Eastern and Western churches joined together by adopting each other's festival, thus establishing the 12-day celebration that lasts from Christmas to the Epiphany. In some places the last day of the celebration is referred to as the festival of the three kings, because it is believed that the magi brought gifts to the Christ child on that day.

Today Christmas is more than a one-day celebration, but rather a part of a lengthy holiday season embracing at least the whole month of December. In the United States the holiday season customarily begins on Thanksgiving Day and ends on January 1.

The reason for this extended holiday period is that Christmas is no longer viewed as strictly a religious festival. It is also the most popular holiday period for everyone in countries where Christianity has become the domiant religion. Even in countries where Christianity is in the minority, Christmas has become a festive, gift-giving holiday time.

Musical Angel

Designed by Cynthia Harris

FINISHED SIZE: About 12" tall.

MATERIALS:
- ❑ Worsted yarn:
    - 3½ oz. white
    - 2 oz. yellow
    - 2 oz. pale pink
    - ½ oz. green
    - 17 yds. brown
- ❑ 1 yd. each yellow and black six-strand embroidery floss
- ❑ Polyester fiberfill
- ❑ Craft glue
- ❑ 4" × 12" Styrofoam® cone
- ❑ 1" square black felt
- ❑ Musical button
- ❑ Tapestry and embroidery needles
- ❑ G hook or hook needed to obtain gauge

GAUGE: 4 sc = 1"; 4 sc rows = 1".

BASIC STITCHES: Ch, sl st, sc, dc.

NOTE: Work in continuous rnds; do not join or turn rnds unless otherwise stated. Mark first st of each rnd.

ANGEL

Rnd 1: Starting at top of Head, with pale pink, ch 3, sl st in first ch to form ring, ch 1, 6 sc in ring. *(6 sc made)*

Rnd 2: sc in each st around. *(12)*

Rnd 3: (sc in next st, 2 sc in next st) around. *(18)*

Rnd 4: (sc in next 2 sts, 2 sc in next st) around. *(24)*

Rnds 5–12: Sc in each st around.

Rnd 13: (sc next 2 sts tog) around. Stuff. *(12)*

Rnds 14–15: For **Neck,** sc in each st around.

Rnd 16: Sc in next 2 sts, 2 sc in next st, (sc in next 3 sts, 2 sc in next st) 2 times, sc in next st changing to white *(see Stitch Guide).* Fasten off pale pink. *(15)*

Rnd 17: For **Body,** sc in next 4 sts, (2 sc in next st, sc in next 4 sts) 2 times, 2 sc in next st. *(18)*

Rnd 18: For **Ruffle,** working this rnd in **front lps** *(see Stitch Guide),* sc in next st, (ch 3, sc in next st) around.

Rnd 19: Working this rnd in **back lps** of rnd 17, (sc in next 5 sts, 2 sc in next st) 3 times. *(21)*

Rnd 20: For **Ruffle,** repeat rnd 18.

Rnd 21: Working this rnd in **back lps** of rnd 19, (ch 3, sc in next st) around.

Rnd 22: (Sc in next 6 sts, 2 sc in next st) 3 times. *(24)*

Rnd 23: Sc in each st around.

Rnd 24: (Sc in next 7 sts, 2 sc in next st) 3 times. *(27)*

Rnd 25: Sc in each st around.

Rnd 26: (Sc in next 8 sts, 2 sc in next st) 3 times. *(30)*

Rnd 27: Sc in each st around.

Rnd 28: (Sc in next 9 sts, 2 sc in next st) 3 times. *(33)*

Rnd 29: Sc in each st around.

Rnd 30: (Sc in next 10 sts, 2 sc in next st) 3 times. *(36)*

Rnd 31: Sc in each st around.

Rnd 32: (Sc in next 11 sts, 2 sc in next st) 3 times. *(39)*

Rnd 33: Sc in each st around.

Rnd 34: (Sc in next 12 sts, 2 sc in next st) 3 times. *(42)*

Rnd 35: Sc in each st around.

Rnd 36: (Sc in next 13 sts, 2 sc in next st) 3 times. *(45)*

Rnd 37: For **Ruffle,** repeat rnd 18.

Rnd 38: Working this rnd in **back lps** of rnd 36, (sc in next 14 sts, 2 sc in next st) 3 times. *(48)*

Rnd 39: Sc in each st around.

Rnd 40: For **Ruffle,** repeat rnd 18.

Rnd 41: Working this rnd in **back lps** of rnd 39, (sc in next 15 sts, 2 sc in next st) 3 times. *(51)*

Rnd 42: Sc in each st around.

Rnd 43: For **Ruffle,** repeat rnd 18.

Rnd 44: Working this rnd in **back lps** of rnd 42, (sc in next 16 sts, 2 sc in next st) 3 times. *(54)*

Rnd 45: Sc in each st around.

Rnd 46: For **Ruffle,** repeat rnd 18.

Rnd 47: Working this rnd in **back lps** of rnd 45, (sc in next 17 sts, 2 sc in next st) 3 times. *(57)*

Rnd 48: Sc in each st around.

Rnd 49: For **Ruffle,** repeat rnd 18.

Rnd 50: Working this rnd in **back lps** of rnd 48, (sc in next 18 sts, 2 sc in next st) 3 times. *(60)*

Rnd 51: Sc in each st around.

Rnd 52: For **Ruffle,** repeat rnd 18.

Rnd 53: Working this rnd in **back lps** of rnd 51, sc in each st around.

Rnd 54: Sc in each st around.

Rnd 55: For **Ruffle,** repeat rnd 18.

Rnd 56: Working this rnd in **back lps** of rnd 54, sc in each st around, sl st in next st. Fasten off.

Cut top end off Styrofoam cone to fit inside of Head and Body.

BOTTOM

Rnd 1: With white, ch 3, sl st in first ch to form ring, ch 1, 6 sc in ring. *(6 sc made)*

Rnds 2–3: 2 sc in each st around. *(12, 24)*

Rnd 4: (Sc in next 2 sts, 2 sc in next st) around. *(32)*

Rnd 5: (Sc in next 3 sts, 2 sc in next st) around. *(40)*

continued on page 20

Musical Angel

continued from page 18

Rnd 6: (Sc in next 4 sts, 2 sc in next st) around. *(48)*
Rnd 7: (Sc in next 7 sts, 2 sc in next st) around. *(54)*
Rnd 8: (Sc in next 8 sts, 2 sc in next st) around. *(60)*
Rnd 9: Insert Styrofoam cone inside Head and Body; matching sts, place wrong side of Bottom over rnd 56 of Angel; working through both thicknesses, ch 1, sc in each st around, join with sl st in first sc.
Rnd 10: For **Ruffle**, working in **front lps**, ch 1, sc in first st, ch 3, (sc in next st, ch 3) around, join with sl st in first sc. Fasten off.

ARM & SLEEVE (make 2)
Rnd 1: For **Hand,** with pale pink, ch 2, 3 sc in second ch from hook. *(3 sc made)*
Rnd 2: 2 sc in each st around. *(6)*
Rnd 3: Sc in each st around.
Rnd 4: For **Thumb,** ch 3, sc in second ch from hook, sc in next ch; sc in next 6 sts.
Rnd 5: Working behind Thumb, sc in next 6 sts. Stuff. Continue stuffing as you work.
Rnds 6–18: For **Arm**, sc in each st around. At end of rnd 18, change to white. Fasten off pale pink.
Rnds 19–21: For **Sleeve**, sc in each st around. **Do not stuff the Sleeve.** At end of rnd 21, **turn.** *(Wrong side of sts will be on outside of work.)*
Rnd 22: (Sc in next 2 sts, 2 sc in next st) around. *(8)*
Rnd 23: Sc in each st around.
Rnd 24: (Sc in next st, 2 sc in next st) around. *(12)*
Rnd 25: Sc in each st around.
Rnd 26: (Sc in next 3 sts, 2 sc in next st) around. *(15)*
Rnd 27: Sc in each st around.
Rnd 28: (Sc in next 4 sts, 2 sc in next st) around. *(18)*
Rnd 29: Sc in each st around.
Rnd 30: (Sc in next 5 sts, 2 sc in next st) around. *(21)*
Rnd 31: Sc in each st around.
Rnd 32: (Sc in next 6 sts, 2 sc in next st) around. *(24)*
Rnd 33: For **Ruffle**, working this rnd in **front lps**, sc in next st, (ch 3, sc in next st) around.
Rnd 34: Working this rnd in **back lps**, sc in each st around.
Rnd 35: Repeat rnd 33, join with sl st in first sc. Fasten off.
Turn rnds 25–35 of Sleeve right side out covering the Arm.
Sew top of Sleeves over rnds 21–24 on each side of Body 2½" apart with Thumbs pointing toward front.

FACIAL FEATURES
For **Eyelashes,** using two strands black floss, embroider straight stitches *(see illustration)* between rnds 8 and 9 on front of Head *(see facial features illustration)* ½" apart.
For **Nose,** with pale pink, embroider satin stitch *(see illustration)* over rnd 9 of Head centered below Eyelashes.
Cut **Mouth** from felt according to pattern piece. Glue Mouth to center front of Head over rnds 10–12 directly below Nose.

FACIAL FEATURE ILLUSTRATION

STRAIGHT STITCH

SATIN STITCH

MOUTH

HAIR
Cut 32 strands each 16" long from brown yarn.
With hairline at rnd 4 centered above Eyelashes, using brown yarn, sew center of strands to top and center back of Head. Separate and arrange strands evenly around sides and back of Head.

HALO
Rnd 1: With yellow, ch 6, sl st in first ch to form ring, ch 3 *(counts as dc),* 13 dc in ring, join with sl st in top of ch-3. *(14 dc made)*
Row 2: Ch 4, dc in next st, (ch 1, dc in next st) 9 times, skip last 3 sts, turn.
Rnd 3: Working in rnds, ch 1, sc in first st, (ch 3, sc in next st) 9 times, ch 3, sc in third ch of ch-4, skip next 2 chs, sc in next worked st, sc in next 3 skipped sts on rnd 1, sc in next worked st, sc in bottom strand *(see illustration)* of dc on row 2, join with sl st in first sc. Fasten off.

Stitching through Hair strands, sew right side at bottom of Halo to back of Head on rnd 8.

WING (make 2)
Row 1: With yellow, ch 3, sl st in first ch to form ring, ch 3 *(counts as dc),* 7 dc in ring, **do not join, turn.** *(8 dc made)*
Row 2: Ch 3, dc in top strand of last dc *(see illustration)* worked on row 1, dc in bottom strand of same dc, dc in

continued on page 21

ring, dc in next 3 chs of ch-3 at beginning of row 1, turn. *(7)*

Row 3: Ch 3, dc in each st across, turn. *(7)*

Row 4: (Ch 3, dc) in first st, dc in each st across to last st, 2 dc in last st, turn. *(9)*

Rows 5–8: Repeat rows 3 and 4 alternately. At end of row 8, **do not turn.** *(13 sts)*

Rnd 9: Working in ends of rows and in sts, ch 3, sc in end of last row, (ch 3, sc in end of next row) 6 times, (ch 3, sc in next unworked st on row 1) 7 times, (ch 3, sc in end of next row) 7 times, ch 3, sc in first st on row 8, (ch 3, skip next st, sc in next st) 6 times, join with sl st in first ch of first ch-3. Fasten off. *Front of rnd 9 is right side of work.*

With wrong side of Wings facing you, tack rows 2–7 of Wings over rnds 21–33 on back of Angel ½" apart.

SONG BOOK

Rnd 1: With green, ch 18, sl st in first ch to form ring, ch 1, sc in each ch around. *(18 sc made)*

Rnds 2–7: Sc in each st around.

Row 8: For **Spine,** flatten rnd 7; working through both thicknesses, ch 1, sc in each st across, turn. *(9) First Side complete.*

Rnd 9: Working in **front lps,** ch 1, sc in each st across; continuing in remaining **back lps** of row 8, sc in each st. **Do not join.** *(18)*

Rnds 10–16: Working in **both lps,** sc in each st around. At end of rnd 16, join with sl st in first sc. Fasten off. *Second Side complete.*

Insert musical button inside First Side and sew opening closed; stuff Second Side and sew opening closed.

Using six strands yellow floss and **outline stitch** *(see Stitch Guide),* embroider two lines down Spine of Book and the word "Joy" on Second Side *(see illustration).* Sew hands to each end of Book. ✽

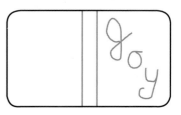

Avoiding Tree Troubles

Although Christmas should be the most joyous of seasons, it can turn so easily to tragedy with little or no warning. Our homes are all decorated with a beautiful tree that we all admire, but sadly, they can also be a very real fire hazard!

Artificial trees are much safer and cleaner, but if Christmas just isn't Christmas without a real tree, then please follow these tips for a safe and secure season!

- A real tree should not lose green needles when you tap it on the ground.
- Leave the tree outside until you are ready to decorate it.
- Cut 1" off the trunk to help the tree absorb water.
- The tree stand should hold at least one gallon of water.
- To improve the tree's water intake, clean the tree stand using one capful of bleach to a cup of water.
- Mix a commercial preservative with the water.
- A 6' tree will use one gallon of water every two days.
- Check the water level every day.
- Secure the tree to the ceiling or walls with wire to keep it from tipping over.
- Keep the tree away from floor heaters, fireplaces or other heat sources.
- Use only UL-approved lights, and link no more than three strands together.
- Use miniature lights which have cool-burning bulbs.
- Turn off the Christmas lights when you sleep or if you leave your home.
- Never use candles—even on artificial trees!
- Dispose of the tree properly—never burn it in a fireplace!

Angel Sachets

Designed by Lucille LaFlamme

Basic Instructions

FINISHED SIZE: Vicki is 4¼" tall. Beth is 4½" tall. Bryony is 5" tall.

MATERIALS FOR ONE:
- ❑ 100 yds. white crochet cotton thread
- ❑ 18" of ⅛" ribbon
- ❑ ½" ribbon rose
- ❑ 2 white 4" circles nylon netting
- ❑ Small amount potpourri
- ❑ Craft glue
- ❑ 2 cotton balls
- ❑ White sewing thread
- ❑ Sewing needle
- ❑ No. 7 steel hook

BASIC STITCHES: Ch, sl st, sc, dc, tr.

Vicki

HEAD & DRESS

Rnd 1: Starting at Head, ch 4, sl st in first ch to form ring, ch 3, 11 dc in ring, join with sl st in top of ch-3. *(12 dc made)*

Rnd 2: (Ch 3, dc) in first st, 2 dc in each st around, join. *(24)*

Rnd 3: Ch 3, dc in each st around, join.

Rnd 4: Ch 3, dc next 2 sts tog, (dc in next st, dc next 2 sts tog) around, join. *(16)* Stuff Head with cotton balls.

Rnd 5: Ch 1, sc in each st around, join with sl st in first sc.

Rnd 6: (Ch 3, dc) in first st, 2 dc in each st around, join. *(32)*

Rnd 7: Working in **back lps** *(see Stitch Guide)*, ch 4, (dc in next st, ch 1) around, join with sl st in third ch of ch-4. *(32 ch sps)*

Rnds 8–10: Sl st in first ch sp, ch 4, (dc in next ch sp, ch 1) around, join.

Rnd 11: Ch 1, sc in first ch sp, ch 3, (sc in next ch sp, ch 3) around, join with sl st in first sc.

Rnds 12–13: Sl st in first ch of first ch sp, sc in same ch sp, ch 3, (sc in next ch sp, ch 3) around, join.

Rnd 14: Ch 1, sc in first st, ch 4, (tr in next ch sp, ch 4, sc in next st, ch 4) around, join.

Rnd 15: Sl st in next 4 chs, sc in next st, ch 3, (skip next st, sc in next st, ch 3) around, join with sl st in first sc.

Rnds 16–17: Sl st in first ch of first ch sp, ch 1, sc in same ch sp, ch 3, (sc in next ch sp, ch 3) around, join.

Rnd 18: Ch 1, 5 sc in each ch sp around, join. Fasten off.

WING COLLAR

Rnd 1: Working in **front lps** of rnd 6 on Head & Dress, join with sc in first st, ch 3, (sc in next st, ch 3) around, join with sl st in first sc. *(32 ch sps made)*

Rnds 2–4: Sl st in first ch of first ch sp, sc in same ch sp, ch 3, (sc in next ch sp, ch 3) around, join.

Rnd 5: Sl st in first ch of first ch sp, sc in same ch sp, (ch 4, sc in next ch sp) around, ch 1, join with dc in first sc.

Rnd 6: Ch 1, sc in first ch sp, ch 4, (sc in next ch sp, ch 4) around, join.

Rnd 7: Ch 1, 6 sc in each ch sp around, join. Fasten off.

FINISHING & ASSEMBLY

1: For **Sachet,** sew both pieces of netting circles together with a running stitch ½" from edge. Pull up thread to gather, forming a pocket. Fill with potpourri, gather tightly at top and secure with thread.

2: Place Sachet inside Head & Dress; gathering as you sew, sew to rnd 10.

3: For **Halo,** ch 40, skip second ch from hook, 3 sc in each ch across. Twist to form curlicue, join with sl st in skipped ch. Fasten off.

4: With sewing thread, tack Halo around top of Head.

5: For **hanger,** tie 8" piece of ribbon to stitch at top of Head.

6: Tie remaining ribbon in bow around neck. Glue or sew ribbon rose to center of bow.

Beth

HEAD & DRESS

Rnd 1: Starting at Head, ch 4, sl st in first ch to form ring, ch 3, 11 dc in ring, join with sl st in top of ch-3. *(12 dc made)*

Rnd 2: (Ch 3, dc) in first st, 2 dc in each st around, join. *(24)*

Rnd 3: Ch 3, dc in each st around, join.

Rnd 4: Ch 3, dc next 2 sts tog, (dc in next st, dc next 2 sts tog) around, join. *(16)* Stuff Head with cotton balls.

Rnd 5: Ch 1, sc in each st around, join with sl st in first sc.

Rnd 6: (Ch 3, dc) in first st, 2 dc in each st around, join. *(32)*

Rnd 7: Working in **back lps** *(see Stitch Guide)*, ch 4, (dc in next st, ch 1) around, join with sl st in third ch of ch-4. *(32 ch sps)*

continued on page 24

Angel Sachets

continued from page 23

Rnds 8–10: Sl st in first ch sp, ch 4, (dc in next ch sp, ch 1) around, join.

Rnd 11: Ch 3, dc in same st, ch 3, sc in next st; for **picot, ch 3, sl st in top of last st made;** ch 3, (2 dc in next st, ch 3, sc in next st, picot, ch 3) around, join with sl st in top of ch-3.

Rnd 12: Ch 1, sc in first dc, sc in next dc, ch 4, (sc in next 2 dc, ch 4) around, join.

Rnd 13: Ch 3, dc in next st, ch 3, sc in next ch sp, picot, ch 3, (dc in next 2 sts, ch 3, sc in next ch sp, picot, ch 3) around, join.

Rnd 14: Ch 1, sc in first dc, sc in next dc, ch 4, (sc in next 2 dc, ch 4) around, join.

Rnd 15: Ch 3, 2 dc in next st, ch 3, sc in next ch sp, picot, ch 3, (dc in next st, 2 dc in next st, ch 3, sc in next ch sp, picot, ch 3) around, join.

Rnd 16: Ch 1, sc in first dc, sc in next 2 dc, ch 4, (sc in next 3 dc, ch 4) around, join.

Rnd 17: Ch 3, dc in next 2 sts, ch 3, sc in next ch sp, picot, ch 3, (dc in next 3 sts, ch 3, sc in next ch sp, picot, ch 3) around, join.

Rnd 18: Ch 1, sc in first dc, sc in next 2 dc, ch 4, (sc in next 3 dc, ch 4) around, join.

Rnd 19: Ch 3, (dc, picot, dc) in next st, dc in next st, ch 3, sc in next ch sp, picot, ch 3, *dc in next st, (dc, picot, dc) in next st, dc in next st, ch 3, sc in next ch sp, picot, ch 3; repeat from * around, join. Fasten off.

WING COLLAR

Rnd 1: Working in **front lps** of rnd 6 on Head & Dress, join with sl st in first st, ch 4, (dc in next st, ch 1) around, join with sl st in third ch of ch-4. *(32 ch sps made)*

Rnd 2: Ch 6, sc in next st, picot, ch 3, (dc in next st, ch 3, sc in next st, picot, ch 3) around, join with sl st in third ch of ch-6.

Rnd 3: Ch 1, sc in first dc, ch 4, (sc in next dc, ch 4) around, join with sl st in first sc.

Rnd 4: Ch 3, dc in same st, ch 3, sc in next ch sp, picot, ch 3, (2 dc in next st, ch 3, sc in next ch sp, picot, ch 3) around, join with sl st in top of ch-3.

Rnd 5: Ch 1, sc in first dc, sc in next dc, ch 5, (sc in next 2 dc, ch 5) around, join.

Rnd 6: Ch 3, dc in same st, picot, 2 dc in next st, ch 3, sc in next ch sp, picot, ch 3, (2 dc in next st, picot, 2 dc in next st, ch 3, sc in next ch sp, picot, ch 3) around, join. Fasten off.

FINISHING & ASSEMBLY

Work Finishing & Assembly for Vicki on page 23.

Bryony

HEAD & DRESS

Rnd 1: Starting at Head, ch 4, sl st in first ch to form ring, ch 3, 11 dc in ring, join with sl st in top of ch-3. *(12 dc made)*

Rnd 2: (Ch 3, dc) in first st, 2 dc in each st around, join. *(24)*

Rnd 3: Ch 3, dc in each st around, join.

Rnd 4: Ch 3, dc next 2 sts tog, (dc in next st, dc next 2 sts tog) around, join. *(16)* Stuff Head with cotton balls.

Rnd 5: Ch 1, sc in each st around, join with sl st in first sc.

Rnd 6: (Ch 3, dc) in first st, 2 dc in each st around, join. *(32)*

Rnd 7: Working in **back lps** *(see Stitch Guide)*, ch 4, (dc in next st, ch 1) around, join with sl st in third ch of ch-4. *(32 ch sps)*

Rnds 8–10: Sl st in first ch sp, ch 4, (dc in next ch sp, ch 1) around, join.

Rnd 11: Ch 1, sc in next ch sp; for **picot, ch 3, sl st in top of last st made;** (ch 4, skip next ch sp, sc in next ch sp, picot) around, ch 1, join with dc in first sc.

Rnd 12: Ch 1, sc in first ch sp, ch 5, (sc in next ch sp, ch 5) around, join with sl st in first sc.

Rnd 13: Ch 1, sc in first st, 5 sc in next ch sp, (sc in next st, 5 sc in next ch sp) around, join.

Rnd 14: Sl st in first 2 sts, ch 1, sc in next st, picot, (ch 5, skip next 5 sts, sc in next st, picot) around, ch 2, join with dc in first sc.

Rnds 15–16: Repeat rnds 12 and 13.

Rnd 17: Sl st in first 2 sts, ch 1, sc in next st, picot, (ch 6, skip next 5 sts, sc in next st, picot) around, ch 3, join with dc in first sc.

Rnd 18: Ch 1, sc in first ch sp, ch 6, (sc in next ch sp, ch 6) around, join with sl st in first sc.

Rnd 19: Ch 1, 7 sc in each ch sp around, join.

Rnd 20: Sl st in next 2 sts, ch 1, sc in next st, picot, ch 6, (skip next 6 sts, sc in next st, picot) around, ch 3, join with dc in first sc.

Rnd 21: Ch 1, sc in first ch sp, ch 7, (sc in next ch sp, ch 7) around, join with sl st in first sc.

Rnd 22: Ch 1, (4 sc, picot, 4 sc) in each ch sp around, join. Fasten off.

WING COLLAR

Rnd 1: Working in **front lps** of rnd 6 on Head & Dress, join with sc in first st, ch 4, (dc in next st, ch 1) around, join with sl st in third ch of ch-4. *(32 ch sps made)*

Rnd 2: Ch 1, sc in first ch sp, ch 3, (sc in next ch sp, ch 3) around, join with sl st in first sc.

Rnd 3: Sl st in first ch of first ch-3, ch 1, sc in same ch, picot, (ch 4, sc in next ch sp, picot) around, ch 1, join with dc in first sc.

Rnd 4: Ch 1, sc in first ch sp, ch 5, (sc in next ch sp, ch 5) around, join with sl st in first sc.

Rnd 5: Ch 1, sc in first st, 5 sc in next ch sp, (sc in next st, 5 sc in next ch sp) around, join.

Rnd 6: Sl st in first 2 sts, ch 1, sc in next st, picot, (ch 5, skip next 5 sts, sc in next st, picot) around, ch 2, join with dc in first sc.

Rnd 7: Ch 1, sc in first ch sp, ch 6, (sc in next ch sp, ch 6) around, join with sl st in first sc.

Rnd 8: Ch 1, sc in first st, (3 sc, picot, 3 sc) in next ch sp, *sc in next st, (3 sc, picot, 3 sc) in next ch sp; repeat from * around, join. Fasten off.

FINISHING & ASSEMBLY

Work Finishing & Assembly for Vicki on page 23. ✻

Frosty Fashions

Christmas Song

Chestnuts roasting on an open fire. Jack Frost nipping at your nose. Yuletide carols being sung by a choir and folks dressed up like Eskimos. Everybody knows a turkey and some mistletoe help to make the season bright. Tiny tots with their eyes all aglow will find it hard to sleep tonight.

Festive Pullover

Designed by Ann Parnell

FINISHED SIZE: Girl's/lady's bust 30"–32".
Finished measurement: 37". **Red yarn:** 13 oz.
Lady's bust 34"–36". Finished measurement: 41".
Red yarn: 14½ oz.
Lady's bust 38"–40". Finished measurement: 45".
Red yarn: 16 oz.
Lady's bust 42"–44". Finished measurement: 49".
Red yarn: 17½ oz.
Lady's bust 46"–48". Finished measurement: 53".
Red yarn: 19 oz.
Lady's bust 50"-52". Finished measurement: 57".
Red yarn: 20½ oz.

MATERIALS:
- ❑ Fingering yarn:
  Red *(see amount listed with size)*
  4 oz. black
  1¼ oz. off-white
- ❑ Tapestry needle
- ❑ F and G hooks or hooks needed to obtain gauges

GAUGES: *F hook* working in **back lps**, 7 sc = 1"; 7 sc rows = 1".
G hook working in **back lps**, 6 sc = 1"; 6 sc rows = 1"; working in **both lps**, 5 sc = 1", 6 sc rows = 1".

BASIC STITCHES: Ch, sl st, sc.

NOTE: Instructions are for girl's/lady's bust 30"–32"; changes for 34"–36", 38"–40", 42"–44", 46"–48" and 50"–52" are in [ ].

BACK
Ribbing
Row 1: With G hook and red, ch 13, sc in second ch from hook, sc in each ch across, turn. *(12 sc)*
Rows 2–92 [2–102, 2–112, 2–122, 2–132, 2–142]: Working these rows in **back lps** *(see Stitch Guide)*, ch 1, sc in each st across. At end of last row, **do not turn.**

Body
Row 1: With G hook, working in ends of Ribbing rows, ch 1, 2 sc in first row, sc in each row across, turn. *(93 sc) [103 sc, 113 sc, 123 sc, 133 sc, 143 sc]*
NOTE: *When changing colors (see Stitch Guide), drop last color to wrong side of work, pick up again when needed. When carrying yarn along back side of work, carefully work every third st around dropped yarn so it does not show on front. Always change to next color in last st made.*

Row 2: Ch 1, sc in first 7 [6, 5, 4, 3, 2] sts; with black, sc in next st; (with red, sc in next 5 sts; with black, sc in next st) across to last 7 [6, 5, 4, 3, 2] sts; with red, sc in each st across turn. Drop black, **do not cut.** *Front of row 2 is right side of work.*
Rows 3–4: Ch 1, sc in each st across, turn.
Row 5: Ch 1, sc in first 4 [3, 2, 7, 6, 5] sts; with black, sc in next st; (with red, sc in next 5 sts; with black, sc in next st) across to last 4 [3, 2, 7, 6, 5] sts; with red, sc in each st across, turn. Drop black, **do not fasten off.**
Rows 6–7: Ch 1, sc in each st across, turn.
NOTE: *Body pattern is established in rows 2-7.*
Rows 8–162 [8–164, 8–166, 8–168, 8–170, 8–172]: Marking each end of row 108 for Sleeve as it is worked, work in body pattern. At end of last row, fasten off red and black.

FRONT
Ribbing
Work same as Back Ribbing.

Body
Rows 1–103: Repeat rows 1–103 of Back Body. At end of last row, fasten off red and black.
Row 104: Join off-white with sc in first st, (ch 1, skip next st, sc in next st) across, **do not turn.** Fasten off.
Row 105: Join black with sc in first st, (ch 1, skip next ch, sc in next sc) across, turn. Fasten off.
Row 106: Working this row in **front lps,** join off-white with sl st in first st, ch 1, hdc in same st, hdc in each st and in each ch across, **do not turn.** Fasten off.
Row 107: Working this row in **front lps,** join black with sc in first st, sc in each st across, turn. Fasten off.
Row 108: Join red with sc in first st, sc in each st across, turn. Mark each end of row for Sleeve.
Row 109: Ch 1, sc in each st across, turn.
Row 110: Ch 1, sc in first 2 sts; changing colors according to color change graphs on page 29, work row 1 of graph A, work row 1 of graph B 2 [2, 2, 4, 4, 4] times, work row 1 of graph C; with red, sc in last 2 sts, turn.
Row 111: Ch 1, sc in first 2 sts, work next row of graph C, work next row of graph B 2 [2, 2, 4, 4, 4] times, work next row of graph A; with red, sc in last 2 sts, turn.
Row 112: Ch 1, sc in first 2 sts, work next row of graph A, work next row of graph B 2 [2, 2, 4, 4, 4]

continued on page 28

Festive Pullover

continued from page 26

times, work next row of graph C; with red, sc in last 2 sts, turn.

Rows 113–136: Repeat rows 111–112 alternately. At end of last row, fasten off red and black.

Row 137: Join black with sc in first st, sc in each st across, **do not turn.** Fasten off.

Row 138: Join off-white with sl st in first st, ch 1, hdc in same st, hdc in each st across, turn.

Row 139: Repeat row 137.

Row 140: Join off-white with sc in first st, (ch 1, skip next st, sc in next st) across, **do not turn.** Fasten off.

Row 141: Join red with sc in first st, (ch 1, skip next ch, sc in next sc) across, turn.

Row 142: Ch 1, sc in each st and in each ch across, turn.

Rows 143–150 [143–150, 143–152, 143–154, 143–154, 143–156]: Repeat rows 2–7 of Back Body consecutively, ending with row 3 [3, 5, 7, 7, 3].

Row 151 [151, 153, 155, 155, 157]: For **first side,** work in body pattern across first 34 [37, 40, 44, 49, 54] sts, sc next 2 sts tog leaving last 57 [64, 71, 77, 82, 87] sts unworked, turn. *(35) [38, 41, 45, 50, 55]*

Row 152 [152, 154, 156, 156, 158]: Ch 1, skip first st, sc next 2 sts tog, work in body pattern across, turn. *(33) [36, 39, 43, 48, 53].*

Row 153 [153, 155, 157, 157, 159]: Work in body pattern across to last 2 sts, sc last 2 sts tog, turn. *(32) [35, 38, 42, 47, 52]*

Rows 154–155 [154–155, 156–157, 158–159, 158–159, 160–161]: Repeat rows 152–153 [152–153, 154–155, 156–157, 156–157, 158–159]. At end of last row, *(29) [32, 35, 39, 44, 49]*

Rows 156–162 [156–164, 158–166, 160–168, 160–170, 162–172]: Work in body pattern. At end of last row, fasten off red and black.

Row 151 [151, 153, 155, 155, 157]: For **neck,** skip next 21 [25, 29, 31, 31, 31] sts on row 150 [150, 152, 154, 154, 156]; for **Second Side,** join red with sl st in next st, ch 1, sc same st and next st tog, work in body pattern across, turn. *(35) [38, 41, 45, 50, 55]*

Rows 152–155 [152–155, 154–157, 156–159, 156–159, 158–161]: Repeat rows 153 and 152 [153 and 152, 155 and 154, 157 and 156, 157 and 156, 159 and 158] of first side alternately. At end of last row, *(29) [32, 35, 39, 44, 49]*

Rows 156–162 [156–164, 158–166, 160–168, 160–170, 162–172]: Work in body pattern. At end of last row, fasten off red and black.

Sew shoulder seams.

NECK RIBBING

Rnd 1: With G hook and right side of neck edge facing you, join red with sl st in shoulder seam, ch 1, sc in each st and in end of each row around ending with odd number of sts, join with sl st in first sc.

Row 2: Working in rows, with F hook, ch 9, sc in second ch from hook, sc in each ch across, skip next st on rnd 1, sl st in next st, turn. *(8 sc)*

Row 3: Working in **back lps,** skip sl st, sc in each sc across, turn.

Row 4: Working in **back lps,** ch 1, sc in each sc across, skip next st on rnd 1; working in **both lps,** sl st in next st on rnd 1, turn.

Next rows: Repeat rows 3 and 4 alternately around rnd 1, ending with row 3. At end of last row, leaving 6" for sewing, fasten off.

Overlap first and last rows to form rib, sew together.

SLEEVE (make 2)
Ribbing

Row 1: With F hook and red, ch 17, sc in second ch from hook, sc in each ch across, turn. *(16 sc made)*

Rows 2–42 [2–44, 2–44, 2–46, 2–50, 2–54]: Working these rows in **back lps,** ch 1, sc in each st across, turn. At end of last row, **do not turn.**

Arm

Row 1: Working in ends of Ribbing rows, with G hook, ch 1, sc in first 2 [1, 1, 4, 6, 2] rows, 2 sc in next row, *sc in next 2 [3, 3, 2, 2, 5] rows, 2 sc in next row; repeat from * across to last 3 [2, 2, 5, 7, 3] rows, sc in each row across, turn. Fasten off red. *(55) [55, 55, 59, 63, 63]*

Rows 2–6: Repeat rows 104–108 of Front Body. Do not mark row.

Row 7: For **inc row,** ch 1, 2 sc in first st, sc in each st across with 2 sc in last st turn. *(57) [57, 57, 61, 65, 65]*

Row 8: Ch 1, sc in first 4 [4, 4, 6, 2, 2] sts; with black, sc in next st; (with red, sc in next 5 sts; with black, sc in next st) across to last 4 [4, 4, 6, 2, 2] sts; with red, sc in each st across, turn. Drop black, **do not fasten off.**

Rows 9–10: Ch 1, sc in each st across, turn.

Row 11: Ch 1, sc in first 1 [1, 1, 3, 5, 5] st; with black, sc in next st; (with red, sc in next 5 sts; with black, sc in next st) across to last 1 [1, 1, 3, 5, 5] st; with red, sc in each st across, turn. Drop black, **do not fasten off.**

Rows 12–13: Ch 1, sc in each st across, turn.

NOTES: Sleeve pattern is established in rows 8–13. When increasing, work each new st in established pattern.

Rows 14–70 [14–78, 14–82, 14–82, 14–82, 14–86]: Working inc row in first row and every following fourth row, work in Sleeve pattern. At end of last row, *(87) [91, 93, 97, 101, 103].*

Rows 71–89 [79–93, 83–97, 83–97, 83–97, 87–97]: Work in Sleeve pattern. At end of last row, fasten off red and black.

Matching center of last row on Sleeve to shoulder seam and ends of row to row 108 on Front and Back, stretching Sleeve slightly to fit, sew Sleeve to Body.

Sew side and Sleeve seams. ✳

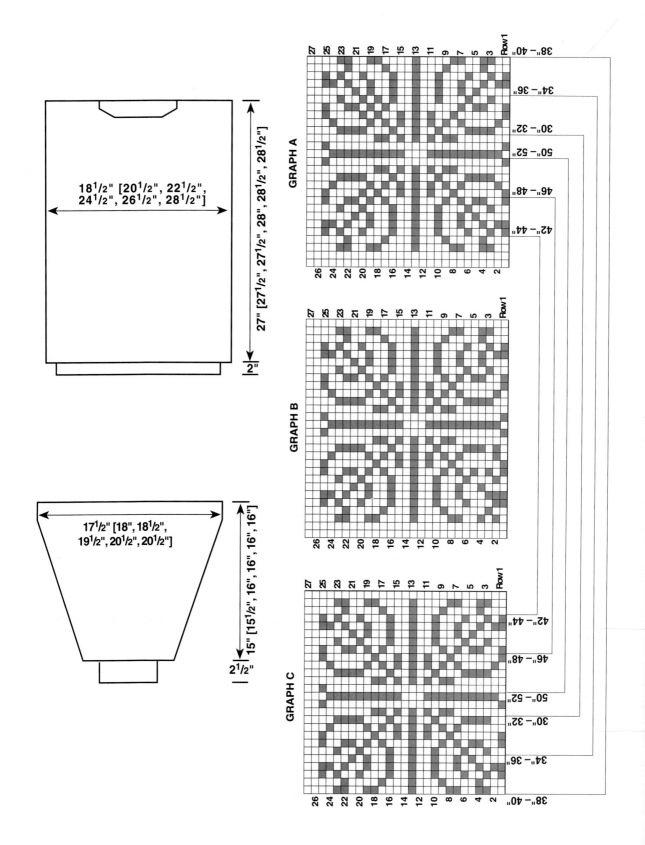

18½" [20½", 22½", 24½", 26½", 28½"]

27" [27½", 27½", 28", 28½", 28½"]

2"

17½" [18", 18½", 19½", 20½", 20½"]

15" [15½", 16", 16", 16", 16"]

2½"

GRAPH A

GRAPH B

GRAPH C

Row 1

38"–40"
34"–36"
30"–32"
50"–52"
46"–48"
42"–44"

42"–44"
46"–48"
50"–52"
30"–32"
34"–36"
38"–40"

Snowflake Sweater

Designed by Ann Parnell

FINISHED SIZES: **Man's chest 34"–36".** Finished measurement: 37½". Yarn 11½ ozs. blue, 9½ ozs. white.

Man's chest 38"–40". Finished measurement: 41¾". Yarn: 12½ ozs. blue, 10½ ozs. white.

Man's chest 42"–44". Finished measurement: 47". Yarn: 13½ ozs. blue, 11½ ozs. white.

Man's chest 46" –48". Finished measurement: 52". Yarn: 15 ozs. blue, 13 ozs. white.

MATERIALS:
- ❑ Sport yarn—colors and amounts listed for Size.
- ❑ Tapestry needle
- ❑ E and F hooks or hooks needed to obtain gauges

GAUGES: **E hook,** 11 sc = 2"; 19 sc **back lp** rows = 4". **F hook,** 23 extended sc = 6"; 13 extended sc rows = 4".

BASIC STITCHES: Ch, sl st, sc.

NOTE: Instructions are for man's chest 34–36"; changes for 38"–40", 42"–44" and 46"–48" are in [ ].

BACK
Ribbing
Row 1: With E hook and blue, ch 15, sc in second ch from hook, sc in each ch across, turn. *(14 sc made)*

Rows 2–72 [2–80, 2–90, 2–100]: Working these rows in **back lps** *(see Stitch Guide)*, ch 1, sc in each st across, turn. At end of last row, **do not turn or fasten off.**

BODY
Row 1: Working in ends of Ribbing rows, with F hook, ch 1; for **extended sc (esc), insert hook in first row, yo, pull through row, yo, pull through 1 lp on hook, yo, pull through 2 lps on hook;** esc in each row across to last row, sc in last row, turn. *(71 esc, 1 sc) [79 esc, 1 sc; 89 esc, 1 sc, 99 esc, 1 sc]*

Row 2 [2–3, 2–4, 2–5]: For **pattern, ch 1, esc in each st across to last st, sc in last st,** turn. At end of last row, **do not turn,** fasten off. *Back of row 2 [3, 4, 5] is right side of work.*

Row 3 [4, 5, 6]: With right side of work facing you, working this row in **back lps,** join white with sl st in first st, work in pattern across, turn.

Row 4 [5, 6, 7]: Work in pattern across. Fasten off.

Rows 5–6 [6–7, 7–8, 8–9]: With blue, repeat rows 3–4, [4–5, 5–6, 6–7].

Row 7 [8–9, 9–10, 10–11]: Repeat row 3 [4–5, 5–6, 6–7]. At end of last row, turn, **do not fasten off.**

Row [12]: For size 46"–48" only, work in pattern across, turn.

NOTE: *When changing colors (see Stitch Guide), drop last color to wrong side of work; carry dropped yarn along back of work, pick up again when needed. Always change to next color in last st made.*

Row 8 [10, 11, 13]: *For row 1 of graph B (see graph on page 33 for size needed),* with blue, ch 1, esc in first st; with white, esc in next 4 [3, 4, 5] sts; with blue, esc in next st; with white, esc in next 5 sts; with blue, esc in next st; with white, esc in next 4 [3, 4, 5] sts; with blue, esc in each of next 2 sts; repeat from * 3 [4, 4, 4] more times across body, turn.

Rows 9–22 [11–24, 12,–25, 14–27]: Changing colors according to graph, beginning with row 2 on graph, working each graph row 4 [5, 5, 5] times across body, work in pattern. At end of last row, fasten off blue.

Row 23 [25, 26, 28]: With white, work in pattern across, turn. For **size 34"–36" only,** fasten off.

Row [26, 27, 29–30]: For **sizes 38"–40", 42–"44", and 46"–48"** only, work in pattern across. Fasten off.

Rows 24–25 [27–28, 28–29, 31–32]: For **all sizes,** with blue, repeat rows 3–4 [4–5, 5–6, 6–7].

Rows 26–27 [29–30, 30–31, 33–34]: Repeat rows 3–4 [4–5, 5–6, 6–7].

Rows 28–44 [31–49, 32–50, 35–55]: Reversing colors, repeat rows 7–23 [8–26, 9–27, 10–30].

Rows 45–69 [50–76, 51–77, 56–84]: With same colors, repeat rows 3–27 [4–30, 5–31, 6–34].

Row 70 [77, 78, 85]: With blue, repeat row 3 [4, 5, 6].

Row 71 [78, 79–81, 86–88]: Work in pattern across, turn. At end of last row, fasten off.

Row 72 [79, 82, 89]: For **first shoulder,** skip first 5 [6, 7, 8] sts, join blue with sc in next st, sc in next 4 [5, 6, 7] sts, sc in next 10 [11, 12, 13] sts, sc in next st leaving last 51 [56, 63, 70] sts unworked, turn. *(16 sts)*

Row 73 [80, 83, 90]: Ch 1, esc in first 5 [6, 7, 8] sts, sc in next 6 sts, sl st in next st leaving last 4 [5, 6 7] sts unworked, turn. Fasten off. *(11) [12, 13, 14] Sl sts are not worked into or counted in st count.*

Row 72 [79, 82, 89]: For **second shoulder,** skip next 30 [32, 36, 40] unworked sts on row 71 [78, 81, 88], join with sl st in next st, ch 1, esc in same st, esc in next 10 [11, 12, 13] sts, sc in next 5 [6, 7, 8] sts, sl st in next st leaving last 4 [5, 6, 7] sts unworked, turn. *(16) [18, 20, 22]*

continued on page 32

Snowflake Sweater

continued from page 31

Row 73 [80, 83, 90]: Ch 1, skip first sl st, sl st in next 5 [6, 7, 8] sts, sc in next 6 sts, esc in next 4 [5, 6, 7] sts, sc in last st. Fasten off. *(11) [12, 13, 14]*

FRONT
Ribbing
Work same as Back Ribbing.

Body
Rows 1–65 [1–72, 1–73, 1–80]: Repeat same rows of Back Body. *(72 sts) [80 sts, 90 sts, 100 sts]*

Row 66 [73, 74, 81]: For **first shoulder,** with right side of work facing you, working this row in **back lps,** join blue with sl st in first st, ch 1, esc in first 25 [28, 33, 36] sts; for **esc 2 sts tog, (insert hook in next st, yo, pull through st, yo, pull through 1 lp on hook) 2 times, yo, pull through last 2 lps on hook;** leaving last 45 [50, 55, 62] sts unworked, turn. *(26) [29, 34, 37]*

Row 67 [74, 75, 82]: Ch 1, esc first 2 sts tog, work in pattern across, turn. Fasten off. *(25) [28, 33, 36]*

Row 68 [75, 76, 83]: With right side of work facing you, working this row in **back lps,** join white with sl st in first st, ch 1, esc in each st across to last 2 sts, esc last 2 sts tog, turn. *(24) [27, 32, 35]*

Row 69 [76, 77, 84]: Ch 1, esc first 2 sts tog, work in pattern across, turn. Fasten off. *(23) [26, 31, 34]*

Rows 70–71 [77–78, 78–79, 85–86]: With blue, repeat rows 68–69 [75–76, 76–77, 83–84]. At end of last row, **do not fasten off.**

Row [80, 87]: For sizes **42"–44"** and **46"–48"** only, work in pattern across to last 2 sts, esc last 2 sts tog, turn. *[28, 31]*

Row [81, 88]: Ch 1, esc first 2 sts tog, work in pattern across, turn. *[27, 30]*

Row 72 [79, 82, 89]: For **all sizes,** for **shoulder shaping,** sl st in first 5 [6, 7, 8] sts, ch 1, sc in next 5 [6, 7, 8] sts, esc in next 10 [11, 12, 13] sts, sc in last st, turn. *(16) [18, 20, 22]*

Row 73 [80, 83, 90]: Ch 1, esc in first 5 [6, 7, 8] sts, sc in next 6 sts, sl st in next st leaving last 4 [5, 6, 7] sc unworked, turn. Fasten off. *(11) [12, 13, 14]*

Row 66 [73, 74, 81]: For **second shoulder,** with right side of work facing you, working this row in **back lps,** skip next 18 [20, 20, 24] unworked sts on row 65 [75, 73, 80], join blue with sl st in next st, ch 1, esc same st and next st tog, work in pattern across, turn. *(26), [29, 34, 37]*

Row 67 [74, 75, 82]: Work in pattern across to last 2 sts, esc last 2 sts tog. Fasten off. *(25) [28, 33, 36]*

Row 68 [75, 76, 83]: With right side of work facing you, working this row in **back lps,** join white with sl st in first st, ch 1, esc same st and next st tog, work in pattern across, turn. *(24) [27, 32, 35]*

Row 69 [76, 77, 84]: Repeat row 67 [74, 75, 82] of second shoulder. *(23) [26, 31, 34]*

Rows 70–71 [77–78, 78–79, 85–86]: With blue, repeat rows 68–69 [75–76, 76–77, 83–84]. At end of last row, **do not fasten off.**

Rows [80–81, 87–88]: For sizes **42–44** and **46"–48"** only, with blue, repeat rows [76–77, 83–84] of second shoulder. At end of last row, **do not fasten off.**

Row 72 [79, 82, 89]: For **all sizes,** work in pattern across first 11 [12, 13, 14] sts; for **shoulder shaping,** sc in next 5 [6, 7, 8] sts, sl st in next st leaving last 4 [5, 6, 7] sts unworked, turn. *(16) [18, 20, 22]*

Row 73 [80, 83, 90]: Ch 1, skip first sl st, sl st in next 5 [6, 7, 8] sts, sc in next 6 sts, esc in next 4 [5, 6, 7] sts, sc in last st. Fasten off. *(11) [12, 13, 14]*.
Sew shoulder seams.

NECK BAND
Rnd 1: Working around neck edge, with right side of work facing you, with E hook and blue, join with sc at shoulder seam, sc in each st and in end of each row around, join with sl st in first sc, **turn.**

Rnd 2: Ch 1, esc in each st around, join with sl st in first esc, **do not** turn.

Rnd 3: Ch 1, sc in each st around, join with sl st in first sc. Fasten off.

SLEEVE (make 2)
Ribbing
Rows 1–36 [1–36, 1–38, 1–40]: Repeat same rows of Back Ribbing. At end of last row, **do not turn or fasten off.**

Arm
Row 1: With F hook, working in ends of Ribbing rows, ch 1, esc in first 1 [1, 3, 0] row; (for **inc, 2 esc in next row;** esc in each of next 2 rows, inc, esc in next row) 7 [7, 7, 8] times, turn. Fasten off. *(49 esc, 1 sc; 51 esc, 1 sc; 55 esc, 1 sc). Back of row 1 is right side of work.*

Row 2: Working this row in **back lps,** join white with sl st in first st, work in pattern across, turn.

Row 3: Ch 1, inc, work in pattern across to last st, (esc, sc) in last st, turn. Fasten off. *(52 sts) [52 sts, 54 sts, 58 sts]*

Rows 4–5: With blue, repeat rows 2–3. *(54) [54, 56, 60]*

Row 6: Repeat row 2.

Row [7, 7, 7–8]: For sizes **38"–40", 42"–44"** and **46"–48"** only, work in pattern across turn.

Row 7 [9]: For **sizes 34"–36 and 46"–48"** only, working in pattern changing colors according to graph for size, work row 1 of graph B 3 times across Sleeve, turn.

Row [8, 8]: For **sizes 38"–40" and 42"–44"** only, working in pattern, changing colors according to graph for size, work row 1 of graph A; work row 1 of graph B 3 times; work row 1 of graph C, turn.

Rows 8–21 [9–22, 10–23]: For **all sizes,** working in pattern, changing colors according to graph, beginning with row 2 on each graph, work next row of graph A; work next row of graph B 3 times; work next row of graph C, turn. At end of last row, *(60) [60, 62, 66].*

Row 22 [23–24, 23–24, 24–26]: Work in pattern across, turn. At end of last row, fasten off.

Rows 23–24 [25–26, 25–26, 27–28]: With blue, repeat rows 2–3. At end of last row, *(62) [62, 64, 68].*

Rows 25–26 [27–28, 27–28, 29–30]: Repeat rows 2–3. Fasten off. At end of last row *(64) [64, 66, 70].*

Row 27 [29, 29, 31]: With blue, repeat row 2.

Row 28 [30, 30, 32]: Ch 1, inc, esc in each st across to last st, (esc, sc) in last st, turn. *(66) [66, 68, 72].*

Rows 29–34 [31–33, 31–33, 33–34]: Work in pattern.

Rows 35–49 [34–52, 34–55, 35–56]: Repeat rows 28–34 [30–33, 30–33, 32–34] consecutively, ending with row 28 [32, 31, 32]. At end of last row, fasten off, *(72) [76, 80, 88] sts.*

Rows 50–53 [53–56, 56–59, 57–60]: Repeat rows 3–6 [4–7, 5–8, 6–9] of Back Body.

Matching center of last row on Sleeves to shoulder seams, being careful not to stretch or gather either piece, sew Sleeves to Body.

Sew Sleeve and side seams. ✳

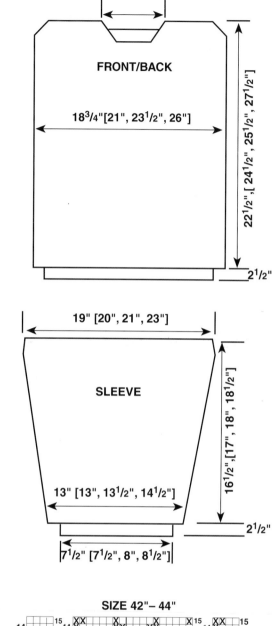

FRONT/BACK

8" [8½", 9½", 10½"]

18¾"[21", 23½", 26"]

22½", [24½", 25½", 27½"]

2½"

19" [20", 21", 23"]

SLEEVE

16½",[17", 18", 18½"]

13" [13", 13½", 14½"]

2½"

7½" [7½", 8", 8½"]

☒ = **BLUE**

☐ = **WHITE**

◪ OR ◩ = **INC**

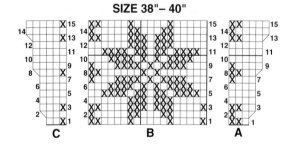

SIZE 34"– 36"

C   B   A

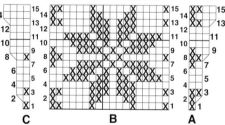

SIZE 38"– 40"

C   B   A

SIZE 42"– 44"

C   B   A

Sweatshirt Fun

Designed by Elizabeth White

FINISHED SIZES: 4½" tall.

MATERIALS FOR BOTH:
- ❏ Size 20 crochet cotton thread:
  - 75 yds. tan
  - 75 yds. white
  - Small amount red
- ❏ 27" red ¼" ribbon
- ❏ Sweatshirt
- ❏ Matching sewing thread
- ❏ Embroidery needle
- ❏ No. 8 steel hook or hook needed to obtain gauge

GAUGE: 10 dc = 1"; 5 dc rows = 1".

BASIC STITCHES: Ch, sl st, sc, dc.

BODY (make 4)

Row 1: With tan, starting at **head**, ch 12, dc in fourth ch from hook, dc in each ch across, turn. *(10 dc made)*

Row 2: (Ch 3, dc) in first st, 2 dc in next st, dc in each st across with 2 dc in each of last 2 sts, turn. *(14)*

Rows 3–4: Ch 3, dc in each st across, turn.

Row 5: Ch 3, (dc next 2 sts tog) 2 times, dc in each st across to last 4 sts; (dc next 2 sts tog) 2 times, turn. *(10)*

Row 6: Ch 3, dc in each st across, turn.

Rows 7–8: Repeat row 2. *(18 sts at end of last row)*

Rows 9–15: Ch 3, dc in each st across, turn.

Row 16: For **First Leg**, ch 3, dc in next 8 sts leaving last 9 sts unworked, turn. *(9)*

Rows 17–21: Ch 3, dc in each st across, turn. At end of last row, **do not turn;** working across ends of rows, ch 3, *(yo, insert hook in same row, yo, pull through, yo, pull through 2 lps on hook) 2 times*, yo, insert hook in end of next row, yo, pull through, yo, pull through 2 lps on hook; repeat between first and second *, yo, pull through all lps on hook. Fasten off.

Row 16: For **Second Leg**, join with sl st in first st at end of row 15, ch 3, dc in last 8 sts, turn. *(9)*

Rows 17–21: Repeat rows 17–21 of First Leg.

Arms

Row 1: Working in ends of rows on one side toward Legs, join tan with sl st in row 7, ch 3, (2 dc in same row, dc in next row) 2 times, turn. *(7 dc)*

Rows 2–3: Ch 3, dc in each st across, turn.

Row 4: Ch 3, (yo, insert hook in next st, yo, pull through st, yo, pull through 2 lps on hook) 6 times, yo, pull through all lps on hook. Fasten off. Repeat on other side.

APRON (for Girl)

Row 1: With white, ch 23, dc in eighth ch from hook, (ch 2, skip next 2 chs, dc in next ch) 5 times, turn. *(6 ch sps, 7 dc)*

Row 2: (Ch 3, dc) in first st, (3 dc in next ch sp, 2 dc in next st) 5 times, 3 dc in last ch sp, 2 dc in sixth ch of ch-8, turn. *(32 dc)*

Row 3: Ch 3, dc in each st across, turn.

Row 4: Repeat row 3 changing to red *(see Stitch Guide)* in last st made. Fasten off white.

Row 5: Repeat row 3 changing to white in last st made. Fasten off red.

Row 6: Ch 3, dc in each st across. Fasten off.

FINISHING

1: With white, using satin stitch *(see Stitch Guide)*, embroider eyes ⅜" apart on row 3.

2: With white using outline stitch *(see Stitch Guide)*, embroider mouth centered below eyes over row 5.

3: For **Boy**, with white, using satin stitch, embroider buttons centered below mouth over rows 8, 10 and 12.

4: For **Boy or Girl**, with wrong sides together, working through both thicknesses, join white with sc in any st, sc in each st and 2 sc in end of each row around, join with sl st in first sc. Fasten off.

5: Tie two 8" pieces of ribbon into bows, tack at center front neck for Boy or left side of head for Girl.

6: For **Girl**, for each strap, cut 3¼" piece ribbon. Sew one end to row 1 of Apron on second dc from end. Run remaining ribbon through row 1 on Apron. Place on Girl and sew all ends together at back.

7: Sew Boy or Girl on sweatshirt as desired. ❊

Child's Trio

Designed by Sue Schult

FINISHED SIZES:
Hat fits approximately 20" diameter head. Scarf is approximately 39" long without fringe. Mittens are approximately 5½" long with edging.

MATERIALS:
❏ Worsted yarn:
  - 8 oz. rose
  - 2½ oz. white
❏ 3" × 21½" piece of fake fur
❏ Sewing thread to match fur
❏ Sewing and tapestry needles
❏ G hook or hook needed to obtain gauge

GAUGE:
4 dc = 1"; 4 dc post st rows = 2".

BASIC STITCHES:
Ch, sl st, sc, dc.

SPECIAL STITCHES:
For **dc increase (dc inc)**, 2 dc in next st.
For **sc increase (sc inc)**, 2 sc in next st.
For **sc decrease (sc dec)**, sc next 2 sts tog.

HAT
Rnd 1: With rose, ch 4, 9 dc in fourth ch from hook, join with sl st in third ch of ch-4. *(10 dc made)*
Rnd 2: (Ch 3—*counts as first dc,* dc) in first st, **dc inc** *(see Special Stitches)* in each st around, join with sl st in top of ch-3. *(20)*
Rnd 3: (Ch 3, dc) in first st, **dc front post *(dc fp— see Stitch Guide)*** around next st, (dc inc, dc fp around next st) 9 times, join. *(30)*
Rnd 4: Ch 3, dc inc, dc fp around next st, (dc in next st, dc inc, dc fp around next st) around, join. *(40)*
Rnd 5: (Ch 3, dc) in first st, dc fp around next st, (dc inc in next st, dc fp around next st) around, join. *(60)*
Rnds 6–16: Ch 3, dc bp around next st, dc fp around next st, (dc bp around each of next 2 sts, dc fp around next st) around, join. At end of last rnd, fasten off.

First Ear Flap
NOTE: *The ch-3 at the beginning of each rnd is back seam on Hat.*
Row 1: Fold Hat in half along back seam *(there with be 10 dc fp showing)*; with back seam to your right, working on one half of Hat, join rose with sc in fourth dc fp after ch-3 on rnd 16, sc in next 9 sts, turn. *(10 sc made)*
Rows 2–4: Ch 1, **sc dec** *(see Special Stitches)*; sc in each st across to last 2 sts, sc dec, turn. *(8, 6, 4)*

Row 5: Ch 1, sc dec 2 times. Fasten off. *(2)*

Second Ear Flap
Row 1: With other side of Hat facing you and back seam to your left, join rose with sc in sixth dc fp before ch-3 on rnd 16, sc in next 9 sts, turn. *(10 sc made)*
Rows 2–4: Ch 1, sc dec, sc in each st across to last 2 sts, sc dec, turn. *(4)*
Row 5: Ch 1, sc dec 2 times, **do not** turn or fasten off. *(2)*
Rnd 6: Working in ends of rows on Ear Flaps and sts on rnd 16 of Hat, sc in end of first 5 rows, sc in next 20 sts on row 16 of Hat, sc in ends of next 5 rows on next Ear Flap, **(sc inc**—*see Special Stitches*—in next st on row 5; for **tie, ch 51, sl st in second ch from hook, sl st in each ch across;** sc inc in next st), sc in end of next 5 rows on same Ear Flap, sc in next 20 sts on row 16 of Hat, sc in next 5 rows on next Ear Flap; repeat between ( ), join with sl st in first sc. Fasten off.

FINISHING
Place wrong side of fur to right side of Hat *(end of fur should meet at back seam),* pin to Hat. While stretching the Hat slightly, with sewing needle and matching thread, sew bottom edge of fur to sc rnds around bottom of Hat, sewing straight across top of Ear Flaps. Sew top edge of fur to Hat.

SCARF
Row 1: With rose, ch 18, dc in third ch from hook, dc in each ch across, turn. *(17 dc made)*
Row 2: Ch 3, (dc fp around next st, dc in next st) across, turn.
Row 3: Ch 3, (dc bp around next st, dc in next st) across, turn.
Rows 4–7: Repeat rows 2 and 3 alternately. At end of last row, fasten off.
Row 8: Join white with sl st in first st, ch 3, (dc fp around next st, dc in next st) across, turn.
Row 9: Ch 3, (dc bp around next st, dc in next st) across, turn. Fasten off.
Row 10: Join rose with sl st in first st, ch 3, (dc fp around next st, dc in next st) across, turn.
Rows 11–88: Repeat rows 2–10 consecutively, ending with row 7.

Finishing
Cut 36 strands from white each 6" long.
To **Fringe,** hold two strands together, fold in half;

continued on page 41

Candy Cane Stockings

Designed by Mary Layfield

FINISHED SIZE: Fits 9" to 9½" sole.

MATERIALS:
- ❏ Worsted yarn:
  - 8 oz. off-white
  - 4½ oz. dk. green
  - 3½ oz. med. green
  - 3½ oz. burgundy
  - 2½ oz. rose
- ❏ G hook or hook needed to obtain gauge

GAUGE: 4 sc = 1"; 9 sc rnds = 2".

BASIC STITCHES: Ch, sl st, sc, dc, tr.

HEEL (make 4)

Row 1: With dk. green, ch 3, sc in second ch from hook, sc in last ch, turn. *(2 sc made)*

Row 2: Ch 1, 2 sc in each st across, turn. *(4)*

Rows 3–5: Ch 1, 2 sc in first st, sc in each st across with 2 sc in last st, turn. *(6, 8, 10)*

Row 6: Ch 1, 2 sc in first st, sc in next 3 sts, 2 sc in next st, sc in next 4 sts, 2 sc in last st, turn. *(13)*

Row 7: Ch 1, sc in first 5 sts, 2 sc in next st, sc in each st across, turn. *(14)*

Rows 8–9: Ch 1, sc in each st across, turn. At end of last row, fasten off.

Match and sew sts on row 9 of two Heel pieces together for seam. Repeat with other two pieces.

SLIPPER SOCK (make 2)

Rnd 1: Starting at toe, with dk. green, ch 10, sc in second ch from hook, sc in next 7 chs, 2 sc in last ch; working on opposite side of ch, sc in next 8 chs, join with sl st in first sc. *(18 sc made)*

Rnd 2: Ch 1, 2 sc in first st, sc in next 8 sts, 2 sc in next st, sc in last 8 sts, join. *(20)*

Rnd 3: Ch 1, 2 sc in first st, sc in next 9 sts, 2 sc in next st, sc in last 9 sts, join. *(22)*

Rnd 4: Ch 1, 2 sc in first st, sc in next 10 sts, 2 sc in next st, sc in last 10 sts, join. *(24)*

Rnd 5: Ch 1, 2 sc in first st, sc in next 11 sts, 2 sc in next st, sc in last 11 sts, join. *(26)*

Rnd 6: Ch 1, 2 sc in first st, sc in next 12 sts, 2 sc in next st, sc in last 12 sts, join. *(28)*

Rnd 7: Ch 1, 2 sc in first st, sc in next 12 sts, 2 sc in each of next 3 sts, sc in next 11 sts, 2 sc in last st, join. Fasten off. *(33)*

Rnd 8: Skip first 9 sts, join off-white with sc in next st, sc in each st around with 2 sc in last st, join. *(34)*

Rnds 9–10: Ch 1, sc in each st around, join. At end of last rnd, fasten off.

Rnd 11: Join dk. green with sc in first st, sc in each st around, join. Fasten off.

Rnd 12: Join med. green with sc in first st, sc in each st around, join. Fasten off.

Rnd 13: Join dk. green with sc in first st, sc in each st around, join. Fasten off.

Rnd 14: Join off-white with sc in first st, sc in each st around with 2 sc in last st, join. *(35)*

Rnd 15: Ch 1, sc in each st around, join.

Rnd 16: Ch 1, sc in each st around with 2 sc in last st, join. Fasten off. *(36)*

Rnd 17: Join burgundy with sc in first st, sc in each st around, join. Fasten off.

Rnd 18: Join rose with sc in first st, sc in each st around, join. Fasten off.

Rnd 19: Join burgundy with sc in first st, sc in each st around with 2 sc in last st, join. Fasten off. *(37)*

Rnd 20: Join off-white with sc in first st, sc in each st around with 2 sc in last st, join. *(38)*

Rnds 21–22: Ch 1, sc in each st around, join. At end of last rnd, fasten off.

Rnd 23: Join dk. green with sc in first st, sc in each st around with 2 sc in last st, join. Fasten off. *(39)*

Rnd 24: Join med. green with sc in first st, sc in each st around, join. Fasten off.

Rnd 25: Join dk. green with sc in first st, sc in each st around with 2 sc in last st, join. Fasten off. *(40)*

Rnd 26: Join off-white with sc in first st, sc in each st around, join.

Rnds 27–28: Ch 1, sc in each st around, join. At end of last rnd, fasten off.

Rnd 29: Join burgundy with sc in first st, sc in each st around with 2 sc in last st, join. Fasten off. *(41)*

Rnd 30: Join rose with sc in first st, sc in each st around, join. Fasten off.

Rnd 31: Join burgundy with sc in first st, sc in each st around, join. Fasten off.

Rnd 32: Join off-white with sc in first st, sc in each st around with 2 sc in last st, join. *(42)*

continued on page 40

Candy Cane Stockings

continued from page 38

Rnds 33–34: Ch 1, sc in each st around, join. At end of last rnd, fasten off.

Rnd 35: For Heel placement, skip first 8 sts, mark next st; skip next 24 sts; for Heel placement, mark next st, skip remaining last 8 sts; with wrong side of sts on Sock facing you, pin row 1 at each end of Heel to marked sts *(see illustration);* working through both thicknesses, join dk. green with sc in last marked st *(remove markers when no longer needed)*, sc in each st across to first marked st; fasten off; turn right side out; to complete Heel, work steps A-F:

 A: Join dk. green with sc in last skipped st on rnd 34 at right-hand side of Heel; working in ends of rows across Heel, evenly space 19 sc across, sc in next skipped st on rnd 34, turn. *(21 sts)*

 B: Ch 1, skip first st, sc in each st across Heel, sc in next skipped st on rnd 34, turn.

 C: Repeat step B 2 times.

 D: Ch 1, sc in each st across Heel, sc in next skipped st on rnd 34, turn. *(22)*

 E: Repeat step D. *(23)*

 F: Ch 1, sc in each st across Heel and in remaining skipped sts on rnd 34, join. Fasten off. *(39)*

Rnd 36: Join med. green with sc in center st on Heel, sc in same st, sc in each st around, join. Fasten off. *(40)*

Rnd 37: Join dk. green with sc in first st, sc in each st around with 2 sc in last st, join. Fasten off. *(41)*

Rnd 38: Join off-white with sc in first st, sc in same st, sc in each st around, join. *(42)*

Rnd 39: Ch 1, sc in each st around, join.

Rnd 40: Ch 1, 2 sc in first st, sc in each st around, join. Fasten off. *(43)*

Rnd 41: Join burgundy with sc in first st, sc in each st around with 2 sc in last st, join. Fasten off. *(44)*

Rnd 42: Join rose with sc in first st, sc in same st, sc in each st around with 2 sc in last st, join. Fasten off. *(46)*

Rnd 43: Join burgundy with sc in first st, sc in each st around, join. Fasten off.

Rnd 44: Join off-white with sc in first st, sc in same st, sc in each st around, join. *(47)*

Rnds 45–46: Ch 1, sc in each st around, join. At end of last rnd, fasten off.

Rnd 47: Join dk. green with sc in first st, sc in each st around, join. Fasten off.

Rnd 48: Join med. green with sc in first st, sc in same st, sc in each st around, join. Fasten off. *(48)*

Rnd 49: Join dk. green with sc in first st, sc in each st around, join. Fasten off.

Rnd 50: Join off-white with sc in first st, sc in same st, sc in each st around with 2 sc in last st, join. *(49)*

Rnd 51: Ch 1, 2 sc in first st, sc in each st around, join. *(50)*

Rnd 52: Ch 1, sc in each st around, join. Fasten off.

Rnd 53: Join burgundy with sc in first st, sc in each st around with 2 sc in last st, join. Fasten off. *(51)*

Rnd 54: Join rose with sc in first st, sc in same st, sc in each st around, join. Fasten off. *(52)*

Rnd 55: Join burgundy with sc in first st, sc in each st around, join. Fasten off.

Rnd 56: Join off-white with sc in first st, sc in each st around with 2 sc in last st, join. *(53)*

Rnds 57–58: Ch 1, 2 sc in first st, sc in each st around, join. At end of last rnd, fasten off. *(54, 55)*

Rnd 59: Join dk. green with sc in first st, sc in each st around with 2 sc in last st, join. Fasten off. *(56)*

Rnd 60: Join med. green with sc in first st, sc in each st around, join. Fasten off.

Rnd 61: Join dk. green with sc in first st, sc in each st around with 2 sc in last st, join. Fasten off. *(57)*

Rnd 62: Join off-white with sc in first st, sc in same st, sc in each st around, join. *(58)*

Rnds 63–64: Ch 1, sc in each st around with 2 sc in last st, join. At end of last rnd, fasten off. *(59, 60)*

Rnd 65: Join burgundy with sc in first st, sc in each st around, join. Fasten off.

Rnd 66: Join rose with sc in first st, sc in each st around with 2 sc in last st, join. Fasten off. *(61)*

Rnd 67: Join burgundy with sc in first st, sc in each st around, join. Fasten off.

Rnd 68: Join off-white with sc in first st, sc in each st around, join.

Rnd 69: Ch 1, sc in each st around, join.

Rnd 70: Ch 1, sc in each st around with 2 sc in last st, join. *(62)*

Rnd 71: (Ch 3—*counts as first dc,* dc) in first st, dc in each st around, join with sl st in top of ch-3. *(63)*

Rnd 72: Ch 1, sc in each st around, join.

Rnd 73: Ch 3, dc in each st around, join.

Rnd 74: Ch 1, sc in each st around, join.

Rnd 75: (Ch 3, dc) in first st, dc in each st around, join. *(64)*

Rnd 76: Ch 1, sc in each st around, join.

Rnds 77–79: Ch 3, dc in each st around, join. At end of last rnd, fasten off.

Rnd 80: With wrong side of rnd 79 facing you, join dk. green with sc in first st, sc in each st around, join.

Rnd 81: Ch 5 *(counts as first tr and ch-1)*, skip next 2 sts, tr in next st; working in front of last tr made, tr in first skipped st *(cross st made),* *ch 1, tr in next st, ch 1, skip next 2 sts, tr in next st; working in front of last tr made, tr in first skipped st *(cross st made)*; repeat from * around, ch 1, join with sl st in fourth ch of ch-5. *(32 ch sps)*

Rnd 82: (Sl st, ch 1, sc) in first ch sp, ch 6, sc in next ch sp, (ch 4, sc in next ch sp, ch 6, sc in next ch sp) around, ch 4, join with sl st in first sc. Fasten off.

Fold last 4 rnds down for cuff. ❄

Child's Trio

continued from page 37

insert hook in st, pull through st, pull ends through fold, tighten *(see illustration)*. Fringe in first and last st and in every other st across first row. Repeat on other end.

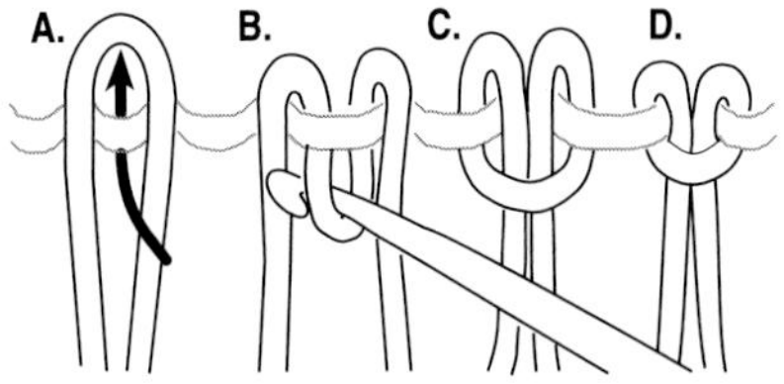

MITTEN (make 2)

Rnd 1: With rose, ch 2, 10 sc in second ch from hook, join with sl st in first sc. *(10 sc made)*

Rnd 2: (Ch 3—*counts as first dc,* dc) in first st, dc inc in each st around, join with sl st in top of ch-3. *(20 dc)*

Rnds 3–9: Ch 3, dc fp around next st, (dc bp around next st, dc fp around next st) around, join.

Rnd 10: Ch 5 *(counts as first dc and ch-2 for thumbhole opening),* dc fp around next st, (dc bp around next st, dc fp around next st) around, join with sl st in third ch of ch-5.

Rnd 11: Ch 3, dc in ch sp of thumbhole opening, dc fp around next st, (dc bp around next st, dc fp around next st) around, join with sl st in top of ch-3. *(21 sts)*

Rnd 12: Ch 3; for **dc dec, dc next 2 sts tog** *(see Stitch Guide);* dc fp around last st of dc dec just worked, (dc bp around next st, dc fp around next st) around, join. *(20)*

Rnd 13: Ch 3, skip dc dec, dc fp around next st, (dc bp around next st, dc fp around next st) around, join. Fasten off.

Rnd 14: For **Edging,** join white with sc in first st, sc in each st around, join with sl st in first sc.

Rnd 15: (Ch 3, 4 dc) in first st, skip next st, sc in next st, skip next st, (5 dc in next st, skip next st, sc in next st, skip next st) around, join with sl st in top of ch-3. Fasten off.

Thumb

NOTE: *Work in continuous rnds; do not turn or join unless otherwise stated. Mark first st of each rnd.*

Rnd 1: Working around thumbhole opening in ends of row and between sts *(see illustration),* join rose with sc between any two sts, evenly space 7 more sc around opening. *(8 sc made)*

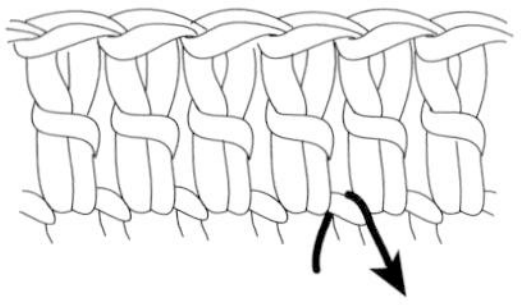

Rnds 2–5: Sc in each st around.

Rnd 6: (Sc dec) around, join with sl st in first sc. Leaving an 8" end, fasten off. *(4 sc)*

With 8" end and tapestry needle, weave end through sts on last rnd, pull to gather, secure end. ❄

Ponder the Poinsettia

The poinsettia is synonymous with the spirit of Christmas, not only because it blooms in wintertime, but because of the legend that associates it with the Christ Child.

This story tells that the poinsettia was once a nondescript roadside weed. Desperate for a gift to offer the baby Jesus, an impoverished little Mexican girl presented the Messiah with an armload of poinsettia branches she had picked and tied together with handwoven twine. Once in His holy presence, the uppermost leaves spontaneously turned a vivid red.

The poinsettia was introduced into the United States by Joel Robert Poinsett, the American Minister to Mexico in the 1920s, for whom the plant was later named.

Snowpeople

Designed by Michele Wilcox

Scarf

FINISHED SIZE: 35" long.

MATERIALS:
- ❑ Worsted yarn:
  - 8 oz. teal
  - 2 oz white
  - Small amount each pink, rust, black and yellow
- ❑ Polyester fiberfill
- ❑ Tapestry needle
- ❑ F and G hooks or hooks needed to obtain gauges

GAUGES: F hook, 9 sc = 2"; 9 sc rows = 2".
G hook, 4 hdc = 1"; 3 hdc rows = 1".

BASIC STITCHES: Ch, sl st, sc, hdc, dc.

FOUNDATION
Row 1: With G hook and teal, ch 26, hdc in second ch from hook, hdc in each ch across, turn. *(25 hdc made)*
NOTE: *Ch-1 at beginning of row is not worked into or counted as a st.*
Rows 2–34: Ch 1, hdc in first st, hdc in each st across, turn.
Row 35: Ch 1, skip first st, hdc in next st, (skip next st, hdc in next st) 11 times, hdc in last st, turn. *(13)*
Rows 36–68: Repeat row 2.
Row 69: Ch 1, 2 hdc in each of first 6 sts, hdc in next st, 2 hdc in each of last 6 sts, turn. *(25)*
Rows 70–104: Repeat row 2. At end of last rnd, fasten off.
For outside edge, mark last st on row 1 and first st on row 104.

HEAD (make 2)
NOTES: *Use F hook for remainder of Scarf.*
Work in continuous rnds; do not join or turn unless otherwise stated. Mark first st of each rnd.
Rnd 1: With white, ch 2, 6 sc in second ch from hook. *(6 sc made)*
Rnd 2: 2 sc in each st around. *(12)*
Rnd 3: (Sc in next st, 2 sc in next st) around. *(18)*
Rnd 4: (Sc in next 2 sts, 2 sc in next st) around. *(24)*
Rnd 5: (Sc in next 3 sts, 2 sc in next st) around. *(30)*
Rnd 6: Sc in first st, 2 sc in next st, (sc in next 4 sts, 2 sc in next st) 5 times, sc in each of last 3 sts. *(36)*
Rnd 7: (Sc in next 5 sts, 2 sc in next st) around. *(42)*
Rnd 8: Sc in first 2 sts, 2 sc in next st, (sc in next 6 sts, 2 sc in next st) 5 times, sc in last 4 sts. *(48)*

Rnd 9: (Sc in next 7 sts, 2 sc in next st) around. *(42)*
Rnd 10: Sc in first 3 sts, 2 sc in next st, (sc in next 8 sts, 2 sc in next st) 5 times, sc in last 5 sts. *(60)*
Rnd 11: (Sc in next 9 sts, 2 sc in next st) around. *(66)*
Rnd 12: Sc in first 4 sts, 2 sc in next st, (sc in next 10 sts, 2 sc in next st) 5 times, sc in last 6 sts, join with sl st in first sc. Fasten off. *(72)*

NOSE (make 2)
Rnd 1: With rust, ch 2, 6 sc in second ch from hook. *(6 sc made)*
Rnd 2: Sc in each st around.
Rnd 3: (Sc in next st, 2 sc in next st) around. *(9)*
Rnds 4–5: Sc in each st around. At end of last rnd, fasten off. Stuff.
Sew one Nose over rnds 1 and 2 on each Head.

LADY'S CHEEK (make 2)
Rnds 1–2: With pink, repeat rnds 1 and 2 of Head. At end of last rnd, join with sl st in first st. Fasten off.
Sew to one Head over rnds 7–11 on each side of Nose.

FINISHING
On each Head, with black, using satin stitch *(see Stitch Guide)*, embroider eyes over two stitches on rnd 6, centered above Nose 1¾" apart.
For **mouth,** with black, embroider seven French knots *(see Stitch Guide)* one stitch apart between rnds 6 and 7 below Nose on each Head.
For **pocket,** leaving 15 sts unsewn on outside edge of each Head, sew one Head over rows 2–18 on each end of Foundation.

HAT (make 2)
Rnds 1–3: With black for Man and teal for Lady, repeat rnds 1–3 of Head.
Rnd 4: Working this rnd in **back lps** *(see Stitch Guide)*, sc in each st around.
Rnds 5–6: Sc in each st around.
Rnd 7: Working this rnd in **front lps**, 2 sc in each st around. *(36)*
Rnd 8: Sc in each st around, join with sl st in first sc. Fasten off. Stuff.

FLOWER
Rnd 1: For **stamen,** with yellow, ch 2, 5 sc in second ch from hook. *(5 sc)*
Rnd 2: Sc in each st around, join with sl st in first sc. Fasten off.

continued on page 44

Snowpeople

continued from page 43

Rnd 3: For **petals,** with white, ch 2, 5 sc in second ch from hook. *(5 sc)*

Rnd 4: Sl st in first st, ch 5, sl st in same st, (sl st, ch 5, sl st) in each st around, join with sl st in first sl st. Fasten off.

Sew rnds 2 and 3 together. Sew Flower over rnds 4–6 on one side of Lady's Hat.

Sew **back lps** of rnd 3 on black Hat over rnds 9–12 above right eye on Man's Head. Sew **back lps** of rnd 3 on teal Hat over rnds 9–12 above left eye on Lady's Head.

Earmuffs

FINISHED SIZE: Cover is 5" across.

MATERIALS:
- ❏ Worsted yarn:
  - 4 oz. white
  - ½ oz. black
  - Small amount each teal, pink, rust, and yellow
- ❏ Thread elastic
- ❏ Earmuffs
- ❏ Polyester fiberfill
- ❏ Tapestry needle
- ❏ F hook or hook needed to obtain gauge

GAUGE: 9 sc = 2"; 9 sc rows = 2".

BASIC STITCHES: Ch, sl st, sc, hdc, dc.

NOTES: Work in continuous rnds; do not join or turn unless otherwise stated. Mark first st of each rnd.

COVER (make 2)

Rnd 1: With white, ch 2, 6 sc in second ch from hook. *(6 sc made)*

Row 2: 2 sc in each st around. *(12)*

Rnd 3: (Sc in next st, 2 sc in next st) around. *(18)*

Rnd 4: (Sc in next 2 sts, 2 sc in next st) around. *(24)*

Rnd 5: (Sc in next 3 sts, 2 sc in next st) around. *(30)*

Rnd 6: (Sc in next 4 sts, 2 sc in next st) around. *(36)*

Rnd 7: (Sc in next 5 sts, 2 sc in next st) around. *(42)*

Rnd 8: (Sc in next 6 sts, 2 sc in next st) around. *(48)*

Rnd 9: (Sc in next 7 sts, 2 sc in next st) around. *(54)*

Rnds 10–13: Sc in each st around.

Rnd 14: (Sc in next 7 sts, sc next 2 sts tog) around. *(48)*

Rnd 15: (Sc in next 6 sts, sc next 2 sts tog) around. *(42)*

Rnd 16: (Sc in next 5 sts, sc next 2 sts tog) around. *(36)*

Rnd 17: (Sc in next 4 sts, sc next 2 sts tog) around, join with sl st in first sc. Fasten off. *(30)*

NOSE (make 2)

Rnd 1: With rust, ch 2, 5 sc in second ch from hook. *(5 sc)*

Rnd 2: Sc in each st around.

Rnds 3–5: 2 sc in first st, sc in each st around. At end of last rnd, join with sl st in first sc. Fasten off. *(8)*

Sew one Nose centered over rnds 2–4 on each Cover.

LADY'S CHEEK (make 2)

Rnd 1: With pink, ch 2, 6 sc in second ch from hook, **do not join.** *(6 sc made)*

Rnd 2: 2 sc in each st around, join with sl st in first st. Fasten off.

Sew to one Cover over rnds 4–7 on each side of Nose.

FINISHING

On each Cover, with black, using satin stitch *(see Stitch Guide),* embroider eyes centered above Nose 1¼" apart over rnds 5–6.

With black, for Man's mouth embroider eight French knots *(see Stitch Guide),* between rnds 5 and 6 centered below Nose one stitch apart on one Cover; for Lady's mouth, embroider six French knots between rnds 4 and 5 centered below Nose one stitch apart on second Cover.

HAT (make 2)

Rnd 1: With black for Man and teal for Lady, ch 2, 6 sc in second ch from hook. *(6 sc made)*

Rnd 2: 2 sc in each st around. *(12)*

Rnd 3: (Sc in next st, 2 sc in next st) around. *(18)*

Rnd 4: (Sc in next 2 sts, 2 sc in next st) around. *(24)*

Rnd 5: (Sc in next 3 sts, 2 sc in next st) around. *(30)*

Rnd 6: Working this rnd in **back lps** *(see Stitch Guide),* sc in each st around.

Rnds 7–9: Sc in each st around.

Rnd 10: Working this rnd in **front lps,** 2 sc in each st around. *(60)*

Rnd 11: Sc in each st around, join with sl st in first sc. Fasten off. Stuff lightly.

FLOWER

Rnd 1: For **stamen,** with yellow, ch 2, 6 sc in second ch from hook. *(6 sc)*

Rnd 2: Sc in each st around, join with sl st in first sc. Fasten off.

Rnd 3: For **petals,** with white, ch 2, 6 sc in second ch from hook. *(6 sc)*

Rnd 4: Sl st in first st, ch 6, sl st in same st, (sl st, ch 6, sl st) in each st around, join with sl st in first sl st. Fasten off.

Sew rnds 2 and 3 together. Sew Flower over rnds 6–9 on side of Lady's Hat.

Sew **back lps** of rnd 8 on black Hat to top of Man's Head over rnds 8–16. Sew **back lps** of rnd 8 on teal Hat to top of Lady's Head over rnds 8–16.

Weave 6½" piece thread elastic in stitches on rnd 17 of each cover. Secure ends.

Place Covers over earmuffs. ❄

Winter Warmers

Sleigh Ride

Our cheeks are nice and rosy and comfy cozy are we. We're snuggled up together like two birds of a feather would be. Let's take the road before us and sing a chorus or two. Come on, it's lovely weather for a sleigh ride together with you.

Angel Afghan

Designed by Ruby Gates

FINISHED SIZE: 53" × 61".

MATERIALS:
- ❑ Worsted yarn:
  - 80 oz. white
  - 10½ oz. lt. rose
- ❑ 700 yds. gold metallic crochet cotton thread
- ❑ C and G hooks or hook needed to obtain gauge

GAUGE: G hook, 4 sc = 1"; 4 sc rows = 1".

BASIC STITCHES: Ch, sl st, sc, dc.

SPECIAL STITCHES: For **cluster (cl)**, yo, insert hook in next st, yo, pull through st, yo, pull through 2 lps on hook, (yo, insert hook in same st, yo, pull through st, yo, pull through 2 lps on hook) 3 times, yo, pull through all 5 lps on hook.

For **sc V st**, (sc, ch 2, sc) in ch sp or st specified in instructions.

For **one corner joining**, sc in ch-2 sp at corner of this Motif, ch 1, drop lp from hook, insert hook in corresponding ch-2 sp at corner of previous Motif, pull dropped lp through ch sp, ch 1, sc in same ch-2 sp on this Motif.

For **ch-2 sp joining**, ch 1, skip next st on this Motif, drop lp from hook, insert hook in corresponding ch-2 sp of previous Motif, pull dropped lp through ch-2 sp, ch 1, sc in next st on this Motif.

For **two corner joining**, sc in ch-2 sp at corner of this Motif, ch 1, drop lp from hook, insert hook in corresponding ch-2 sp of previous Motif, pull dropped lp through ch-2 sp, ch 1, insert hook in corresponding ch-2 sp of adjacent Motif, pull dropped lp through ch sp, ch 1, sc in same ch-2 sp on this Motif.

FIRST ROW
First Angel Motif
Row 1: With G hook and white, ch 62, sc in second ch from hook, sc in each ch across, turn. *(61 sc made)*

Rows 2–5: Ch 1, sc in each st across, turn.

Row 6: Ch 1, sc in first 21 sts, *cl *(see Special Stitches)* in next st, sc in next st; repeat from * 5 more times, sc in each st across, turn.

Rows 7–75: Ch 1, work across according to corresponding rows on graph on page 48, turn. At end of last row, **do not turn**.

Rnd 76: Working around outer edge, ch 1, sc in end of first 75 rows, ch 2; working in remaining lps on

opposite side of starting ch, sc in each ch across, ch 2, sc in end of last 75 rows, ch 2, working across row 75, sc in each st across, ch 2, join with sl st in first sc. Fasten off. *(272)*

Body Trim
Rnd 1: With right side of Motif facing you, with two strands of metallic thread held together and C hook, working between sts around Angel, join with sc at bottom of Angel, sc between each of next 2 sts around Angel to first sc, join with sl st in first sc.

Rnd 2: Ch 1, **sc V st** *(see Special Stitches)* in each st around, join. Fasten off.

Halo Trim
Beginning at one end of Halo, repeat rnds 1 and 2 of Angel Body Trim.

Angel Motif Border
Rnd 1: With right side of Motif facing you, with G hook and one strand of lt. rose and two strands of metallic thread held together, join with sc in first ch-2 sp at top right hand corner of rnd 76, ch 2, sc in same ch-2 sp, sc in each st around with sc V st in each ch-2 sp at corner, join with sl st in first sc. *(280 sc made—63 sc across top and bottom between corner ch sps, 77 sc across each side between corner ch sps)*

Rnd 2: Ch 1, sc in each st around with sc V st in each ch-2 sp at corner, join. *(284 sc—65 sc across each top and bottom, 79 sc across each side)*

Rnd 3: Ch 1, sc in first st, ch 2, skip next st, sc V st in ch-2 sp, *ch 2, skip next st, (sc in next st, ch 2, skip next st) across to next ch-2 sp at corner, sc V st in ch-2 sp at corner; repeat from * 2 more times, ch 2, skip next st, (sc in next st, ch 2, skip next st) around, join. Fasten off.

First Cross Motif
Row 1: With G hook and white, ch 62, sc in second ch from hook, sc in each ch across, turn. *(61 sc made)*

Rows 2–7: Ch 1, sc in each st across, turn.

Row 8: Ch 1, sc in first 28 sts, *cl in next st, sc in next st; repeat from * 2 more times, sc in each st across, turn.

Rows 9–75: Ch 1, work across according to corresponding rows on graph on page 49, turn. At end of last row, **do not turn**.

Rnd 76: Working around outer edge, ch 1, sc in end of first 75 rows, ch 2; working in remaining lps

continued on page 48

Snowflake Afghan

Designed by Kathryn Clark

FINISHED SIZE: Approximately 51" × 51".

MATERIALS:
- ❏ Sport yarn:
  - 30 oz. white
  - 25 oz. blue
- ❏ E hook or hook needed to obtain gauge

GAUGE: Snowflake = ¾" across. Motif rnds 1–3 = 2¾" across.

BASIC STITCHES: Ch, sl st, sc, hdc, dc, tr.

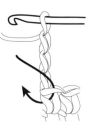

SPECIAL STITCHES: For **picot,** sl st in **back lp** and **left bar** of last sc made *(see illustration).*

NOTE: Label each Snowflake as it is completed.

SNOWFLAKE NO. 1 (make 15)
Rnd 1: With white, ch 6, sl st in first ch to form ring, (sc in ring, ch 2) 6 times, join with sl st in first sc. *(6 ch sps made)*

Rnd 2: Ch 1, *sc in sc, (ch 3, picot—*see Special Stitch*) 2 times, (hdc, dc) in next ch sp, ch 6, sc in fourth ch from hook, ch 5, picot—*corner formed,* ch 4, picot, sl st in next 2 chs of ch-6, sl st in last dc made, hdc in same ch sp as dc; repeat from * around, join. Fasten off. *(6 corners)*

SNOWFLAKE NO. 2 (make 15)
With white, ch 6, sl st in first ch to form ring, ch 10, sc in fourth ch from hook, ch 5, picot—*corner formed,* ch 4, picot, sl st in next 4 chs of ch-10, (*dc in ring, ch 3, sl st in second ch from hook, ch 1*, dc in ring, ch 7, sc in fourth ch from hook, ch 5, picot—*corner formed,* ch 4, picot, sl st in next 3 chs of ch-7, sl st in last dc made) 5 times; repeat between first and second *, join with sl st in third ch of ch-10. Fasten off. *(6 corners)*

SNOWFLAKE NO. 3 (make 14)
With white, ch 6, sl st in first ch to form ring, ch 10, sc in fourth ch from hook, ch 5, picot—*corner formed,* ch 4, picot, ch 3, (dc in ring, ch 3, sl st in last dc made, dc in ring, ch 7, sc in fourth ch from hook, ch 5, picot—*corner formed,* ch 4, picot, ch 3) 5 times, dc in ring, ch 3, sl st in last dc made, join with sl st in third ch of ch-10. Fasten off. *(6 corners)*

SNOWFLAKE NO. 4 (make 15)
With white, ch 6, sl st in first ch to form ring, ch 1, *sc in ring, ch 3, sc in ring, (ch 5, sc in fourth ch from hook) 2 times, ch 5, picot—*corner formed,* ch 4, picot, sl st in next ch, (sl st, ch 4, sl st) in **back lp** and **left bar** of next sc, sl st in next ch; repeat from * 5 more times, join with sl st in first sc. Fasten off. *(6 corners)*

SNOWFLAKE NO. 5 (make 15)
Rnd 1: With white, ch 6, sl st in first ch to form ring, ch 1, (2 sc in ring, ch 3, picot) 6 times, join with sl st in first sc. *(12 sc made)*

Rnd 2: Ch 6, sl st in fourth ch from hook, (ch 7, sc in fourth ch from hook, ch 5, picot—*corner formed,* ch 4, picot, sl st in next ch of ch-7, ch 2, skip next sc on rnd 1, dc in next sc, ch 3, sl st in last dc made) 5 times, ch 7, sc in fourth ch from hook, ch 5, picot—*corner formed,* ch 4, picot, sl st in next ch of ch-7, ch 2, skip last sc on rnd 1, join with sl st in third ch of ch-6. Fasten off. *(6 corners)*

SNOWFLAKE NO. 6 (make 15)
Rnd 1: With white, ch 6, sl st in first ch to form ring, ch 4 *(counts as first dc and ch-1 sp),* (dc in ring, ch 1) 11 times, join with sl st in third ch of ch-4. *(12 ch sps made)*

Rnd 2: Ch 1, *(sc, ch 3, sc) in next ch sp, sc in next ch sp, ch 6, sc in fourth ch from hook, ch 5, picot—*corner formed,* ch 4, picot, sl st in next 2 chs of ch-6, sc in same ch sp on rnd 1; repeat from * 5 more times, join with sl st in first sc. Fasten off. *(6 corners)*

SNOWFLAKE NO. 7 (make 15)
Rnd 1: With white, ch 6, sl st in first ch to form ring, ch 4 *(counts as first sc and ch-3),* (sc in ring, ch 3) 5 times, join with sl st in first ch of ch-4. *(6 ch sps made)*

Rnd 2: Sl st in next ch, *(sc in next ch sp, ch 3, picot, ch 8, sc in fourth ch from hook, ch 5, picot—*corner formed,* ch 4, picot, sl st in next ch of ch-8, ch 3) 6 times, join with sl st in first sc. Fasten off. *(6 corners)*

MOTIF (make one for each Snowflake)
Rnd 1: With blue, ch 6, sl st in first ch to form ring, ch 3 *(counts as first dc),* 11 dc in ring, join with sl st in top of ch-3. *(12 dc made)*

Rnd 2: (Ch 3, dc) in first st, dc in next st, (3 dc in next st, dc in next st) 5 times, dc in same st as ch-3, join. *(24)*

continued on page 55

Santas Afghan

FINISHED SIZE: 44" × 61".

MATERIALS:
- ❑ Worsted yarn:
  - 42 oz. emerald green
  - 16 oz. red
  - 16 oz. white
  - 3½ oz. black
  - 3½ oz. off-white
  - 3½ oz. pink
  - 9 yds. yellow
  - 9 yds. blue
- ❑ Tapestry needle
- ❑ G hook or hook needed to obtain gauge

GAUGE: 4 sc = 1"; 4 sc rows = 1".

BASIC STITCHES: Ch, sl st, sc, tr.

AFGHAN

Motif (make 9)

Row 1: With green, ch 38, sc in second ch from hook and in each ch across, turn. *(37 sc made)*

Rows 2–60: Ch 1, sc in each st across, turn. At end of last row, **do not turn.**

Rnd 61: Working around outer edge, ch 1, sc in each st and in end of each row around with 3 sc in each corner, join with sl st in first sc. Fasten off.

Each square on graph equals one sc. Using cross st *(see illustration)*, embroider each Motif according to graph.

CROSS STITCH

2 4
3 1

Edging

Rnd 1: Join white with sc in any center corner st, (ch 2, sc) in same st as first sc, sc in each st around with (sc, ch 2, sc) in each center corner st, join with sl st in first sc, **turn.** Fasten off.

Rnd 2: Join red with sl st in any corner ch sp, (ch 4, tr, ch 2, 2 tr) in same ch sp as sl st, tr in each st around with (2 tr, ch 2, 2 tr) in each corner ch sp, join with sl st in top of ch-4, **turn.** Fasten off.

Rnd 3: Join white with sc in any corner ch sp, (ch 2, sc) in same ch sp as first sc, sc in each st around with (sc, ch 2, sc) in each corner ch sp, join, **turn.** Fasten off.

Rnd 4: Join green with sl st in any corner ch sp, (ch 4, tr, ch 2, 2 tr) in same ch sp as sl st, tr in each st around with (2 tr, ch 2, 2 tr) in each corner ch sp, join, **turn.** Fasten off.

Rnd 5: Join white with sc in any corner ch sp, 2 sc in same ch sp as first sc, sc in each st around with 3 sc in each corner ch sp, join. Fasten off.

With white, sew **back bars** *(see Stitch Guide)* of stitches on Motifs together three Motifs wide and three Motifs long. Block if desired.

BORDER

Rnd 1: With wrong side facing you, join white with sc in any center corner st, (ch 2, sc) in same st as first sc, sc in each st and in each seam around with (sc, ch 2, sc) in each center corner st, join with sl st in first sc, **turn.**

Rnd 2: Ch 1, sc in first 3 sts, ch 2, sl st in third ch from hook, (sc in next 3 sts, ch 2, sl st in third ch from hook) around with 3 sc in each corner ch sp, join. Fasten off. ❄

CROSS STITCH KEY:

- ■ = RED
- ☐ = WHITE
- ▨ = BLACK
- ▩ = OFF-WHITE
- ▦ = PINK
- ☐ = YELLOW
- ■ = BLUE

Santas & Snowmen Afghans

Designed by Eleanor Albano-Miles

Snowmen Afghan

continued from page 52

Snowmen Afghan

FINISHED SIZE: 49" × 58".

MATERIALS:
- ❏ Worsted yarn:
  - 40 oz. blue
  - 16 oz. white
  - 3½ oz. brown
  - 3½ oz. red
  - 3½ oz. green
  - 3½ oz. orange
  - 3½ oz. black
- ❏ Tapestry needle
- ❏ G hook or hook needed to obtain gauge

GAUGE: 4 sc = 1"; 4 sc rows = 1".

BASIC STITCHES: Ch, sl st, sc, tr.

AFGHAN
Motif (make 9)
Row 1: With blue, ch 43, sc in second ch from hook and in each ch across, turn. *(42 sc made)*

Rows 2–57: Ch 1, sc in each st across, turn. At end of last row, **do not turn.**

Rnd 58: Working around outer edge, ch 1, sc in each st and in end of each row around with 3 sc in each corner, join with sl st in first sc. Fasten off.

Each square on graph equals one sc. Using cross st *(see illustration on page 52)*, embroider each Motif according to graph.

Edging
Rnd 1: Join white with sc in any center corner st, (ch 2, sc) in same st as first sc, sc in each st around with (sc, ch 2, sc) in each center corner st, join with sl st in first sc, **turn.** Fasten off.

Rnd 2: Join green with sl st in any corner ch sp, (ch 4, tr, ch 2, 2 tr) in same ch sp as sl st, tr in each st around with (2 tr, ch 2, 2 tr) in each corner ch sp, join with sl st in top of ch-4, **turn.** Fasten off.

Rnd 3: Join white with sc in any corner ch sp, (ch 2, sc) in same ch sp as first sc, sc in each st around with (sc, ch 2, sc) in each corner ch sp, join, **turn.** Fasten off.

Rnd 4: Join red with sl st in any corner ch sp, (ch 4, tr, ch 2, 2 tr) in same ch sp as sl st, tr in each st around with (2 tr, ch 2, 2 tr) in each corner ch sp, join, **turn.** Fasten off.

Rnd 5: Join white with sc in any corner ch sp, 2 sc in same ch sp as first sc, sc in each st around with 3 sc in each corner ch sp, join. Fasten off.

With white, sew **back lps** *(see Stitch Guide on page 160)* of stitches on Motifs together three Motifs wide and three Motifs long. Block if desired.

BORDER
Rnd 1: With wrong side facing you, join white with sc in any center corner st, (ch 2, sc) in same st as first sc, sc in each st and in each seam around with (sc, ch 2, sc) in each center corner st, join with sl st in first sc, **turn.**

Rnd 2: Ch 1, sc in first 3 sts, ch 2, sl st in second ch from hook, (sc in next 3 sts, ch 2, sl st in second ch from hook) around with 3 sc in each ch sp, join. Fasten off. ❋

CROSS STITCH KEY:

- ☐ = WHITE
- ☐ = BROWN
- ☐ = RED
- ☐ = GREEN
- ☐ = ORANGE
- ☐ = BLACK

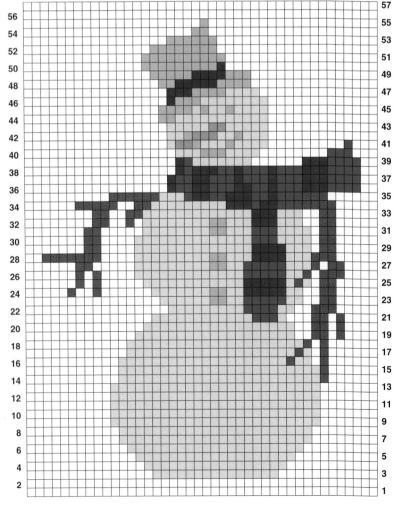

Snowflake Afghan

continued from page 51

Rnd 3: (Ch 3, dc) in first st, dc in next 3 sts, (3 dc in next st, dc in next 3 sts) 5 times, dc in same st as ch-3, join. *(36)*

Rnd 4: (Ch 3, dc) in first st, dc in next 5 sts, (3 dc in next st, dc in next 5 sts) 5 times, dc in same st as ch-3, join. *(48)*

Rnd 5: Ch 1; for **joining sc, with right sides of both pieces facing you, insert hook in any corner on Snowflake and in first st on rnd 4 at same time, complete as sc;** ch 2, skip next st on rnd 4, (sc in next st, ch 2, skip next st) 3 times, *work joining sc, ch 2, skip next st on rnd 4, (sc in next st, ch 2, skip next st) 3 times; repeat from * 4 more times, join with sl st in first sc. *(24 ch sps)*

Rnd 6: Ch 1, *sc in joining sc *(corner st)*, ch 3, (sc in next ch sp, ch 3) 4 times; repeat from * around, join. Fasten off. *(30 ch sps)*

ASSEMBLY

Work Motif Borders positioning Snowflakes to match numbers shown on illustration.

Motif Border No. 1 (make 1)

Join white with sl st in ch sp to the right of any corner st on first Motif, (ch 2, hdc, 2 dc) in same ch sp, tr in corner st, (2 dc, 2 hdc) in next ch sp, *sc in next ch sp, (hdc, 3 dc, hdc) in next ch sp, sc in next ch sp, (2 hdc, 2 dc) in next ch sp, tr in corner st, (2 dc, 2 hdc) in next ch sp; repeat from * 4 more times, sc in next ch sp, (hdc, 3 dc, hdc) in next ch sp, sc in next ch sp, join with sl st in top of ch-2. Fasten off. *(6 tr, 42 dc made)*

Motif Border No. 2 (joins on one, two or three sides)

NOTE: *To* ***work joining,*** *drop lp from hook; with right sides of both pieces facing you, insert hook in corresponding tr or dc on adjacent Motif, return dropped lp to hook, pull through st, sl st in top of last st made on this Motif.*

Join white with sl st in ch sp to the right of any corner st, (ch 2, hdc, 2 dc) in same ch sp; *to **join side,** tr in corner st, work joining *(see Note)*, (2 dc, 2 hdc) in next ch sp, sc in next ch sp, (hdc, 2 dc, work joining, dc, hdc) in next ch sp, sc in next ch sp, (2 hdc, 2 dc) in next ch sp, tr in corner st, work joining; repeat from * one or two more times as needed to join according to assembly illustration; [to complete rnd, (2 dc, 2 hdc) in next ch sp, sc in next ch sp, (hdc, 3 dc, hdc) in next ch sp, sc in next ch sp, (2 hdc, 2 dc) in next ch sp, tr in corner st]; repeat between [ ] around to last 4 ch sps, (2 dc, 2 hdc) in next ch sp, sc in next ch sp, (hdc, 3 dc, hdc) in next ch sp, sc in next ch sp, join with sl st in top of ch-2. Fasten off. *(6 tr, 42 dc made)*

Repeat Motif Border No. 2 until all Motifs are joined according to illustration.

BORDER

Rnd 1: Working around outer edge of assembled Motifs, join white with sc in second st past any joined tr, *(ch 2, sc) in each st around to next joined tr, skip next joined tr; sc in next st on next Motif, ch 2; repeat from * around, join with sl st in first sc.

Rnds 2-4: (Sl st, ch 1, sc) in next ch sp, ch 2, (sc in next ch sp, ch 2) around, join.

Rnd 5: Ch 1, (sc, ch 2, sc) in each ch sp around, join. Fasten off. ❄

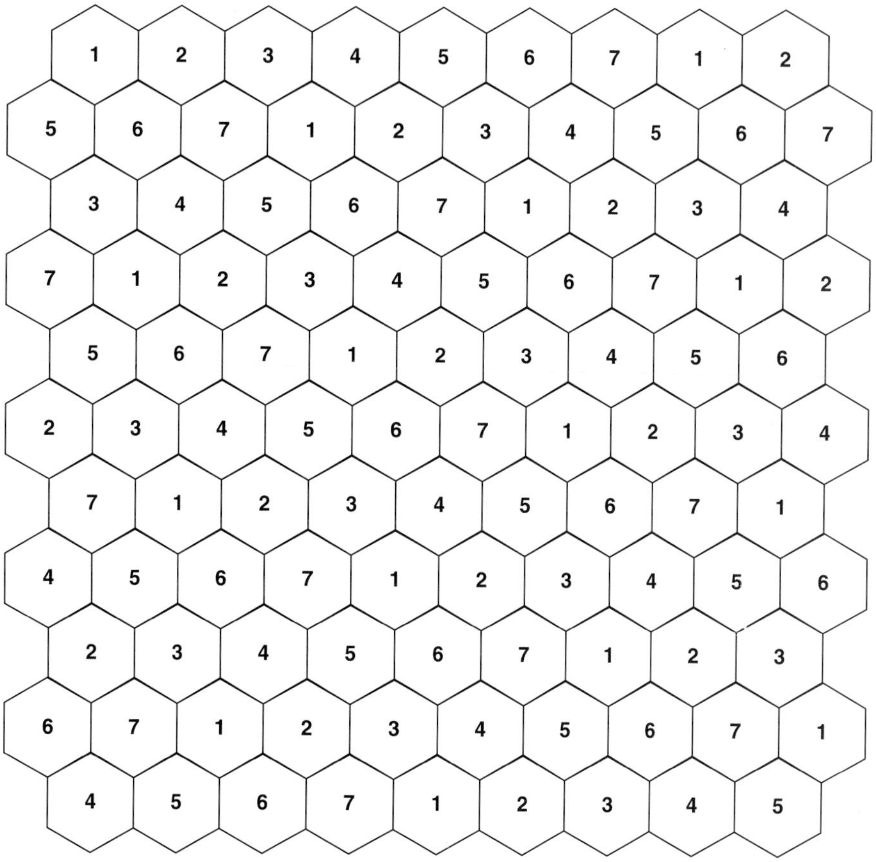

Quick & Easy Holiday Afghan

Designed by Carolyn Christmas

FINISHED SIZE: About 54" × 62".

MATERIALS:
- ❏ Worsted yarn:
  - 35 oz. red
  - 18 oz. white
  - 3 oz. green
  - 3 oz. yellow
- ❏ P Hook or size needed to obtain gauge

GAUGE: With two strands yarn held together, Block rnds 1–2 = 4" across; 3 dc = 2"; 2 dc rows = 3".

BASIC STITCHES: Ch, sl st, sc, hdc, dc.

SPECIAL STITCHES: For **picot**, ch 3, sl st in third ch from hook.

For **popcorn (pc)**, 5 dc in next sc, drop lp from hook, insert hook in top of first dc, pull dropped lp through.

NOTE: Afghan is worked with two strands same-color yarn held together throughout.

SIDE STRIP (make 2)
First Block
Rnd 1: With yellow, ch 2, 8 sc in second ch from hook, join with sl st in first sc. Fasten off. *(8 sc made)*

Rnd 2: Join red with sl st in any st, (ch 3, 4 dc) in same st as sl st, drop lp from hook, insert hook in top of ch-3, pull dropped lp through *(beginning pc made)*, ch 2, **pc** *(see Special Stitches)* in next st, ch 2, (pc, ch 2) in each st around, join with sl st in top of beginning pc. Fasten off. *(8 pc)*

Rnd 3: Join green with sl st in any ch-2 sp, ch 1, (sc, **picot**—see Special Stitches, sc) in same ch-2 sp as sl st, *sc in top of next pc, (sc, picot, sc) in next ch-2 sp; repeat from * around, sc in last pc, join with sl st in first sc. Fasten off. *(24 sc, 8 picots)*

Rnd 4: Working behind picots, join white with sc in first sc after any picot, sc in next 2 sc, ch 1, (sc in next 3 sc, ch 1) around, join.

Rnd 5: Ch 1, sc in first st, (ch 3, skip next st or ch, sc in next st) around, ch 1, join with dc in first sc *(joining ch sp made)*. *(16 ch-sps)*

Rnd 6: Ch 1, sc in joining ch sp, ch 5, sc in same ch sp, *ch 3, (sc in next ch-3 sp, ch 3) 3 times, (sc, ch 5, sc) in next ch sp; repeat from * 3 more times, ch 3, (sc in next ch-3 sp, ch 3) 3 times, join with sl st in first sc. Fasten off.

Second Block
Rnds 1–5: Repeat rnds 1–5 of First Block.

Rnd 6: Ch 1, sc in joining ch sp, ch 2, sl st in any ch-5 sp on last Block made, ch 2, sc in joining sp on Second Block, (ch 1, sl st in next ch-3 sp on last Block, ch 1, sc in next ch-3 sp on Second Block) 4 times, ch 2, sl st in next ch-5 sp on last Block, ch 2, sc in same ch-5 sp on Second Block, *ch 3, (sc in next ch-3 sp, ch 3)

3 times, (sc, ch 5, sc) in next ch-3 sp; repeat from *, ch 3, (sc in next ch-3 sp, ch 3) 3 times, join. Fasten off.

Third–Sixth Blocks
Working on side of Block opposite last joined edge, repeat Second Block.

EDGING
Panels
Row 1: Working across one long edge of one Side Strip, join red with sl st in bottom right corner sp, ch 3, dc in same sp, 2 dc in each sp across ending with 2 dc in corner sp at end of Side Strip, turn.

Rows 2–7: Ch 3, dc in each dc across, turn. At end of row 7, fasten off.

Beginning at top left corner sp and working across remaining long edge of Side Strip, repeat rows 1–7.

ASSEMBLY
To join Side Strips, hold Strips wrong sides together matching sts; join red with sl st in first st on first Side, sl st in first st on second Side, (sl st in next st on first Side, sl st in next st on second Side) across. Fasten off.

BORDER
Rnd 1: Working around outer edge, join red with sc in first st of last Edging row on either Side, 2 sc in same st, sc around all edges, working 2 sc in end of each dc row, 2 sc in each ch sp of Blocks, sc in each dc along sides and 3 sc in each corner, join with sl st in first sc. Fasten off.

NOTE: *On next rnd, it may be necessary to skip one more or fewer stitches than indicated before corners to place (sc, ch 3, sc) in center st of each corner.*

Rnd 2: Join yellow with sc in center sc at any corner, ch 3, sc in same corner, (ch 2, skip 2 sts, sc in next st) around with (sc, ch 3, sc) in center st of each corner, join. Fasten off.

Rnd 3: Join red in sl st in first corner ch-3 sp, ch 3 *(counts as dc)*, 4 dc in same sp as ch-3, (3 dc in next ch-2 sp) around with 5 dc in each corner, join with sl st in top of ch-3. Fasten off.

Rnd 4: Join green with sl st in third dc of 5-dc group at any corner, (ch 4, dc, ch 1, dc) in same st, *[ch 1, skip next 2 sts, sc in next sp between 3-dc groups, (ch 1, skip next st, dc in next st, ch 1, skip next st, sc in next sp between 3-dc groups) across to next corner, ch 1], (dc, ch 1, dc, ch 1, dc) in center dc of 5-dc group at corner; repeat from * 2 times; repeat between [ ], join with sl st in third ch of ch-4. Fasten off.

Rnd 5: Join white with sl st in first dc of any corner, (ch 3, picot, dc) in same st; skipping ch-1 sps, (dc, picot, dc) in each of next 2 dc, *[hdc in each ch-1 sp, sc in each sc and (dc, picot, dc) in each dc across to next corner]; skipping ch-1 sps, (dc, picot, dc) in each of next 3 dc at corner; repeat from * 2 more times; repeat between [ ], join with sl st in top of ch-3. Fasten off. ✺

Poinsettia Afghan

Designed by Shirley Zebrowski

FINISHED SIZE: 60" × 62".

MATERIALS:
- ❑ Worsted yarn:
    - 40 oz. winter white
    - 20 oz. each red and green
- ❑ Tapestry needle
- ❑ H and J hooks or hook needed to obtain gauge

GAUGE: H hook, 9 sc = 3"; 9 sc rows = 3". Each Motif is 7¾" × 7½".

BASIC STITCHES: Ch, sl st, sc.

MOTIF (make 32 white/red; 32 white/green)

NOTE: *When **changing colors** (see Stitch Guide), always change color in last st made, drop unused color to wrong side of work, pick up when needed.*

Row 1: With H hook and white, ch 24, sc in second ch from hook, sc in next 21 chs changing to next color *(see Note)*, sc in last ch, turn. *(23 sc made)*

Row 2: Ch 1, sc in first 2 sts changing to white, sc in last 21 sts, turn.

Row 3: Ch 1, sc in first 20 sts changing to next color, sc in last 3 sts, turn.

Row 4: Ch 1, sc in first 4 sts changing to white, sc in last 19 sts, turn.

Row 5: Ch 1, sc in first 18 sts changing to next color, sc in last 5 sts, turn.

Row 6: Ch 1, sc in first 6 sts changing to white, sc in last 17 sts, turn.

Row 7: Ch 1, sc in first 16 sts changing to next color, sc in last 7 sts, turn.

Row 8: Ch 1, sc in first 8 sts changing to white, sc in last 15 sts, turn.

Row 9: Ch 1, sc in first 14 sts changing to next color, sc in last 9 sts, turn.

Row 10: Ch 1, sc in first 10 sts changing to white, sc in last 13 sts, turn.

Row 11: Ch 1, sc in first 12 sts changing to next color, sc in last 11 sts, turn.

Row 12: Ch 1, sc in first 12 sts changing to white, sc in last 11 sts, turn.

Row 13: Ch 1, sc in first 10 sts changing to next color, sc in last 13 sts, turn.

continued on page 60

Poinsettia Afghan

continued from page 58

Row 14: Ch 1, sc in first 14 sts changing to white, sc in last 9 sts, turn.

Row 15: Ch 1, sc in first 8 sts changing to next color, sc in last 15 sts, turn.

Row 16: Ch 1, sc in first 16 sts changing to white, sc in last 7 sts, turn.

Row 17: Ch 1, sc in first 6 sts changing to next color, sc in last 17 sts, turn.

Row 18: Ch 1, sc in first 18 sts changing to white, sc in last 5 sts, turn.

Row 19: Ch 1, sc in first 4 sts changing to next color, sc in last 19 sts, turn.

Row 20: Ch 1, sc in first 20 sts changing to white, sc in last 3 sts, turn.

Row 21: Ch 1, sc in first 2 sts changing to next color, sc in last 21 sts, turn.

Row 22: Ch 1, sc in first 22 sts changing to white, sc in last st. Fasten off both colors.

ASSEMBLY

Arrange Motifs according to assembly illustration, matching sts to sts and rows to rows; with tapestry needle and matching colors, sew Motifs together.

EDGING

Working around outer edge, with J hook and one strand each of red and green held together as one, join with sc in any st at corner, 2 sc in same st, sc in each st, in end of each row and in each remaining lp on opposite side of starting ch around with 3 sc in each corner, join with sl st in first sc. Fasten off. ❈

ASSEMBLY ILLUSTRATION

Home for the Holidays

I'll Be Home For Christmas

I'll be home for Christmas.
You can count on me.
Please have snow and mistletoe
and presents on the tree.
Christmas Eve will find me
where the love light gleams.
I'll be home for Christmas
if only in my dreams.

Designed by Cynthia Harris

Baby Jesus & Manger

FINISHED SIZES: Baby Jesus is approximately 3" long. Manger is approximately 3" × 5".

MATERIALS:
- ❑ Worsted yarn:
    - 2 oz. gold
    - 1 oz. med. brown
    - Small amount each peach, white and dk. tan
- ❑ Pink and black embroidery floss
- ❑ 5" square cardboard
- ❑ Polyester fiberfill
- ❑ Craft glue
- ❑ Embroidery and tapestry needles
- ❑ F hook or hook needed to obtain gauge

GAUGE: 9 sc = 2"; 9 sc rows = 2".

BASIC STITCHES: Ch, sl st, sc, hdc.

NOTE: Work in continuous rnds; do not join or turn unless otherwise stated. Mark first st of each rnd.

BABY JESUS

Rnd 1: With peach, ch 2, 6 sc in second ch from hook. *(6 sc made)*

Rnd 2: 2 sc in each st around. *(12)*

Rnd 3: (Sc in next 3 sts, 2 sc in next st) around. *(15)*

Rnds 4–6: Sc in each st around. Stuff. Continue stuffing as you work.

Rnd 7: (Sc in next 3 sts, sc next 2 sts tog) around. *(12)*

Rnd 8: (Sc in next st, sc next 2 sts tog) around, join with sl st in first sc. *(8)* Fasten off.

Rnd 9: Join white with sc in first st, 2 sc in next st, (sc in next st, 2 sc in next st) around. *(12)*

Rnd 10: (Sc in next 2 sts, 2 sc in next st) around. *(16)*

Rnds 11–14: Sc in each st around.

Rnd 15: (Sc in next 2 sts, sc next 2 sts tog) around. *(12)*

Rnd 16: (Sc in next st, sc next 2 sts tog) around. *(8)*

Rnd 17: (Sc next 2 sts tog) around, join with sl st in first sc. Leaving an 8" strand for sewing, fasten off. Sew opening closed.

Facial Features

With black floss, using straight stitch *(see Stitch Guide)*, embroider eyes between rnds 4 and 5 of Head one stitch apart. With peach, embroider nose between rnds 5 and 6 centered between eyes. With pink floss, embroider mouth between rnds 6 and 7 centered below nose.

SWADDLING CLOTH

Row 1: With white, ch 10, sc in second ch from hook, sc in each ch across, turn. *(9 sc)*

Row 2: Ch 1, sc in each st across, turn.

Row 3: Ch 1, sc in first st, (sc in next st on row before last, skip st on last row behind last sc, sc in next st) across, turn.

Rows 4–6: Ch 1, sc in each st across, turn.

Row 7: Ch 1, sc in first st, *sc around post of next st on row before last *(see illustration)*, skip st on last row behind last sc, sc in next st; repeat from * across, turn.

POST OF SC

Rows 8–10: Ch 1, sc in each st across, turn.

Rows 11–40: Repeat rows 3–10 consecutively, ending with row 8. Fasten off.

Fold in half crosswise. Sew rows 1 and 40 together. Sew ends of rows together on one side. Place Baby inside.

Tie

Cut a strand of dk. tan 52" long. Fold in half, tie knot in ends. Place one end over doorknob; holding ends securely, twist very tightly in one direction. Still holding ends, fold in half and let twist from fold naturally. Cut from doorknob, tie knot 1" from each end. Trim ends even.

Tie around Swaddling Cloth under Baby's chin.

MANGER

Side (make 2)

Row 1: With med. brown, ch 21, sc in second ch from hook, sc in each ch across, turn. *(20 sc)*

Row 2: Working this row in **back lps** *(see Stitch Guide)*, ch 1, sc in each st across, turn.

Row 3: Working this row in **front lps**, ch 2 *(counts as first hdc)*, hdc in each st across, turn.

Rows 4–7: Repeat rows 2 and 3 alternately. At end of last row, fasten off.

End (make 2)

Row 1: With med. brown, ch 13, sc in second ch from hook, sc in each ch across, turn. *(12 sc)*

Rows 2–7: Repeat rows 2–7 of Side.

Bottom

Row 1: With med. brown, ch 21, sc in second ch from hook, sc in each ch across, turn. *(20 sc)*

Rows 2–12: Ch 1, sc in each st across, turn. At end of last row, fasten off.

continued on page 64

Crochet Creche

continued from page 63

Using Bottom for pattern, cut piece of cardboard. Lay aside.

Sew short edges of Sides and Ends together forming a box. Sew Bottom to bottom of Sides and Ends.

Corner (make 4)
Row 1: With med. brown, ch 10, sc in second ch from hook, sc in each ch across. Fasten off. *(9 sc)*

Row 2: Working in starting ch on opposite side of row 1, join with sc in first ch, sc in each ch across. Fasten off.

Sew one Corner over each corner seam through **back lps.**

Lining Side (make 2)
Row 1: With gold, ch 20, sc in second ch from hook, (ch 1, skip next ch, sc in next ch) across, turn. *(10 sc, 9 ch sps made)*

Rows 2–7: Ch 1, sc in first st, (ch 1, skip next ch, sc in next st) across, turn. At end of last row, fasten off.

Lining End (make 2)
Row 1: With gold, ch 12, sc in second ch from hook, (ch 1, skip next ch, sc in next ch) across, turn. *(6 sc, 5 ch sps made)*

Rows 2–7: Repeat rows 2–7 of Lining Side.

Lining Bottom
Row 1: With gold, ch 20, sc in second ch from hook, sc in each ch across, turn. *(19 sc made)*

Rows 2–7: Ch 1, sc in each st across, turn. At end of last row, fasten off.

Hay
For each fringe, cut one strand of gold 4½" long. Fold in half, insert hook in ch sp, pull fold through sp, pull ends through fold, tighten.

Fringe in each ch–1 sp on each Side and End.

Finishing
With Hay on inside, sew short edges of Lining Sides and Lining Ends together forming a box. Sew Lining Bottom to bottom of Lining Sides and Lining Ends.

Glue cardboard in bottom of Manger, cover with 1" of fiberfill. Insert Lining into Manger, with med. brown, easing to fit, sc top edge of Lining to top edge of Manger. Place Baby in Manger.

Mary

FINISHED SIZE: Approximately 9" tall.

MATERIALS:
- ❏ Worsted yarn:
  - 2½ oz. lt. purple
  - 1 oz. orchid
  - Small amount each peach, white, black, med. brown and lt. rose
- ❏ Polyester fiberfill
- ❏ 3" plastic or cardboard circle
- ❏ Tapestry needle
- ❏ F and G hooks or hook needed to obtain gauges

GAUGES: **F hook,** 9 sc = 2"; 9 sc rows = 2". **G hook,** 4 sc = 1"; 4 sc rows = 1".

BASIC STITCHES: Ch, sl st, sc.

NOTE: Work in continuous rnds; do not join or turn unless otherwise stated. Mark first st of each rnd.

HEAD & BODY
Rnd 1: With G hook and peach, ch 2, 8 sc in second ch from hook. *(8 sc made)*

Rnd 2: 2 sc in each st around. *(16)*

Rnd 3: (Sc in next st, 2 sc in next st) around. *(24)*

Rnds 4–7: Sc in each st around.

Rnd 8: Sc in first 9 sts, (sc next 2 sts tog) 3 times, sc in last 9 sts. *(21)*

Rnd 9: Sc in first 8 sts; for **Cheek,** 3 sc in each of next 2 sts; sc in next st; for **Cheek,** 3 sc in each of next 2 sts; sc in last 8 sts. *(29)*

Rnd 10: Sc in each st around.

Rnd 11: (Sc in next st, sc next 2 sts tog) 9 times, sc last 2 sts tog. *(19)* Stuff Head shaping Cheeks. Continue stuffing as you work.

Rnd 12: (Sc next 2 sts tog) 9 times, sc last st and first st of same rnd tog. *(9)*

Rnds 13–14: Sc in each st around. At end of last rnd, join with sl st in first sc. Fasten off.

Rnd 15: With F hook and lt. purple, join with sc in any st, sc in same st, sc in next 2 sts, (2 sc in next st, sc in next 2 sts) 2 times. *(12)*

Rnd 16: (Sc in next st, 2 sc in next st) around. *(18)*

Rnd 17: Sc in each st around.

Rnd 18: (Sc in next 5 sts, 2 sc in next st) around. *(21)*

Rnd 19: Sc in each st around.

Rnd 20: (Sc in next 6 sts, 2 sc in next st) around. *(24)*

Rnd 21: Sc in each st around.

Rnd 22: (Sc in next 7 sts, 2 sc in next st) around. *(27)*

Rnd 23: Sc in each st around.

Rnd 24: (Sc in next 8 sts, 2 sc in next st) around. *(30)*

Rnd 25: Sc in each st around.

Rnd 26: (Sc in next 9 sts, 2 sc in next st) around. *(33)*

Rnd 27: Sc in each st around.

Rnd 28: (Sc in next 10 sts, 2 sc in next st) around. *(36)*

Rnd 29: Sc in each st around.

Rnd 30: (Sc in next 11 sts, 2 sc in next st) around. *(39)*

Rnd 31: Sc in each st around.

Rnd 32: (Sc in next 12 sts, 2 sc in next st) around. *(42)*

Rnd 33: Sc in each st around.

Rnd 34: (Sc in next 13 sts, 2 sc in next st) around. *(45)*

Rnd 35: Sc in each st around.

Rnd 36: (Sc in next 14 sts, 2 sc in next st) around. *(48)*

Rnds 37–39: Sc in each st around. At end of last rnd, join with sl st in first sc. Fasten off.

continued on page 65

BASE

Rnd 1: With F hook and lt. purple, ch 2, 6 sc in second ch from hook. *(6 sc)*

Rnds 2–3: 2 sc in each st around. *(12, 24)*

Rnd 4: (Sc in next 2 sts, 2 sc in next st) around. *(32)*

Rnd 5: (Sc in next 3 sts, 2 sc in next st) around. *(40)*

Rnd 6: (Sc in next 4 sts, 2 sc in next st) around, join with sl st in first sc. Fasten off. *(48)*

Hold Base and Body wrong sides together with plastic or cardboard circle between, matching sts; working through both thicknesses, join lt. purple with sc in any st; for **reverse sc (see Stitch Guide), working from left to right, insert hook in next st to right, complete as sc;** reverse sc in each st around, join with sl st in first sc. Fasten off.

ARM (make 2)

Rnd 1: With F hook and lt. purple, ch 2, 6 sc in second ch from hook. *(6 sc made)*

Rnd 2: (Sc in next st, 2 sc in next st) around. *(9)*

Rnds 3–8: Sc in each st around.

Rnd 9: (Sc in next 2 sts, 2 sc in next st) around. *(12)*

Rnd 10: (Sc in next 3 sts, 2 sc in next st) around. *(15)*

Rnd 11: (Sc in next 4 sts, 2 sc in next st) around. *(18)*

Rnd 12: Sc in each st around, join with sl st in first sc. Fasten off.

Hand

Rnd 1: Working this rnd in **back lps** *(see Stitch Guide),* with F hook and peach, join with sc in second st of rnd 12 on Arm, sc in next 5 sts leaving remaining sts unworked, join with sl st in first sc. *(6 sc)*

Rnd 2: Ch 1, sc in each st around.

Rnd 3: Sc in each st around. At end of last rnd, join with sl st in first sc. Leaving an 8" strand for weaving, fasten off.

Weave strand through sts of rnd 3, pull to gather. Secure strand.

Sew Arms to sides of Body.

EYES & NOSE

With peach, using satin stitch *(see Stitch Guide),* embroider Nose on rnd 9 of Head between Cheeks.

To sculpture face, with peach, insert needle from back of Head to one side of Nose on row above, make small stitch, pull needle out at beginning, pull slightly for eye indentation. Insert needle back through Head to other side of Nose on row above, make small stitch, pull needle out at beginning, pull slightly for other eye indentation, secure ends.

With white, using satin stitch, working side to side, embroider Eyes on eye indentations. With black, working up and down, embroider pupil at center of each Eye.

MOUTH

With lt. rose, using satin stitch, embroider Mouth centered one row below Nose.

HAIR

Cut 14 strands med. brown each 8" long. Starting at rnd 3 in front of Head, sew center of strands down center top of Head forming a part.

Gather strands together on each side of Head and sew in place.

MANTLE

Row 1: With G hook and orchid, ch 55, sc in second ch from hook, sc in each ch across, turn. *(54 sc)* Fasten off.

Row 2: Join lt. purple with sc in first st, sc in each st across, turn. Fasten off.

Row 3: Join orchid with sc in first st, sc in next st on row before last, (sc in next st on last row, sc in next st on row before last) across, **do not turn.** Fasten off.

Rnd 4: Join lt. purple with sc in first st, sc in next st, ch 2, (sc in next 2 sts, ch 2) across, 2 sc in end of row 2, ch 2; working in starting ch on opposite side of row 1, (sc in next 2 chs, ch 2) across, 2 sc in end of row 2, ch 2, join with sl st in first sc. Fasten off.

Place Mantle around one shoulder and tack ends together in front.

HOODED CAPE

Row 1: With G hook and lt. purple, ch 72, sc in second ch from hook, sc in each ch across, turn. *(71 sc made)*

Row 2: Ch 1, sc in each st across, turn. Fasten off.

Row 3: Join orchid with sc in first st, sc in each st across, turn.

Row 4: Ch 1, sc in each st across, turn. Fasten off.

Row 5: Join lt. purple with sc in first st, sc in next st three rows below, (sc in next st on last row, sc in next st three rows below) across to last st on last row, sc in last st, turn.

Row 6: Ch 1, sc in each st across, turn. Fasten off.

Rows 7–13: Repeat rows 3–6 consecutively, ending with row 5. At end of last row, fasten off.

Fold last row in half matching sts, starting at fold sew together through **back lps,** leaving 10 sts at each end unsewn.

Row 14: Working in starting ch on opposite side of row 1, join orchid with sc in first ch, sc in next ch, ch 2, (sc in each of next 2 ch, ch 2) across to last ch, sc in last ch. Fasten off.

Place Cape on Mary and tack in place as shown in photo.

Joseph

FINISHED SIZE: Approximately 8½" tall.

MATERIALS:

❑ Worsted yarn:
   2 oz. burgundy
   Small amount each peach, black, white, rust and dk. tan
❑ Polyester fiberfill
❑ 3" plastic or cardboard circle
❑ Tapestry needle
❑ F and G hooks or hook needed to obtain gauge

continued on page 66

Crochet Creche

continued from page 65

GAUGES: F hook, 9 sc = 2"; 9 sc rows = 2".
G hook, 4 sc = 1"; 4 sc rows = 1".

BASIC STITCHES: Ch, sl st, sc, dc.

NOTE: Work in continuous rnds; do not join or turn unless otherwise stated. Mark first st of each rnd.

HEAD & BODY
Rnds 1–34: With peach and burgundy, work rnds 1–34 of Mary's Head & Body. At end of last rnd, join with sl st in first sc. Fasten off.
Rnd 35: Join dk. tan with sc in first st, sc in each st around.
Rnd 36: (Sc in next 14 sts, 2 sc in next st) around, join with sl st in first sc. *(48)* Fasten off.
Rnd 37: Join burgundy with sc in first st, sc in each st around.
Rnds 38–39: Sc in each st around. At end of last rnd, join with sl st in first sc. Fasten off.

BASE, ARM & HANDS
With peach and burgundy, work same as Mary's Base, Arm and Hands.

EYES & NOSE
Work same as Mary's Eyes and Nose.

HAIR
With rust, using satin stitch, embroider top, sides and back of Head until completely covered, framing face; embroider rnds 10–13 for beard as shown in photo.

MUSTACHE
With F hook and rust, ch 2, sl st in second ch from hook, ch 3, dc in same ch as sl st, ch 3, dc in top of last dc made, ch 1, sl st in top of last dc made. Fasten off.
Tack below Nose.

MANTLE
Row 1: With G hook and burgundy, ch 41, sc in second ch from hook, sc in each ch across, turn. *(40 sc made)*
Rows 2–4: Ch 1, sc in each st across, turn. At end of last row, fasten off.
Row 5: Join dk. tan with sc in first st, sc in each st across, turn.
Row 6: Ch 1, sc in each st across, turn. Fasten off.
Row 7: Working in starting ch on opposite side of row 1, join dk. tan with sc in first ch, sc in each ch across, turn.
Row 8: Ch 1, sc in each st across. Fasten off.
Place Mantle around one shoulder and tack ends together in front.

Ram, Ewe & Lambs

FINISHED SIZES: Ram is approximately 5½" tall. Ewe is approximately 4¼" tall. Lambs are approximately 3½" tall.

MATERIALS:
❑ Worsted yarn:
    4½ oz. off-white
    Small amount tan
❑ Sport yarn:
    3 oz. off-white
    Small amount black
❑ Polyester fiberfill
❑ Tapestry needle
❑ E and F hooks or hooks needed to obtain gauges

GAUGES: E hook and sport yarn, 5 berry sts and 4 sc = 2"; 5 berry st rows = 1".
F hook and worsted yarn, 2 berry sts and 2 sc = 1"; 4 berry st rows = 1".

BASIC STITCHES: Ch, sl st, sc.

NOTES: Work in continuous rnds; do not join or turn unless otherwise stated. Mark first st of each rnd.
Work Ram and Ewe with F hook. Work Lamb with E hook.

RAM
Body
Rnd 1: Starting at chest, with off-white worsted, ch 2, 6 sc in second ch from hook. *(6 sc)*
NOTE: *For* **berry st (bs)**, *insert hook in st, yo, pull through st (2 lps on hook, keep first lp on hook); working with second lp only, ch 3; yo, pull through 2 lps on hook, pushing bs to right side of work.*
Rnd 2: *Sc in next st, **bs** (see Note) in same st as last sc; repeat from * around. *(12 sts).*
Rnd 3: *Sc in next st, (bs, sc) in next st, bs in next st, (sc, bs) in next st; repeat from * 2 more times. *(18 sts)*
Rnd 4: *Sc in next st, bs in next st, (sc, bs) in next st; repeat from * 4 more times, sc in next st, bs in next st, sc in last st. *(23 sts)*
Rnd 5: (Bs in next st, sc in next st) around to last st, bs in last st.
Rnd 6: (Sc in next st, bs in next st) around to last st, sc in last st.
Rnds 7–16: Repeat rnds 5 and 6 alternately.
Rnd 17: (Bs in next st, sc in next st, bs in next st, sc next 2 sts tog) 4 times, bs in next st, sc last 2 sts tog. *(18)*. Stuff.
Rnd 18: (Bs in next st, sc next 2 sts tog) around, join with sl st in first st. Leaving an 8" strand for weaving, fasten off.
Weave strand through sts of last rnd, pull to gather. Secure strand.

Head
Rnd 1: With off-white worsted, ch 2, 6 sc in second ch from hook. *(6 sc)*

Rnd 2: (Sc in next st, 2 sc in next st) around. *(9)*

Rnd 3: (Sc in next 2 sts, 2 sc in next st) around. *(12)*

Rnds 4–5: Sc in each st around.

Rnd 6: (2 sc in next st, sc in next 3 sts) around. *(15)*

Rnd 7: (2 sc in next st, sc in next 6 sts) 2 times, sc in last st. *(17)*

Rnds 8–9: Sc in each st around.

Rnds 10–13: Repeat rnds 6 and 5 of Body alternately.

Rnd 14: (Sc in next st, bs in next st) 3 times, sc next 2 sts tog, (sc in next st, bs in next st) 3 times, sc in next st, sc last 2 sts tog. *(15 sts)* Stuff.

Rnd 15: (Bs in next st, sc next 2 sts tog) around, join with sl st in first sc. Leaving an 8" strand for weaving, fasten off.

Weave strand through sts of last rnd, pull to gather. Secure strand.

Sew rnds 10–13 of Head to Body.

Leg (make 4)

Rnd 1: With off-white worsted, ch 2, 6 sc in second ch from hook. *(6 sc)*

Rnd 2: (Sc in next st, 2 sc in next st) around. *(9)*

Rnds 3–8: Sc in each st around.

Rnds 9–11: Repeat rnds 6 and 5 of Body alternately, ending with rnd 6. At end of last rnd, join with sl st in first sc. Leaving an 8" strand for weaving, fasten off. Stuff.

Weave strand through sts of last rnd, pull to gather. Secure strand.

Sew two Legs to bottom front of Body; sew two to bottom back of Body.

Ear (make 2)

With off-white worsted, ch 6, sc in second ch from hook, sc in each ch across. Fasten off.

With back side of sts facing you, sew Ears to top of Head 2" apart.

Horn (make 2)

Row 1: With tan, ch 11, sc in second ch from hook, sc in each ch across, turn. *(10 sc)*

Row 2: Ch 1, sc in each st across. Fasten off.

Fold lengthwise, sew sts of row 2 and starting ch together.

Sew to top of Head in front of Ears 1" apart. Curl Horns under.

Tail

Rnd 1: With off-white, ch 2, 6 sc in second ch from hook. *(6 sc)*

Rnds 2–3: Sc in each st around. At end of last rnd, join with sl st in first sc.

Row 4: Flatten last rnd; working through both thicknesses, ch 1, sc in each st across. Fasten off.

With back side of last row facing you, sew to back of Body.

Facial Features

With black, using French knot *(see Stitch Guide)*, embroider eyes on rnd 8 of Head ¾" apart. Using fly stitch *(see illustration)*, embroider mouth centered between eyes on rnd 1.

FLY STITCH

1.   2.

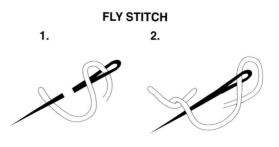

EWE

Body

Rnds 1–3: Work rnds 1–3 of Ram's Body.

Rnd 4: *(Bs in next st, sc in next st) 2 times, (bs, sc) in next st; repeat from * 2 more times, bs in next st, sc in next st, bs in last st. *(21 sts)*

Rnds 5–13: Work rnds 6 and 5 of Ram's Body alternately, ending with rnd 6.

Rnd 14: (Bs in next st, sc next 2 sts tog) around, join with sl st in first sc. *(14)* Leaving an 8" strand for weaving, fasten off. Stuff.

Weave strand through sts of last rnd, pull to gather. Secure strand.

Head

Rnds 1–5: Work rnds 1–5 of Ram's Head.

Rnd 6: *Sc in next st, bs in next st, sc in next st, (bs, sc) in next st*, bs in next st, sc in next st, bs in next st, (sc, bs) in next st; repeat between first and second *. *(15 sts)*

Rnds 7–11: Work rnds 5 and 6 of Ram's Body alternately, ending with rnd 5. Stuff.

Rnd 12: (Sc next 2 sts tog, bs in next st) around, join with sl st in first sc. Leaving an 8" strand for weaving, fasten off. *(10)*

Weave strand through sts of last rnd, pull to gather. Secure strand.

Sew rnds 8–10 of Head to Body.

Leg (make 4)

Rnd 1: With off-white worsted, ch 2, 6 sc in second ch from hook. *(6 sc)*

Rnd 2: 2 sc in first st, sc in last 5 sts. *(7)*

Rnds 3–6: Sc in each st around.

Rnds 7–9: Repeat rnds 6 and 5 of Ram's Body alternately, ending with rnd 6. At end of last rnd, join with sl st in first sc. Leaving an 8" strand for weaving, fasten off. Stuff.

Weave strand through sts of last rnd, pull to gather. Secure strand.

Sew two Legs to bottom front of Body; sew two to bottom back of Body.

Ear (make 2)

With off-white, ch 5, sc in second ch from hook, sc in each ch across. Fasten off.

With back side of sts facing you, sew Ears to top of Head 1¾" apart.

Tail

Work same as Ram's Tail.

continued on page 68

 **67**

Crochet Creche

continued from page 67

Facial Features

With black, using French knot, embroider eyes on rnd 5 of Head ½" apart. Using fly stitch, embroider mouth centered between eyes on rnd 1.

LAMB

With sport yarn, work same as Ewe.

BLACK-FACED LAMB

Body

With sport yarn, work same as Ewe's Body.

Head

Rnds 1–5: With black, work rnds 1–5 of Ram's Head. At end of last rnd, change to off-white sport *(see Stitch Guide)* in last st made.

Rnds 6–12: Work rnds 6–12 of Ewe's Head.

Leg (make 4)

Rnds 1–6: With black, work rnds 1–6 of Ewe's Leg. At end of last rnd, change to off-white sport in last st made.

Rnds 7–9: Work rnds 7–9 of Ewe's Leg.

Ear & Tail

With black, work same as Ewe's Ear and Ram's Tail.

Donkey

FINISHED SIZE: Approximately 5" tall.

MATERIALS:
- ❑ Worsted yarn:
  - 2 oz. lt. gray
  - Small amount each dk. gray, off-white and dk. brown
- ❑ Dk. brown sewing thread
- ❑ Polyester fiberfill
- ❑ Sewing and tapestry needles
- ❑ F hook or hook needed to obtain gauge

GAUGE: 9 sc = 2"; 9 sc rows = 2".

BASIC STITCHES: Ch, sl st, sc, hdc.

NOTE: Work in continuous rnds; do not join or turn unless otherwise stated. Mark first st of each rnd.

BODY

Rnd 1: Starting at neck, with lt. gray, ch 16, sl st in first ch to form ring, ch 1, sc in each ch around. *(16 sc made)*

Rnd 2: 3 sc in first st, sc in each st around. *(18)*

Rnd 3: Sc in first st, 3 sc in next st, sc in next 8 sts, sc next 2 sts tog, sc in last 6 sts. *(19)*

Rnds 4–5: Sc in each st around.

Rnd 6: (2 sc in next st, sc in next st) 4 times, sc in each st around. *(23)*

Rnd 7: Sc in first 10 sts, (2 sc in next st, sc in next st) 2 times, 2 sc in next st; for **Back,** sl st in next 5 sts; 2 sc in next st, sc in next st, 2 sc in last st. *(28)*.

Rnd 8: Sc in first 18 sts, sl st in next 5 sts, sc in last 5 sts.

Rnds 9–15: Sc in each st around.

Rnd 16: Sc in first 21 sts, sc next 2 sts tog, sc in last 5 sts. *(27)*

Rnds 17–22: Sc in each st around.

Rnds 23–24: (Sc next 2 sts tog, sc in next st) around. *(18, 12)*

Rnd 25: (Sc next 2 sts tog) around, join with sl st in first sc. Leaving an 8" strand for sewing, fasten off. Sew rnd 25 closed. Stuff.

HEAD

Rnd 1: Starting at muzzle, with off-white, ch 2, 6 sc in second ch from hook. *(6 sc)*

Rnd 2: 2 sc in each st around. *(12)*

Rnd 3: Sc in each st around changing to lt. gray *(see Stitch Guide)* in last st made.

Rnd 4: (Sc in each of next 3 sts, 2 sc in next st) around. *(15)*

Rnds 5–8: Sc in each st around.

Rnd 9: 2 sc in each of first 2 sts, sc in next 11 sts, 2 sc in each of last 2 sts. *(19)*

Rnds 10–12: Sc in each st around.

Rnd 13: Sc in first 7 sts, sc next 2 sts tog, sc in next st, sc next 2 sts tog, sc in last 7 sts. *(17)*

Rnd 14: (Sc in next st, sc next 2 sts tog) 5 times, sc in last 2 sts. *(12)* Stuff.

Rnd 15: (Sc next 2 sts tog) around, join with sl st in first sc. Leaving an 8" strand for sewing, fasten off. Sew opening closed.

Sew rnds 11–15 of Head to rnd 1 of Body.

EAR (make 2)

Row 1: With lt. gray, ch 10, sc in second ch from hook, sc in next 7 chs, 3 sc in last ch; continuing on opposite side of starting ch, sc in next 8 chs, **do not turn.** *(19)* Fasten off.

Row 2: Working this row in **back lps** *(see Stitch Guide),* join dk. gray with sl st in first st, sl st in each st around. Fasten off.

Sew first and last sts of row 1 together.

Sew Ears to top of Head 1" apart.

LEG (make 2 Left Legs, 2 Right Legs)

Rnd 1: With lt. gray, ch 2, 8 sc in second ch from hook. *(8 sc made)*

Rnd 2: Working this rnd in **back lps,** sc in first 3 sts, sc next 2 sts tog, sc in last 3 sts. *(7)*

Rnds 3–4: Sc in each st around.

Rnd 5: Sc in first 2 sts, 2 sc in each of next 3 sts, sc in last 2 sts. *(10)*

Rnd 6: Sc in first 2 sts, (sc next 2 sts tog) 3 times, sc in last 2 sts. *(7)*

Rnd 7: Sc in each st around.

Rnd 8: (Sc in next st, 2 sc in next st) 3 times, sc in last st. *(10)*

Rnd 9: (Sc in next 3 sts, 2 sc in next st) 2 times, sc in last 2 sts. *(12)*

Rnds 10–11: For **Left Leg,** sc in first 4 sts, hdc in next 5 sts, sc in last 3 sts. At end of last rnd, join with sl st in first sc. Fasten off. Stuff.

Rnds 10–11: For **Right Leg**, sc in first st, hdc in next 5 sts, sc in last 6 sts. At end of last rnd, join with sl st in first sc. Fasten off. Stuff.

Sew one Left Leg and one Right Leg to bottom of Body over rnds 6–10 with hdc to outside for **Front Legs.** Tack rnd 9 of Legs together at bottom of Body.

Repeat with remaining Legs over rnds 18–22 of Body for **Back Legs.**

FORELOCK & MANE

For each **Fringe,** cut one strand of dk. gray 3" long; fold in half, insert hook in st, pull fold through st, pull ends through fold. Tighten.

Fringe 4 sts between Ears for Forelock. Fringe sts from back of Forelock down back of Head to rnd 6 of Body for Mane.

TAIL

Cut three strands of dk. gray each 12" long; tie separate 6" strand dk. gray around center of all strands held together leaving ends for sewing. Fold strands in half; make braid 2" long; secure ends. Trim. Sew fold to back of Body.

FACIAL FEATURES

With dk. brown yarn, using satin stitch *(see Stitch Guide),* embroider eyes on rnd 9 of Head three sts apart; using straight stitch *(see Stitch Guide),* embroider mouth on rnds 1–2.

HALTER

With three strands dk. brown yarn, braid a 4⅜" strap and two 5½" straps. With sewing thread, tack ends of 4⅜" piece together, place around muzzle. Sew one end of one 5½" piece to each side of muzzle strap, pull center of strap behind Ears. Sew ends of remaining 5½" strap together. Place around Head in front of Ears. Tack to Head strap on each side.

Ox

FINISHED SIZE: Approximately 4½" tall sitting.

MATERIALS:
- ❑ Worsted yarn:
    - 2 oz. tan
    - Small amount each dk. brown and cream
- ❑ Black, ecru and lt. brown embroidery floss
- ❑ Polyester fiberfill
- ❑ Embroidery and tapestry needles
- ❑ F hook or hook needed to obtain gauge

GAUGE: 9 sc = 2"; 9 sc rows = 2".

BASIC STITCHES: Ch, sl st, sc, hdc.

NOTE: Work in continuous rnds; do not join or turn unless otherwise stated. Mark first st of each rnd.

HEAD

Rnd 1: Starting at nose, with tan, ch 4, 2 sc in second ch from hook, sc in next ch, 4 sc in last ch; continuing on opposite side of starting ch, sc in next ch, 2 sc in same ch as first sc. *(10 sc)*

Rnd 2: 2 sc in first st, sc in next 4 sts, 2 sc in next st, sc in last 4 sts. *(12)*

Rnd 3: (Sc in next 2 sts, 2 sc in next st) around. *(16)*

Rnds 4–5: Sc in each st around.

Rnd 6: (Sc in next 3 sts, 2 sc in next st) around. *(20)*

Rnds 7–8: Sc in each st around.

Rnd 9: (Sc in next 4 sts, 2 sc in next st) around. *(24)*

Rnds 10–12: Sc in each st around.

Rnd 13: (Sc in next 2 sts, sc next 2 sts tog) around. *(18)* Stuff.

Rnd 14: (Sc in next st, sc next 2 sts tog) around. *(12)*

Rnd 15: (Sc next 2 sts tog) around, join with sl st in first sc. Leaving an 8" strand for sewing, fasten off. Sew opening closed.

FACIAL FEATURES

With ecru floss, using satin stitch, working side to side, embroider eyes on rnd 7 of Head 1" apart. With black, working up and down, embroider pupil at center of each eye.

With lt. brown, using satin stitch, embroider nostrils on rnd 2 of Head three sts apart.

BODY

Rnd 1: Starting at chest, with tan, ch 2, 6 sc in second ch from hook. *(6 sc)*.

Rnd 2: 2 sc in each st around, *(12)*

Rnd 3: (Sc in next st, 2 sc in next st) around. *(18)*

Rnd 4: (Sc in next 2 sts, 2 sc in next st) around. *(24)*

Rnd 5: (Sc in next 3 sts, 2 sc in next st) around. *(30)*

Rnds 6–13: Sc in each st around. Stuff. Continue stuffing as you work.

Rnd 14: (Sc in next 8 sts, sc next 2 sts tog) around. *(27)*

Rnd 15: Sc in each st around.

Rnd 16: (Sc in next 7 sts, sc next 2 sts tog) around. *(24)*

Rnds 17–23: Sc in each st around.

Rnd 24: (Sc in next 6 sts, sc next 2 sts tog) around. *(21)*

Rnd 25: (Sc in next 5 sts, sc next 2 sts tog) around. *(18)*

Rnd 26: (Sc in next st, sc next 2 sts tog) around. *(12)*.

Rnd 27: (Sc next 2 sts tog) around, join with sl st in first sc. *(6)* Leaving an 8" strand for sewing, fasten off. Sew opening closed.

NECK

Rnd 1: With tan, ch 24, sl st in first ch to form ring, ch 1, sc in each ch around. *(24 sc)*

Rnds 2–3: Sc in each st around. At end of last rnd, join with sl st in first sc, fasten off.

Sew rnd 1 of Neck over rnds 7–14 of Head. Sew rnd 3 of Neck over rnds 2–10 on top of Body.

HORN (make 2)

Row 1: With cream, ch 7, sc in second ch from hook, sc in each ch across, turn. *(6 sc)*.

Row 2: Ch 1, sc first 2 sts tog, sc in next 2 sts, sc last 2 sts tog, turn. *(4)*

Row 3: Ch 1, sc first 2 sts tog, sc last 2 sts tog, turn. *(2)*

continued on page 73

Christmas Kitchen

Designed by Mary Jo Cook

FINISHED SIZES: Potholder is 8" × 8½". Hot Pad is 12½" × 13½".

MATERIALS:
- ❑ Worsted yarn:
  - 7½ oz. white
  - 1 oz. green
  - 5 yds. red
  - Small amount each yellow, blue and pink
- ❑ Tapestry needle
- ❑ I crochet hook and I afghan hook or hook needed to obtain gauge.

GAUGE: 4 afghan sts = 1", 7 afghan rows = 2".

BASIC STITCHES: Ch, sl st, sc.

POT HOLDER
Side (make 2)
Row 1: With afghan hook and white, ch 29; for first row of **afghan st,** insert hook in second ch from hook, yo, pull through ch, (insert hook in next ch, yo, pull through ch) across leaving all lps on hook; to **work lps off hook,** yo, pull through first lp on hook, (yo, pull through next 2 lps on hook — *see illustration 1)* across. Lp or vertical bar remaining on hook at end of first lp of next row. *(29 sts made)*

Rows 2–22: Skip first vertical bar, (insert hook under next vertical bar—*see illustration 2,* yo, pull through bar) across to last bar; for last lp, insert hook under last bar and lp directly behind it *(see illustration 3),* yo, pull through bar and lp, work lps off hook.

Row 23: Skip first vertical bar, sl st in each vertical bar across. Fasten off.

Row 24: For **bottom trim,** working in remaining lps on opposite side of starting ch on row 1, with I crochet hook, join white with sc in first ch, sc in each ch across. Fasten off.

Using cross stitch *(see illustration)* and straight stitch *(see Stitch Guide),* embroider one Side according to graph on page 72.

For **ornaments,** with tapestry needle,

embroider pink, yellow and blue French knots *(see Stitch Guide)* randomly spaced on Tree.

Cut two 6" strands of red. Tie one strand to bar between the center two red cross stitches at top and bottom edges *(see photo).*

Edging
Rnd 1: Hold embroidered and plain sides wrong sides together, with embroidered side facing you, working through both thicknesses around outer edge, with I crochet hook, join white with sc in end of row 1 at bottom right-hand side, 3 sc in same row, evenly space 20 more sc across to last row, 4 sc in end of last row, sc in next 28 sl sts on row 23; working in ends of rows, 4 sc in end of next row, evenly sp 20 more sc across to row 1, 4 sc in end of row 1; working across sts on row 24 at bottom of embroidered side only, sc in each st across, join with sl st in first sc. Fasten off. *(112 sc made)*

Rnd 2: With I crochet hook, join green with sc in first st, sc in next 3 sts; for **picot, ch 3, sl st in left bar** *(see illustration)* of last sc made; (sc in next 4 sts, picot) around, join with sl st in first sc. Fasten off.

HOT PAD
Side (make 2)
Row 1: With ch 50, repeat row 1 of Potholder Side.

Rows 2–37: Repeat row 2 of Potholder.

Rows 38–39: Repeat rows 23 and 24 of Potholder Side.

Using graph on page 72, work embroidery in same manner as Potholder.

Edging
Rnd 1: Hold embroidered and plain sides wrong sides together, with embroidered side facing you; working through both thicknesses, with I crochet hook, join white with sc in end of row 1 at bottom right-hand side, 3 sc in same row, evenly space 31 more sc across to last row, 4 sc in end of last row, sc in next 49 sts on row 38; working in ends of rows, 4 sc in end of next row, evenly space 31 more sc across to row 1, 4 sc in end of row 1; working across sts on row 39 at bottom, sc in each st across, join with sl st in first sc. Fasten off. *(176 sc made)*

Rnd 2: With embroidered side facing you, with I crochet hook, join green with sc in first st, sc in next 3 sts, picot, (sc in next 4 sts, picot) around, join with sl st in first sc. Fasten off. ❈

graphs on page 72

Christmas Kitchen

continued from page 70

HOT PAD

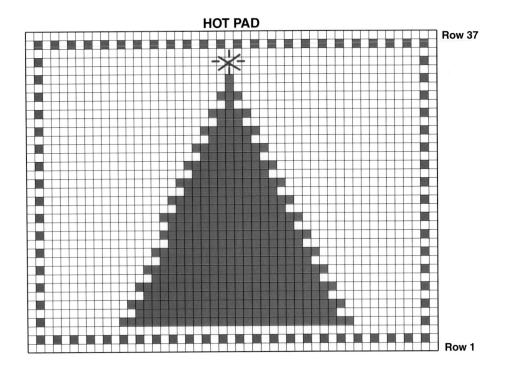

Row 37

Row 1

POT HOLDER

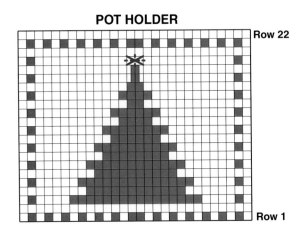

Row 22

Row 1

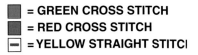

■ = GREEN CROSS STITCH
■ = RED CROSS STITCH
⊟ = YELLOW STRAIGHT STITCH

Crochet Creche

continued from page 69

Row 4: Ch 1, sc next 2 sts tog. Fasten off.
Sew ends of rows together stuffing lightly.
Sew row 1 of Horns to top of Head 1" apart.

EAR (make 2)

With tan, ch 6, sl st in second ch from hook, sc in next ch, hdc in next 2 chs, sc in last ch. Leaving an 8" strand for sewing, fasten off.
With right side of sts facing you, sew to each side of Head below Horns.

FRONT LEG (make 2)

Rnd 1: With dk. brown, ch 2, 6 sc in second ch from hook. *(6 sc)*
Rnd 2: Sc in each st around changing to tan *(see Stitch Guide)* in last st made.
Rnds 3–8: Sc in each st around. Stuff. Continue stuffing as you work.
Rnd 9: 2 hdc in each of first 3 sts, sc in last 3 sts. *(9)*
Rnds 10–11: Hdc in first 6 sts, sc in last 3 sts.
Rnds 12–17: Sc in each st around.
Rnd 18: (Sc in next st, sc next 2 sts tog) around, join with sl st in first sc. Leaving an 8" strand for sewing, fasten off. Sew opening closed.

BACK LEG (make 2)

Rnd 1: With dk. brown, ch 2, 6 sc in second ch from hook. *(6 sc)*
Rnd 2: (Sc in next st, 2 sc in next st) around. *(9)*
Rnd 3: Sc in each st around changing to tan in last st made.
Rnds 4–13: Sc in each st around. Stuff. Continue stuffing as you work.
Rnd 14: (Sc in next st, sc next 2 sts tog) around *(6)*
Rnd 15: (Skip next st, sl st in next st) around. Fasten off.
Sew Legs to each side of Body according to illustration.

TAIL

Row 1: With tan, ch 25, sc in second ch from hook, sc in next 18 chs, hdc in last 5 chs, turn. *(24 sts)*
Row 2: Ch 2, hdc in next 4 sts, sc in last 19 sts. Fasten off.
Sew hdc end to center back of Body.
Cut two strands tan each 3" long. With both strands held together, fold in half, insert hook in st at end of Tail, pull fold through, pull ends through fold, tighten. Trim to 1". ✳

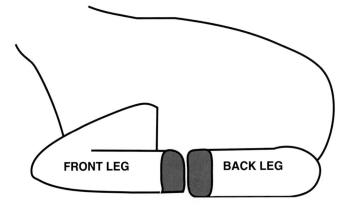

FRONT LEG   BACK LEG

Away in a Manger

Many surmise Christ was likely born in a hillside cave used as a livestock feeding enclosure, and rugged shepherds in the dark fields near the compound were frightened by the light and heavenly voices of angels rejoicing at His birth.

The *creche*, a French word meaning *manger* or *crib*, is a depiction of the Nativity in the stable at Bethlehem. A reminder to us of our Savior's humble beginnings, it has become a universal holiday decorating scheme.

But according to some historians, the familiar creche scene is more fable than fact. They say that if the shepherds were tending their flocks in the fields that night as the gospel reports, it probably wasn't winter, for in Palestine sheep were penned up close to town for the winter.

Gingerbread House Tissue Cover

An Original by Annie

FINISHED SIZE: Fits boutique-style tissue box.

MATERIALS:
- ❏ Worsted yarn:
  - 4½ oz. rust
  - 3 oz. white
  - Small amount each tan, dk. brown, lt. yellow, dk. yellow, rose, teal, purple, orange and red
- ❏ Polyester fiberfill
- ❏ Tapestry needle
- ❏ G hook or hook needed to obtain gauge

GAUGE: 4 sc = 1"; 4 sc rows = 1".

BASIC STITCHES: Ch, sl st, sc, hdc, dc.

HOUSE
Side A (make 2)
Row 1: Starting at bottom, with rust, ch 21, sc in second ch from hook, sc in each ch across, turn. *(20 sc made)*

Rows 2–22: Ch 1, sc in each st across, turn. *Front of row 2 is right side of work.*

Row 23: For **gable,** ch 1, sc first 2 sts tog, sc in each st across to last 2 sts, sc last 2 sts tog, turn. *(18)*

Rows 24–26: Ch 1, sc first 2 sts tog, sc next 2 sts tog, sc in each st across to last 4 sts, (sc next 2 sts tog) 2 times, turn. *(14, 10, 6)*

Row 27: Ch 1, sc first 2 sts tog, (sc next 2 sts tog) 2 times, turn. *(3)*

Row 28: Ch 1, sc 3 sts tog. Fasten off.

Side B (make 2)
Row 1: Starting at bottom, with rust, ch 19, sc in second ch from hook, sc in each ch across, turn. *(18 sc made)*

Rows 2–22: Ch 1, sc in each st across, turn. At end of last row, fasten off. *Front of row 2 is right side of work.*

Ceiling
Row 1: With rust, ch 21, sc in second ch from hook, sc in each ch across, turn. *(20 sc made)*

Rows 2–5: Ch 1, sc in each st across, turn.

Row 6: For **first side,** ch 1, sc in first 6 sts leaving last 14 sts unworked, turn. *(6)*

Rows 7–12: Ch 1, sc in each st across, turn. At end of last row, fasten off.

Row 6: For **chimney opening,** skip next 8 unworked sts on row 5; for **second side,** join rust with sc in next unworked st, sc in each st across, turn. *(6)*

Rows 7–12: Ch 1, sc in each st across, turn.

Row 13: Ch 1, sc in first 6 sts, ch 8, sc in next 6 sts on first side, turn. *(12 sc, 8 chs)*

Row 14: Ch 1, sc in each st and in each ch across, turn. *(20)*

Rows 15–18: Ch 1, sc in each st across, turn. At end of last row, fasten off.

Chimney
NOTE: *Work in continuous rnds, do not join or turn unless otherwise stated. Mark first st of each rnd.*

Rnd 1: Join rust with sc in first unworked st on row 5 of Ceiling, sc in next 8 sts; working in ends of rows, sc in next 7 rows; working in remaining lps on opposite side of ch-8 on row 13, sc in next 8 chs; working in ends of rows, sc in last 7 rows. *(30 sc made)*

Rnds 2–4: Dc front post *(dc fp—see Stitch Guide)* around post of first st, dc fp around each st around.

Rnd 5: Sc in each st around, join with sl st in first sc. Fasten off.

Rnd 6: For **snow trim,** join white with sc in first st, 3 dc in next st, (sc in next st, 3 dc in next st) around, join. Fasten off.

ASSEMBLY
Matching long edges, working through both thicknesses and in ends of rows, alternating Sides, with white, sc Side pieces wrong sides together forming a box.

With tan and Chimney facing up, sew Ceiling to top edges on Side B pieces and to row 22 on gable of Side A pieces.

Window (make 2)
Row 1: With lt. yellow, ch 8, sc in second ch from hook, sc in each ch across, turn. *(7 sc made)*

Rows 2–8: Ch 1, sc in each st across, turn. At end of last row, fasten off.

Rnd 9: Working in rnds, starting at bottom, join white with sc in end of first row, sc in end of next 7 rows, 3 sc in first st, sc in next 5 sts, 3 sc in last st; working in ends of rows, sc in last 8 rows; for

continued on page 79

Pineapple Centerpiece

Designed by Mrs. L.V. Johnson

FINISHED SIZE: 21" across.

MATERIALS:
- ❑ 575 yds. white size 10 crochet cotton
- ❑ No. 8 steel hook or hook needed to obtain gauge.

GAUGE: 10 sts = 1"; bullion stitch = $\frac{5}{8}$" tall.

SPECIAL STITCHES: For **bullion stitch (bs)**, yo 20 times on hook, insert hook in st, yo, pull lp through st, yo, pull through all 21 lps on hook at same time *(if pulling through all lps is difficult, try pulling hook through 1 or 2 lps at a time until all lps have been worked off)*, ch 1. If making this stitch for the first time, practice before starting instructions. **A (dtr, ch 1) can be substituted for the bullion stitch** if desired.
For **shell**, 3 bs in next sc, ch 3, skip next sc, 3 bs in next sc.
For **bs shell**, (bs, ch 1) 6 times in st or ch.

CENTERPIECE
Rnd 1: Ch 7, sl st in first ch to form ring, ch 4, 38 tr in ring, join with sl st in top of ch-4. *(38 tr)*
Rnd 2: Ch 7, **bs** *(see Special Stitches)* in each st around, join with sl st in first bs.
Rnd 3: *Ch 6, skip next 2 bs, sc in next sp between bs, (ch 6, skip next bs, sc in next sp between bs) 2 times; repeat from * around to last st, ch 6, join with sl st in joining sl st of last rnd. *(28 ch lps)*
Rnds 4–6: Sl st across to center of first ch lp, (ch 6, sc in next ch sp) around, joining last ch lp where first started.
Rnd 7: Sl st to center of first ch lp, *13 tr in next ch lp, sc in next ch lp, (ch 6, sc in next ch lp) 2 times; repeat from * around, joining last ch lp where first started.
Rnd 8: (Ch 7, bs in next 13 tr, ch 7, sc in next ch lp, ch 6, sc in next ch lp) around, ch 7, joining last ch-7 in top of first bs.
Rnd 9: *Ch 5, (sc in next sp between bs, ch 5) 12 times, skip next ch lp, 3 bs in next ch lp, ch 5, sc in next bs; repeat from * around, joining last ch-5 where first started.

continued on page 78

Plaid Place Mat

Designed by Suzanne Echols

FINISHED SIZE: Approximately 11½" × 16½".

MATERIALS:
- ❏ Worsted yarn:
    - 2 oz. white
    - Small amount each red and green
- ❏ Tapestry needle
- ❏ G hook or hook needed to obtain gauge

GAUGE: 2 dc and 2 ch-1 sps = 1"; 2 dc rows = 1".

BASIC STITCHES: Ch, sl st, dc.

PLACE MAT
Row 1: With white, ch 48, dc in sixth ch from hook, (ch 1, skip next ch, dc in next ch) across, turn. *(First 3 chs count as first dc—23 dc, 22 ch sps made.)*

Rows 2–5: Ch 4, skip next ch sp, dc in next st, (ch 1, skip next ch sp, dc in next st) across, turn. At end of last row, fasten off.

Row 6: Join red with sl st in first st, ch 4, skip next ch sp, dc in next st, (ch 1, skip next ch sp, dc in next st) across, turn.

Rows 7–10: Ch 4, skip next ch sp, dc in next st, (ch 1, skip next ch sp, dc in next st) across, turn. At end of last row, fasten off.

Rows 11–35: Following color sequence of white, green, white, red, white, repeat rows 6–10 consecutively.

FINISHING
With two strands red held together, leaving 2½" at each end for fringe, working from bottom to top of Place Mat, weave yarn under and over first row of ch-1 sps.

Alternating the weaving pattern over and under then under and over, weave three more rows of red, five rows of white, four rows of green, five rows of white and four rows of red.

Tie fringe ends together in knots to secure. ✻

Tree Trimming

One of the most deeply rooted traditions of the Christmas season is the embellishing of our homes and public places with a decorated evergreen tree.

This modern custom undoubtedly sprang from ancient winter festivals held in Northern European countries which upheld the evergreen as a symbol of immortality. Holly and pine branches were brought indoors to guard the home from evil spirits during the long, dark winter, and decorated holly trees were placed in the village common or square.

By the 16th century, the church gave new meaning to the Christmastime tree by hanging it with apples to symbolize the fruit of knowledge for Adam and Eve and using it as a prop in "Passion" plays. Eventually, families began to add decorations of paper roses, stars, angels, hearts, flowers and bells to signify the birth of Christ.

In Germany, the tree of choice was a silver fir or balsam tree, with branches spaced far enough apart to support candles without creating a fire hazard. The candles represented Christ as the Light of the World. And it was here that the custom of gift-giving began, as holiday celebrants hung oranges and bags of nuts or small trinkets such as dolls, pens, drums and needlecases on the tree for guests to take home with them.

Our modern Christmas trees borrow from these traditions to create a stunning individual statement of beauty that can range from simple to extravagant. While many families decorate their trees with the same ornaments from year to year, adding each holiday season to their heirloom look, others of us turn to a new theme each year.

For ideas, we can turn to craft or Christmas-store displays or own ingenuity. Try these for starters:

• An outdoor birdwatcher's tree decorated simply with velvet ribbons and a variety of foodstuffs attractive to our feathered friends

• A "family" tree decked predominately with family portraits

• Trees for children including a teddy bear tree, a fairy tale tree complete with Little Red Riding Hood, Snow White, and other characters, or a circus-theme tree

• A sophisticated New Orleans-style tree hung with carnival masks, bottles of hot sauce and sheets of jazz music

• Themed trees for golfers, fishermen or cooking enthusiasts

But what about those fantastically lush decorator trees? We turned to professionals to discover some of their secrets!

First, whether you are using a natural or artificial tree, reshape the tree. Think of how a tree grows, with each frond leaning towards the sun, and work from bottom to top and back to front, giving each branch a lift up and out.

Next, add lights, the more the merrier! For light coverage, use 150 lights per foot of tree, for moderate coverage, 200 lights per foot, and for an all-out glow, 250 lights per foot of tree. The new light webs are easiest to use, or weave strings of lights from trunk to tip and back again. Or string lights like garlands, horizontally or vertically, for a different effect.

Finally, add decorations and garlands. Start with bows, ribbons and larger ornaments, and fill in with smaller ornaments and silk flowers.

The chart below is helpful for planning the number and size of ornaments you may need for moderate coverage of average size trees. For light or full coverage, adjust the number of ornaments accordingly.

	4' Tree	6' Tree	7' Tree	8' Tree	10' Tree	12' Tree
Small Size Ornaments	24	36	48	54	86	108
Medium Size Ornaments	16	24	32	36	54	72
Large Size Ornaments	24	36	48	54	86	108

Snow Flurry

Frosty the Snowman

Frosty the snowman was a jolly happy soul with a corncob pipe and a button nose and two eyes made out of coal. Frosty the snowman is a fairy tale they say. He was made of snow but the children know how he came to life one day. There must have been some magic in that old silk hat they found. For when they placed it on his head he began to dance around.

Frosty the Snowman

Designed by Michele Wilcox

FINISHED SIZE: 16" high without hat.

MATERIALS:
- ❏ Worsted yarn:
  - 6 oz. white
  - 1 oz. green
  - Small amount dk. peach
- ❏ 2 black ¼" pom-poms *(for eyes)*
- ❏ Four ¾" buttons in assorted colors
- ❏ 4" × 30" piece of flannel fabric
- ❏ Decorative Christmas pick
- ❏ Small craft pipe
- ❏ Black felt craft top hat
- ❏ Hot glue gun
- ❏ Two cups uncooked rice or popcorn in a small plastic bag
- ❏ Musical button *(optional)*
- ❏ 32 × 50-hole piece of 7-mesh plastic canvas
- ❏ Polyester fiberfill
- ❏ Tapestry needle
- ❏ G hook or hook needed to obtain gauge

GAUGE: 4 sc = 1"; 4 sc rows = 1".

BASIC STITCHES: Ch, sl st, sc.

BODY SIDE (make 2)

Row 1: Starting at top of head, with white, ch 11, sc in second ch from hook, sc in each ch across, turn. *(10 sc made)*

Rows 2–3: Ch 1, 2 sc in first st, sc in each st across to last st, 2 sc in last st, turn. *(12, 14)*

Row 4: Ch 1, sc in each st across, turn.

Row 5: Ch 1, 2 sc in first st, sc in each st across to last st, 2 sc in last st, turn. *(16)*

Rows 6–7: Ch 1, sc in each st across, turn.

Row 8: Ch 1, 2 sc in first st, sc in each st across to last st, 2 sc in last st, turn. *(18)*

Rows 9–21: Ch 1, sc in each st across, turn.

Rows 22–26: Ch 1, 2 sc in first st, sc in each st across to last st, 2 sc in last st, turn. *(28 sc at end of row 26)*

Rows 27–30: Ch 1, sc in each st across, turn.

Row 31: Ch 1, 2 sc in first st, sc in each st across to last st, 2 sc in last st, turn. *(30)*

Rows 32–34: Ch 1, sc in each st across, turn.

Row 35: Ch 1, 2 sc in first st, sc in each st across to last st, 2 sc in last st, turn. *(32)*

Rows 36–51: Repeat rows 32–35 consecutively. *(40 sc at end of row 51)*

Rows 52–69: Ch 1, sc in each st across, turn. At end of last row, fasten off.

Matching ends of rows 1–69, sew Body Sides together, leaving sts of row 69 unsewn for bottom opening.

BASE

Row 1: With white, ch 10, sc in second ch from hook, sc in each ch across, turn. *(9 sc made)*

Row 2: Ch 1, 2 sc in first st, sc in each st across to last st, 2 sc in last st, turn. *(11)*

Row 3: Ch 1, sc in each st across, turn.

Rows 4–10: Repeat rows 2 and 3 alternately, ending with row 2. *(19 sc at end of row 10)*

Rows 11–19: Ch 1, sc in each st across, turn.

Row 20: Ch 1, sc first 2 sts tog, sc in each st across to last 2 sts, sc last 2 sts tog, turn. *(17)*

Row 21: Ch 1, sc in each st across, turn.

Rows 22–28: Repeat rows 20 and 21 alternately, ending with row 20. *(9 sts at end of row 28)*

Row 29: Ch 1, sc in each st across. Fasten off.

Using Base as a pattern, cut plastic canvas. Stuff Body. Place bag of popcorn or rice inside Body to weight bottom.

Easing to fit, sew Base to row 69 of Body Sides, inserting plastic canvas before closing.

Sew four buttons to one Side as shown in photo for front.

ARM SIDE (make 4)

Row 1: With green, for mitten, ch 6, sc in second ch from hook, sc in each ch across, turn. *(5 sc made)*

Row 2: Ch 1, 2 sc in first st, sc in each st across to last st, 2 sc in last st, turn. *(7)*

Row 3: Ch 1, sc in each st across, turn.

Row 4: Ch 1, 2 sc in first st, sc in each st across to last st, 2 sc in last st, turn. *(9)*

Rows 5–10: Ch 1, sc in each st across, turn. At end of last row, change to white.

Rows 11–26: For **Arm,** ch 1, sc in each st across, turn.

Row 27: Ch 1, sc first 2 sts tog, sc in each st across to last st, sc last 2 sts tog. Fasten off.

Matching ends of rows, sew two Arm Sides together, inserting music button in mitten and stuffing before closing.

Repeat with remaining Arm Sides, omitting music button.

Sew Arms to side seams of Body, curving right Arm toward front as shown in photo.

THUMB (make 2)

NOTE: Work in continuous rnds, do not join or turn unless otherwise stated. Mark first st of each rnd.

Rnd 1: With green, ch 2, 6 sc in second ch from hook. *(6 sc made)*

continued on page 89

Galaxy Tablecloth

Designed by Gloria Coombes

FINISHED SIZE: Approximately 65".

MATERIALS:
- ❏ 2,820 yds. white size 10 crochet cotton
- ❏ Size 9 hook or hook needed to obtain gauge

GAUGE: Motif is 4¾" across.

BASIC STITCHES: Ch, sl st, sc, dc, dtr.

SPECIAL STITCHES: For **double crochet cluster (dc cl)**, *yo, insert hook in st, yo, pull lp through, yo, pull through 2 lps on hook leaving last lps on hook; working in same st, repeat from * number of times needed for number of dc in cluster, yo and pull through all lps on hook.

For **double treble (dtr)**, yo 3 times, insert hook in st, yo, pull loop through, (yo, pull through 2 loops on hook) 4 times.

FIRST ROW
Motif A
Rnd 1: Ch 6, sl st in first ch to form ring, ch 3, 11 dc in ring, join with sl st in top of ch-3. *(12 dc made)*

Rnd 2: Ch 1, sc in first st, ch 9, *skip next st, sc in next st; for **picot, ch 5, sl st in first ch of ch-5;** ch 9; repeat from * 4 more times, skip next st, join with sl st in first sc, picot.

Rnd 3: Sl st to fifth ch of next ch-9, ch 1, sc in same ch, ch 11, (sc in fifth ch of next ch-9, ch 11) 5 times, join with sl st in first sc.

Rnd 4: Ch 1, sc in first st, *(7 sc, ch 7, 7 sc) in next ch-11 sp, sc in next sc; repeat from * 4 more times, (7 sc, ch 7, 7 sc) in next ch-11 sp, join with sl st in first sc.

Rnd 5: Ch 1, sc in first st, picot, ch 7, *(3 sc, ch 3, 3 sc) in ch-7 sp, ch 7, skip next 7 sc, sc in next sc, picot, ch 7; repeat from * 4 more times, (3 sc, ch 3, 3 sc) in ch-7 sp, ch 3, join with dtr *(see Special Stitches)* in first sc.

Rnd 6: Ch 1, sc in top of dtr, *[ch 7, sc in fourth ch of next ch-7 sp, ch 5, **3-dc cl** *(see Special Stitches)* in next ch-3 sp, (ch 3, 3-dc cl, picot, ch 3, 3-dc cl) in same ch-3 sp, ch 5], sc in fourth ch of next ch-7 sp; repeat from * 4 more times; repeat between [ ], join with sl st in first sc. Fasten off.

Motif B
Rnd 1: Ch 6, sl st in first ch to form ring, ch 3, 11 dc in ring, join with sl st in top of ch-3. *(12 dc made)*

Rnd 2: Ch 1, sc in first st, ch 9, *skip next st, sc in next st; for **picot, ch 5, sl st in first ch of ch-5;** ch 9; repeat from * 4 more times, skip next st, join with sl st in first sc, picot.

Rnd 3: Sl st to fifth ch of next ch-9, ch 1, sc in same ch, ch 11, (sc in fifth ch of next ch-9, ch 11) 5 times, join with sl st in first sc.

Rnd 4: Ch 1, sc in first st, *(7 sc, ch 7, 7 sc) in next ch-11 sp, sc in next sc; repeat from * 4 more times, (7 sc, ch 7, 7 sc) in next ch-11 sp, join with sl st in first sc.

Rnd 5: Ch 1, sc in first st, picot, ch 7, *(3 sc, ch 3, 3 sc) in ch-7 sp, ch 7, skip next 7 sc, sc in next sc, picot, ch 7; repeat from * 4 more times, (3 sc, ch 3, 3 sc) in ch-7 sp, ch 3, join with dtr in first sc.

Rnd 6: Ch 1, sc in top of dtr, ch 7, sc in fourth ch of next ch-7 sp, ch 5, 3-dc cl in next ch-3 sp, (ch 3, 3-dc cl; for **joining picot, ch 2, sl st in any picot of last Motif made *(see assembly illustration)*, ch 2, sl st in first ch of first ch-2;** ch 3, 3-dc cl) in same ch-3 sp, ch 5, sc in fourth ch of next ch-7 sp, ch 7, sc in fourth ch of next ch-7 sp, ch 5, 3-dc cl in next ch-3 sp, (ch 3, 3-dc cl, joining picot, ch 3, 3-dc cl) in same ch-3 sp, ch 5, sc in fourth ch of next ch-7 sp, *ch 7, sc in fourth ch of next ch-7 sp, ch 5, 3-dc cl in next ch-3 sp, (ch 3, 3-dc cl, picot, ch 3, 3-dc cl) in same ch-3 sp, ch 5, sc in fourth ch of next ch-7 sp; repeat from * 3 more times ending with sl st in first sc. Fasten off.

Repeat Motif B six more times.

SECOND ROW
Motif B
Joining as shown in Assembly illustration, work same as First Row Motif B.

Motif C
Rnd 1: Ch 6, sl st in first ch to form ring, ch 3, 11 dc in ring, join with sl st in top of ch-3. *(12 dc made)*

Rnd 2: Ch 1, sc in first st, ch 9, *skip next st, sc in next st; for **picot, ch 5, sl st in first ch of ch-5;** ch 9; repeat from * 4 more times, skip next st, join with sl st in first sc, picot.

Rnd 3: Sl st to fifth ch of next ch-9, ch 1, sc in same ch, ch 11, (sc in fifth ch of next ch-9, ch 11) 5 times, join with sl st in first sc.

Rnd 4: Ch 1, sc in first st, *(7 sc, ch 7, 7 sc) in next ch-11 sp, sc in next sc; repeat from * 4 more times, (7 sc, ch 7, 7 sc) in next ch-11 sp, join with sl st in first sc.

Rnd 5: Ch 1, sc in first st, picot, ch 7, *(3 sc, ch 3, 3 sc) in ch-7 sp, ch 7, skip next 7 sc, sc in next sc, picot, ch 7; repeat from * 4 more times, (3 sc, ch 3, 3 sc) in ch-7 sp, ch 3, join with dtr in first sc.

continued on page 88

Galaxy Tablecloth

continued from page 86

Rnd 6: Ch 1, sc in top of dtr, ch 7, sc in fourth ch of next ch-7 sp, ch 5, 3-dc cl in next ch-3 sp, (ch 3, 3-dc cl; for **joining picot, ch 2, sl st in corresponding picot of last Motif made (see Assembly Illustration), ch 2, sl st in first ch of ch-2;** ch 3, 3-dc cl) in same ch-3 sp, ch 5, sc in fourth ch of next ch-7 sp, *ch 7, sc in fourth ch of next ch-7 sp, ch 5, 3-dc cl in next ch-3 sp, (ch 3, 3-dc cl, joining picot in joined picots, ch 3, 3-dc cl) in same ch-3 sp, ch 5, sc in fourth ch of next ch-7 sp; repeat from * 2 more times, [ch 7, sc in fourth ch of next ch-7 sp, ch 5, 3-dc cl in next ch-3 sp, (ch 3, 3-dc cl, picot, ch 3, 3-dc cl) in same ch-3 sp, ch 5, sc in fourth ch of next ch-7 sp]; repeat between [ ] 1 more time ending with sl st first sc. Fasten off.

Repeat Motif C six more times.

Motif D

Rnd 1: Ch 6, sl st in first ch to form ring, ch 3, 11 dc in ring, join with sl st in top of ch-3. *(12 dc made)*

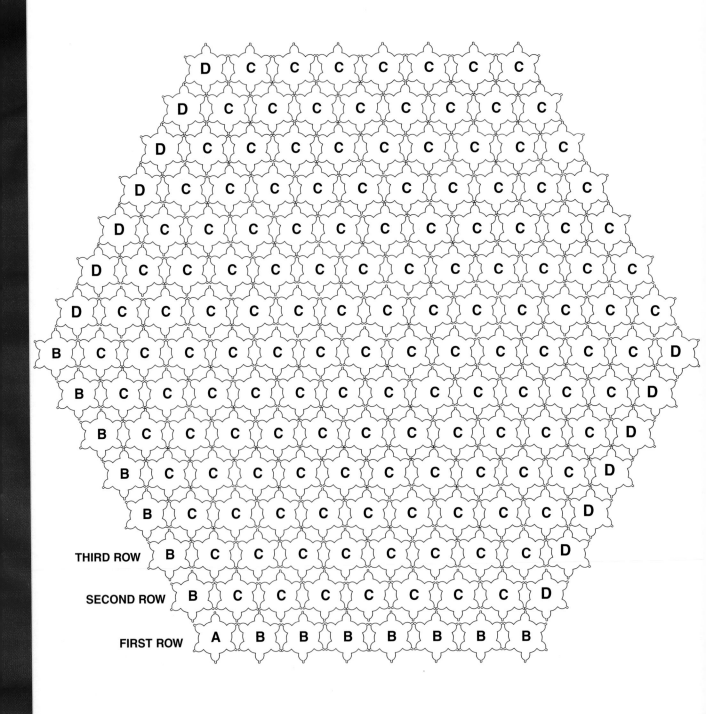

THIRD ROW

SECOND ROW

FIRST ROW

Rnd 2: Ch 1, sc in first st, ch 9, *skip next st, sc in next st; for **picot, ch 5, sl st in first ch of ch-5;** ch 9; repeat from * 4 more times, skip next st, join with sl st in first sc, picot.

Rnd 3: Sl st to fifth ch of next ch-9, ch 1, sc in same ch, ch 11, (sc in fifth ch of next ch-9, ch 11) 5 times, join with sl st in first sc.

Rnd 4: Ch 1, sc in first st, *(7 sc, ch 7, 7 sc) in next ch-11 sp, sc in next sc; repeat from * 4 more times, (7 sc, ch 7, 7 sc) in next ch-11 sp, join with sl st in first sc.

Rnd 5: Ch 1, sc in first st, picot, ch 7, *(3 sc, ch 3, 3 sc) in ch-7 sp, ch 7, skip next 7 sc, sc in next sc, picot, ch 7; repeat from * 4 more times, (3 sc, ch 3, 3 sc) in ch-7 sp, ch 3, join with dtr in first sc.

Rnd 6: Ch 1, sc in top of dtr, ch 7, sc in fourth ch of next ch-7 sp, ch 5, 3-dc cl in next ch-3 sp, (ch 3, 3-dc cl; for **joining picot, ch 2, sl st in corresponding picot of last Motif made (see Assembly Illustration), ch 2, sl st in first ch of ch-2;** ch 3, 3-dc cl) in same ch-3 sp, ch 5, sc in fourth ch of next ch-7 sp, *ch 7, sc in fourth ch of next ch-7 sp, ch 5, 3-dc cl in next ch-3 sp, (ch 3, 3-dc cl, joining picot in joined picots, ch 3, 3-dc cl) in same ch-3 sp, ch 5, sc in fourth ch of next ch-7 sp; repeat from * once, [ch 7, sc in fourth ch of next ch-7 sp, ch 5, 3-dc cl in next ch-3 sp, (ch 3, 3-dc cl, picot, ch 3, 3-dc cl) in same ch-3 sp, ch 5, sc in fourth ch of next ch-7 sp]; repeat between [ ] 1 more time ending with sl st first sc. Fasten off.

THIRD–EIGHTH ROWS
Work same as Second Row.

NINTH–FIFTEENTH ROWS
Motif D
Joining as shown in Assembly Illustration work same as Second Motif D.

Motif C
Work same as Second Row Motif C. ❋

Frosty the Snowman

continued from page 85

Rnd 2: (Sc in next 2 sts, 2 sc in next st) 2 times. *(8 sc)*

Rnds 3–5: Sc in each st around. At end of last rnd, join with sl st in first sc. Fasten off.
Stuff lightly, flatten rnd 5 and sew to front seam at row 9 of Arm.

NOSE
Rnd 1: With dk. peach, ch 2, 6 sc in second ch from hook, **do not** join rnds. *(6 sc made)*

Rnd 2: Sc in each st around.

Rnd 3: 2 sc in next st, sc in each st around. *(7)*

Rnd 4: Sc in each st around.

Rnd 5: 2 sc in next st, sc in each st around. *(8)*

Rnd 6: Sc in each st around.

Rnd 7: 2 sc in next st, sc in each st around, join with sl st in first sc. Fasten off.

FINISHING
1: For **scarf,** make ten 1½" cuts in each short end of fabric for fringe; tie scarf around Body as shown in photo.

2: Glue hat to top of Body.

3: Stuff Nose lightly. Sew to front of Body between scarf and Hat.

4: Glue pom-poms and pipe in place as shown in photo.

5: Place decorative pick in Body at curve of right Arm as shown. ❋

Santa's Better Half

Frosty the Snowman, Rudolf the Red-Nosed Reindeer, the little drummer boy, Santa and his elves—they are all actors in the grand pageant we call Christmas.

But, we ask, what about Mrs. Claus? The custom closest to a female personification of Santa is the Italian tradition of La Befaña, the kindly old woman with the power of a fairy queen, who gives children gifts on the eve of Epiphany, January sixth.

We have our suspicions about the real Mrs. Santa. She's so much more than the mystic mate of Father Christmas. She works, she cooks, she carpools, then at bedtime, tucks in the covers and gives us a huge hug. And of course she crochets! Recognize her? She is the hallowed spirit of motherhood who offers us eternal love from a pure heart.

Pinecone & Snowflake Wreath

An Original by Annie

FINISHED SIZE: 12" wreath

MATERIALS:
- ❏ Worsted-weight yarn:
    - 8 ozs. brown
    - 2 ozs. green
- ❏ 120 yds. white size 10 crochet cotton thread
- ❏ 12" Styrofoam® ring
- ❏ 3 yds. plaid 2⅝" wired ribbon
- ❏ 1½ yds. blue ¹⁄₁₆" ribbon
- ❏ Low-temp hot glue
- ❏ Fabric stiffener
- ❏ T-pins and rust-proof small head straight pins
- ❏ Plastic wrap
- ❏ Three 6" pieces of 22-gauge floral wire
- ❏ Tapestry needle
- ❏ No. 7 steel hook; F, G, H and J hooks or hooks needed to obtain gauges.

GAUGES: **F hook** and single strand yarn, 4 sc = 1".
H hook and single strand yarn, 7 dc = 2"; 2 dc **back loop** rows = 1½".
J hook and 2 strands yarn, 3 ch = 1".

SPECIAL STITCH: For **loop stitch (lp st),** insert hook in st, wrap yarn over finger from back to front *(see illustration)* forming a loop the length needed, cross hook over front strand of loop, pick up back strand and pull through st, drop loop from finger, yo, pull through both loops on hook.

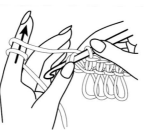

WREATH COVER
Rnd 1: With H hook and single strand brown yarn, ch 105, sl st in first ch to form ring, ch 3, dc in each ch around, join with sl st in top of ch-3. *(105 dc made)*
Rnds 2–8: Working these rnds in **back lps** *(see Stitch Guide),* ch 3, dc in each st around, join with sl st in top of ch-3. At end of last rnd, fasten off. *(Cover should stretch just a little when fitting around ring.)*

Place Cover over Styrofoam ring *(use T-pins to hold Cover on ring as you work);* with H hook and brown yarn, sl st first and last rnds together, keeping seam on back of ring where it will not show.

VINES
First Vine (make 4)
With J hook and two strands brown yarn held together as one, ch 10; for **picot, sl st in third ch from hook;** ch 20, picot, ch 15, picot, ch 20, picot, ch 25, picot, ch 15, picot, ch 20, picot, ch 10. Fasten off.

Second Vine (make 4)
With J hook and two strands brown yarn held together as one, ch 5, picot, ch 20, picot, ch 15, picot, ch 20, picot, ch 25, picot, ch 15, picot, ch 20, picot, ch 15. Fasten off.

Third Vine (make 3)
With J hook and two strands brown yarn held together as one, ch 13, picot, ch 20, picot, ch 15, picot, ch 20, picot, ch 25, picot, ch 15, picot, ch 20, picot, ch 7. Fasten off.
To join Vines, work a sc in one end of each of 10 Vines connecting them side by side.
Using T-pins, pin joined ends to front of covered Wreath. Loosely intertwine Vines and arrange around front of Wreath to resemble grapevine, using small-head pins to hold where needed.
Sc in other end of each Vine in same manner as first ends; using T-pins, pin in place next to first end of Vines.
Pin one end of remaining Vine to wrong side of Wreath; spacing evenly, wrap Vine around, securing other Vines to Front of Wreath. Pin other end to wrong side of Wreath.

EVERGREEN BRANCHES
Short Branch (make 4)
Row 1: With I hook and brown yarn, ch 9. Fasten off.
Row 2: With F hook and two strands green yarn held together as one, join with sl st in first ch, ch 1, work **loop st** *(see Special Stitches)* in each ch of last row, ch 1; working on opposite side of ch-9, loop st in each loop across. Fasten off. Cut loops.

continued on page 95

Five-in-One
Doily

Designed by Sue Penrod

Five-in-One Doily

continued from page 93

FINISHED SIZE: Doily is 9" across. Bowl is 5½" across. Window hangers are 9", 7" and 5" across.

MATERIALS:
- ❑ 250 yds. white size 10 crochet cotton
- ❑ ½ yd. ⅛" ribbon
- ❑ 5", 7" and 9" metal rings
- ❑ Plastic margarine or glass container 4" across bottom, 5½" across top and 2¼" deep
- ❑ Nylon fishing line
- ❑ E hook or hook needed to obtain gauge

GAUGE: Rnd 1 is 1¾" across; 2 shell rows = 1".

BASIC STITCHES: Ch, sl st, sc, dc.

SPECIAL STITCHES: For **beginning shell (beg shell),** sl st in next st, (sl st, ch 3, dc, ch 2, 2 dc) in next ch sp.
For **shell,** (2 dc, ch 2, 2 dc) in next ch sp.

DOILY

Rnd 1: Ch 12, sl st in first ch to form ring, ch 3, dc in ring, ch 2, (2 dc in ring, ch 2) 9 times, join with sl st in top of ch-3. *(20 dc, 10 ch sps)*

Rnd 2: Beg shell *(see Special Stitches)*, ch 2, *shell *(see Special Stitches)* in next ch sp; ch 2; repeat from * around, join with sl st in top of ch-3. *(10 shells)*

Rnd 3: Beg shell, ch 4, (shell in ch sp of next shell, ch 4) around, join.

Rnd 4: Sl st in next st, (sl st, ch 3, 2 dc, ch 2, 3 dc) in next ch sp, ch 3, *(3 dc, ch 2, 3 dc) in next shell, ch 3; repeat from * around, join.

Rnd 5: Sl st in next 2 sts, (sl st, ch 3, 2 dc, ch 3, 3 dc) in next ch sp, ch 3, sc around next 3 ch sps of last 3 rnds, ch 3, *(3 dc, ch 3, 3 dc) in next ch sp, ch 3, sc around next 3 chs of last 3 rnds, ch 3; repeat from * around, join.

Rnd 6: Sl st in next 2 sts, (sl st, ch 3, 3 dc, ch 3, 4 dc) in next ch sp, ch 5, skip next 2 ch sps and sc, *(4 dc, ch 3, 4 dc) in next ch sp, ch 5, skip next 2 ch sps and sc; repeat from * around, join.

Rnd 7: Sl st in next 3 sts, (sl st, ch 3, 4 dc, ch 3, 5 dc) in next ch sp, ch 5, skip next ch sp, *(5 dc, ch 3, 5 dc) in next ch sp, ch 5, skip next ch sp; repeat from * around, join.

Rnd 8: Sl st in next 4 sts, (sl st, ch 3, 4 dc, ch 3, 5 dc) in next ch sp, ch 4, sc around next 2 chs of last 2 rnds, ch 4, *(5 dc, ch 3, 5 dc) in next ch sp, ch 4, sc around next 2 chs of last 2 rnds, ch 4; repeat from * around, join. Fasten off.

LARGE WINDOW HANGER

Work same as Doily.

Working around 9" ring *(see illustration)*, 20 sc around ring, sc around ring and any ch-3 sp on Hanger, (20 sc around ring, sc around ring and next ch-3 sp on Hanger) around, join with sl st in first sc. Fasten off.
Hang from window with nylon line.

MEDIUM WINDOW HANGER

Rnds 1–6: Work rnds 1–6 of Doily. At end of last rnd, fasten off.

Working around 7" ring *(see illustration)*, 12 sc around ring, sc around ring and any ch-3 sp on Hanger, (12 sc around ring, sc around ring and next ch-3 sp on Hanger) around, join with sl st in first sc. Fasten off.
Hang from window with nylon line.

SMALL WINDOW HANGER

Rnds 1–3: Work rnds 1–3 of Doily.

Rnd 4: Sl st in next st, (sl st, ch 3, 2 dc, ch 2, 3 dc) in next ch sp, ch 3, sc around next 2 chs of last 2 rnds, ch 3, *(3 dc, ch 2, 3 dc) in next shell, ch 3, sc around next 2 chs of last 2 rnds, ch 3; repeat from * around, join. Fasten off.

Working around 5" ring *(see illustration)*, 8 sc around ring, sc around ring and any ch-2 sp on Hanger, (8 sc around ring, sc around ring and next ch-2 sp on Hanger) around, join with sl st in first sc. Fasten off.
Hang from window with nylon line.

BOWL

Work same as Doily.

Cover bottom of container with plastic wrap. Apply fabric stiffener to bowl, shape over bottom of container. Let dry completely. Remove from container. Weave ribbon through ch-5 sps on rnd 6. Tie in bow. ✳

SC AROUND RING

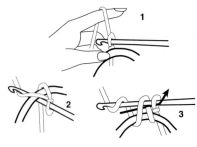

Pinecone Wreath

continued from page 91

Medium Branch (make 4)
Row 1: With I hook and brown yarn, ch 15. Fasten off.
Row 2: With F hook and two strands green held together as one, join with sl st in first ch, work loop st in each ch on last row. Fasten off. Cut loops.

Long Branch (make 4)
With ch 20, repeat Medium Evergreen Branch.

LARGE PINE CONE (make 5)
With G hook and brown yarn, ch 18; for **picot, sl st in third ch from hook**; skip next 2 chs, (dc, ch 3, picot) 2 times in next ch, (dc, ch 3, picot) 3 times in each ch across. Leaving 6" end, fasten off.
Beginning at center top, roll strand of scales into cone shape, tacking together through center with 6" end *(see illustration).*

SMALL PINE CONE
With F hook, repeat Large Pine Cone.

SNOWFLAKES
Flake A (make 2)
Rnd 1: With No. 7 steel hook and white thread, ch 6, sl st in first ch to form ring, ch 3, 2-dc cluster *(see Special Stitches)* in ring, (ch 5, 3-dc cluster) 5 times in ring, ch 2, dc in top of first cluster.
Rnd 2: *Ch 10, (sc, ch 5, sc) in next ch loop; repeat from * 4 more times, ch 10, sc in ch-2 sp, ch 5, join with sl st in first ch of ch-10. Fasten off.
To stiffen, apply undiluted fabric stiffener to item, place on surface covered with plastic wrap. Pin to shape. Let dry completely.

Flake B
Rnd 1: Repeat rnd 1 of Flake A.
Rnd 2: *Ch 15, (sc, ch 5, sc) in next ch loop; repeat from * 4 more times, ch 15, sc in ch-2 sp, ch 5, join with sl st in first ch of ch-15. Fasten off.
Stiffen same as Flake A.

Flake C (make 2)
Rnd 1: Repeat rnd 1 of Flake A.
Rnd 2: *For **picot loop,** (ch 5, sc in third ch from hook) 5 times, sl st in same ch as first sc of loop, ch 2; (sc, ch 10, sc) in next ch loop; repeat from * around, ending with sl st in dc. Fasten off.
Stiffen same as Flake A.

FINISHING
For **Bow,** with right side facing you, hold ribbon in one hand 3" from one end, measure 10" on ribbon and fold over toward the back forming first loop, gather up width of ribbon at point of loop where you are holding it between thumb and fingers.
Measure another 10" on ribbon, fold up toward the front to gathering point of first loop, gather end of second loop and hold next to end of first loop between thumb and fingers.
Gathering ends of loops at center as tightly as possible, continue measuring 10" lengths and folding loops, alternating the direction of the loops until desired number for bow are made. **Do not** let go of center.
Fold a 6" piece of wire around center and tightly twist ends together directly behind loops. Cut remaining ribbon from back of bow.
From ribbon, cut one short and one long piece of desired lengths for center loop and streamers.
Fold short piece for center loop in a tube overlapping ends about ½". Gather up width of ribbon at overlapped ends, place at center of bow and secure in place with a 6" piece of wire.
Fold long piece in half for streamers, gather ribbon at fold, attach to back of bow with remaining ends of wire. Trim ends of streamers as shown in photo.
For narrow ribbon, cut remaining wide ribbon into ¾"-wide strips and use to make a 5" bow.
Glue or pin Evergreen Branches to bottom of Wreath according to diagram.
Glue or pin small bow and three Large Pine Cones over Branches as shown in photo.
Cut 1/16" ribbon in 12", 10" and 8" pieces. Tie 1½" bow in one end of each piece, glue to bottom of each remaining Pine Cone. Glue or pin other end to Wreath behind group of Cones.
Glue or pin large bow, streamers and Snowflakes on Wreath as shown in photo. ❄

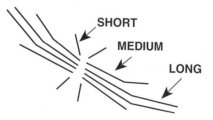

Snowman Kitchen Set

Designed by Maggie Weldon

FINISHED SIZES: Towel Holder is 5½" × 5½"; Pot Holder is 7" × 7".

MATERIALS FOR BOTH:
- ❏ Worsted yarn:
    - 100 yds. each of white and blue
    - 10 yds. black
- ❏ 7-mesh plastic canvas:
    - One 34 × 34-hole piece
    - One 6 × 34-hole piece
- ❏ Scrap orange felt
- ❏ Ten 6mm black beads
- ❏ Dish towel
- ❏ Hot glue and glue gun or craft glue
- ❏ Tapestry needle
- ❏ H hook or hook needed to obtain gauge

GAUGE: 7 sc = 2"; 4 sc rows = 1".

BASIC STITCHES: Ch, sc and sl st.

NOTE: For **color change** *(see Stitch Guide),* always change to next color in last st worked. Carry dropped yarn loosely across back of work.

TOWEL HOLDER
Row 1: With blue, ch 18, sc in second ch from hook and in each ch across, turn. *(17 sc made)*
Rows 2–18: Following graph on page 98 for color changes, ch 1, sc in each st across, turn. At end of last row, leaving 20" length for sewing, fasten off.
Rnd 19: For **Border,** with right side facing you, join white with sl st in first st of row 18, *(ch 3, skip next st, sl st in next st) 8 times, (ch 3, sl st) in same end st; working in ends of rows, (ch 3, skip next row, sl st in next row) 8 times*, ch 3, sl st in first ch of starting ch on row 1, ch 3, sl st in same st; repeat between first and second *, ch 3, join with sl st in first sl st. **Do not turn or fasten off.**
For **First Tie,** ch 75. Fasten off.
For **Second Tie,** join white with sl st in opposite top corner, ch 75. Fasten off.

FINISHING
1: With black and tapestry needle, embroider **straight stitches** *(see Stitch Guide)* for mouth according to graph.
2: From orange felt, cut nose according to pattern on page 98 and glue in place according to graph.
3: Glue beads in place according to graph.
4: With tapestry needle and blue, sew short ends of 6 × 34-hole plastic canvas piece to last 6 holes on each side of one edge on 34 × 34-hole piece.
5: Using 20" length, sew 34 × 34-hole piece to wrong side of Towel Holder with 6 × 34-hole piece on bottom edge and facing out. Insert towel between plastic canvas pieces.

POT HOLDER
Front
Row 1: With blue, ch 22, sc in second ch from hook and in each ch across, turn. *(21 sc made)*
Rows 2–24: Following graph for color changes, ch 1, sc in each st across, turn. At end of last row, fasten off.

Back
Row 1: Repeat row 1 of Front.
Rows 2–24: Ch 1, sc in each st across, turn. At end of last row, fasten off.

BORDER
Holding Front and Back wrong sides together and working through both thicknesses, with front facing you, join white with sl st in first st of row 24, ch 1, (sc, ch 3, sc) in same st, (ch 3, skip next st, sc in next st) 5 times, ch 15, sl st in sc just made *(hanger made),* (ch 3, skip next st, sc in next st) 5 times, ch 3, sc in same st; *working down end of rows, (ch 3, skip next row, sc in next row) 11 times, ch 3*; working in opposite side of starting ch, (sc, ch 3, sc) in first st, (ch 3, skip next st, sc in next st) 10 times, (ch 3, sc) in same st; repeat between first and second *, join with sl st in first sc. Fasten off.

FINISHING
Repeat steps 1–3 of Towel Holder Finishing. ❄

graphs on page 98

Snowman Kitchen Set

continued from page 96

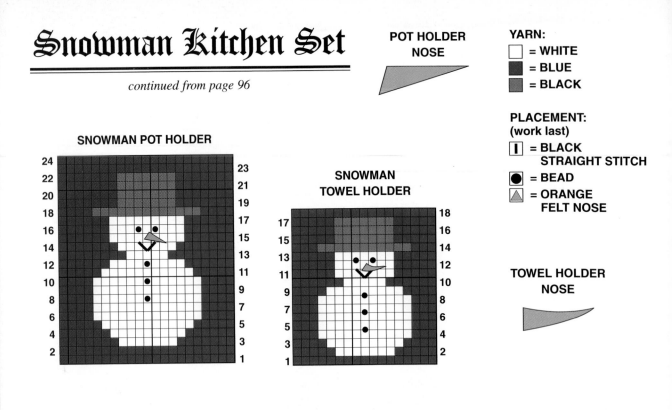

POT HOLDER NOSE

SNOWMAN POT HOLDER

SNOWMAN TOWEL HOLDER

YARN:
☐ = WHITE
■ = BLUE
■ = BLACK

PLACEMENT:
(work last)
Ⅰ = BLACK STRAIGHT STITCH
● = BEAD
△ = ORANGE FELT NOSE

TOWEL HOLDER NOSE

Favorite Foods

What invokes beloved Christmas memories most? The sanctity of a candlelit service? Traditional carols floating on the frosty air? A family gathering for gift unwrapping? Yes, but how about the food?

The feasting that serves a centerpiece of celebrations springs originally from ancient festivals observing the symbolic "return of light" signified by the winter solstice. After December 25 was declared the official date for celebrating Christmas by Pope Julius I in A.D. 350, the celebration gradually became the "great feast" of the year, especially in England. In 1252, King Henry III roasted 600 oxen for a Christmas menu that also included salmon pies and roasted peacocks. By the time of the great feudal lords, roast suckling pig and stuffed boar's head highlighted the delicacies consumed during twelve full days of Christmas merriment. Lavish meals that included mulled wine for toasts, stuffed roast goose, bread puddings and fruit-filled cakes were popularized by Queen Victoria.

This Victorian legacy lives on, especially in the form of two dishes synonymous with Christmas: eggnog and fruitcake.

Eggnog, traditionally a cold punch made rich with eggs, cream, sugar and some form of alcohol, enjoys modern twists that involve egg substitute and "light" cream, or the use of apple juice instead of alcohol. At the other end of the scale is an old colonial American recipe that lists ingredients as three dozen eggs, one gallon thick cream, one pint each whisky, rum, gin and brandy (to "cook" the eggs) and sugar, from one to one-and-a-half pounds, to taste.

The recipe calls for whipping the egg whites and yolks separately until light, and dividing the sugar between the whites and yolks, beating again until light, then combining the two egg mixtures and adding the whiskey. Next, the cook should whip the cream, folding it gradually into the egg mixture and beating in, at intervals, the rum, gin and brandy. The nog is then ready to be served--in very small portions we assume!

Fruitcake, that confection of dried fruits, nuts and spirits, though seemingly consumed by the few and ridiculed by the many, is considered the queen of cakes in some countries, and is honored as the traditional wedding cake in England even today.

Santa's Workshop

Santa Claus is Coming to Town

You better watch out.
You better not cry.
Better not pout,
I'm telling you why.
Santa Claus is coming to town.
He's making a list
and checking it twice;
gonna find out
who's naughty and nice.
Santa Claus is coming to town.

Rocking Horse

Designed by Michele Wilcox

FINISHED SIZE: 12" × 14".

MATERIALS:
- ❏ Worsted yarn:
  - 4½ oz. brown
  - 2½ oz. red
  - 1 oz. off-white
  - Small amounts blue and black
- ❏ Polyester fiberfill
- ❏ 2 small jingle bells
- ❏ Tapestry needle
- ❏ F hook or size needed to obtain gauge

GAUGE: 9 sc = 2"; 9 sc rows = 2".

BASIC STITCHES: Ch, sl st, sc.

BODY SIDE (make 2)

Row 1: With brown, ch 28, 2 sc in second ch from hook, sc in next 25 chs, 2 sc in last ch, turn. *(29 sc made)*

Rows 2–3: Ch 1, 2 sc in first st, sc in each st across to last st, 2 sc in last st, turn. *(31, 33)*

Rows 4–11: Ch 1, sc in each st across, turn.

Row 12: Ch 1, sc first 2 sts tog, sc in each st across, turn. *(32)*

Row 13: Ch 1, sc in each st across to last 2 sts, sc last 2 sts tog, turn. *(31)*

Row 14: Ch 1, sc first 2 sts tog, sc in next 10 sts, sl st in next 6 sts, sc next 2 sts tog, sc in next 8 sts, sc next 2 sts tog, sc in last st, turn. *(22 sc, 6 sl sts)*

Row 15: For **neck,** ch 1, sc in first 10 sts, sc next 2 sts tog leaving last 16 sts unworked, turn. *(11)*

Row 16: Repeat row 4.

Row 17: Repeat row 13. *(10)*

Rows 18–20: Repeat row 4.

Row 21: Repeat row 13. *(9)*

Rows 22–23: Repeat row 4.

Row 24: Ch 1, sc first 2 sts tog, sc in last 7 sts; for **head,** ch 5; turn. *(8 sc, 5 ch)*

Row 25: Sc in second ch from hook, sc in next 3 chs, sc in last 8 sts, turn. *(12)*

Row 26: Ch 1, sc first 2 sts tog, sc in next 9 sts, 2 sc in last st; for **nose,** ch 4; turn. *(12 sc, 4 chs)*

Row 27: 2 sc in second ch from hook, sc in next 2 chs, sc in last 12 sts, turn. *(16)*

continued on page 106

Old-Time Teddy

Designed by Janie Heffel

FINISHED SIZE: Approximately 23" tall.

MATERIALS:
- ❑ Worsted yarn:
    - 12 oz. tan
    - ½ oz. brown
    - Small amount black
- ❑ 1 yd. of ribbon
- ❑ Polyester fiberfill
- ❑ 1 pair brown 15mm animal eyes with washers
- ❑ 2 pair 30mm doll joints
- ❑ Tapestry and sculpture needles
- ❑ G hook or hook needed to obtain gauge

GAUGE: 4 sc = 1"; 4 sc rows = 1".

BASIC STITCHES: Ch, sl st, sc.

SPECIAL STITCHES: For **sc decrease (sc dec)**, sc next 2 sts tog *(see Stitch Guide)*.
For **3-sc dec**, (insert hook in next st, yo, pull through st) 3 times, yo, pull through all 4 lps on hook.

HEAD SIDE (make 2)
Row 1: Starting at bottom of neck, with tan, ch 16, sc in second ch from hook, sc in each ch across, turn. *(15 sc made)*
Row 2: Ch 1, sc in each st across, turn.
Row 3: Ch 1, 2 sc in first st, sc in each st across with 2 sc in last st, turn. *(17)*
Row 4: Ch 1, sc in each st across with 2 sc in last st, turn. *(18)*
Row 5: Ch 1, 2 sc in first st, sc in each st across, turn. *(19)*
Row 6: Ch 1, sc in each st across with 2 sc in last st, turn. *(20)*
Rows 7–14: Repeat rows 5 and 6 alternately. *(28 sts at end of row 14.)*
Row 15: Ch 1, **sc dec** *(see Special Stitches)*, sc in each st across, turn. *(27)*
Row 16: Ch 1, sc in next 25 sts, sc dec, turn. *(26)*
Row 17: Ch 1, sc dec, sc in each st across, turn. *(25)*
Row 18: Ch 1, sc dec, sc in next 15 sts, sl st in next 2 sts leaving remaining 6 sts unworked for front of face, turn. *(18)*
Row 19: Ch 1, sc dec 2 times, sc in each st across to last 2 sts, sc dec, turn. *(15 sc)*
Rows 20–23: Ch 1, sc dec, sc in each st across to last 2 sts, sc dec, turn. At end of last row, fasten off. *(7 sts at end of last row.)*

HEAD GUSSET
Row 1: Starting at bottom back of neck, with tan,

ch 8, sc in second ch from hook, sc in each ch across, turn. *(7 sc made)*
Rows 2–4: Ch 1, sc in each st across, turn.
Row 5: Ch 1, sc in first 3 sts, 2 sc in next st, sc in last 3 sts, turn. *(8)*
Row 6: Ch 1, sc in each st across, turn.
Row 7: Ch 1, sc in first 4 sts, 2 sc in next st, sc in each st across, turn. *(9)*
Row 8: Ch 1, sc in each st across, turn.
Rows 9–12: Repeat rows 7 and 8 alternately. *(11 sts at end of last row.)*
Rows 13–14: Ch 1, sc in first 6 sts, 2 sc in next st, sc in each st across, turn. *(12, 13)*
Rows 15–16: Ch 1, sc in first 6 sts, 2 sc in next st, sc in each st across, turn. *(14, 15)*
Row 17: Ch 1, sc in first 3 sts, (2 sc in next st, sc in next 3 sts) across, turn. *(18)*
Row 18: Ch 1, sc in each st across, turn.
Row 19: Ch 1, sc in first 8 sts, 2 sc in next st, sc in each st across, turn. *(19)*
Rows 20–23: Ch 1, sc in each st across, turn.
Row 24: Ch 1, sc in first 9 sts, sc dec, sc in each st across, turn. *(18)*
Row 25: Ch 1, sc in each st across, turn.
Row 26: Ch 1, sc in first 4 sts, sc dec, (sc in next 4 sts, sc dec) across, turn. *(15)*
Rows 27–29: Ch 1, sc in each st across, turn.
Row 30: Ch 1, sc in first 7 sts, sc dec, sc in each st across, turn. *(14)*
Row 31: Ch 1, sc in each st across, turn.
Row 32: Ch 1, sc in first 6 sts, sc dec, sc in each st across, turn. *(13)*
Row 33: Ch 1, sc in first 3 sts, (sc dec, sc in next 3 sts) across, turn. *(11)*
Row 34: Ch 1, sc in first 2 sts, sc dec, sc in next 2 sts, sc dec, sc in last 3 sts, turn. *(9)*
Row 35: Ch 1, sc in first 2 sts, sc dec, sc in next 2 sts, sc dec, sc in last st, turn. *(7)*
Rows 36–37: Ch 1, sc in each st across, turn.
Row 38: Ch 1, sc in first 3 sts, sc dec, sc in each st across, turn. *(6)*
Row 39: Ch 1, sc in each st across, turn.
Row 40: Ch 1, sc in first 2 sts, sc dec, sc in last 2 sts, turn. *(5)*
Row 41: Ch 1, sc dec, sc in next st, sc dec, turn. *(3)*
Row 42: Ch 1, sc dec, sc in last st, turn. *(2)*
Row 43: Ch 1, sc dec, fasten off. *(1)*

ASSEMBLY
Starting on front at bottom of neck *(see illustration)*, with tan yarn and tapestry needle, sew matching ends of rows 1–17 on Head Sides together.

continued on page 104

Old-Time Teddy

continued from page 102

Starting at bottom back of neck, with tan yarn and tapestry needle, easing to fit, sew Head Gusset to Head Sides with row 43 at end of row 17 on front of Head *(see assembly illustration)*.

ASSEMBLY ILLUSTRATION

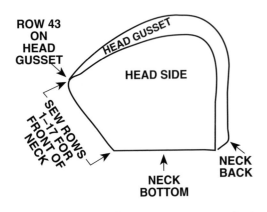

Attach eyes on seam between rows 18 and 19 on Head Sides 2" apart. Stuff Head firmly.

With black yarn, using satin stitch *(see Stitch Guide)*, embroider nose over rows 42–43 on Head Gusset and over rows 15–17 on front of Head Sides *(see Facial Feature illustration)*.

With black yarn, using straight stitch *(see Stitch Guide)*, embroider mouth below nose.

FACIAL FEATURE ILLUSTRATION

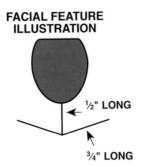

½" LONG

¾" LONG

EAR (make 2)
Row 1: With tan, ch 9, sc in second ch from hook, sc in each ch across, turn. *(8 sc made)*

Row 2: Ch 1, sc in first 3 sts, 2 sc in next st, sc in each st across, turn. *(9)*

Rows 3–4: Ch 1, sc in first 4 sts, 2 sc in next st, sc in each st across, turn. *(10, 11)*

Row 5: Ch 1, sc in first 5 sts, 2 sc in next st, sc in each st across, turn. *(12)*

Row 6: Ch 1, sc in each st across, turn.

Rows 7–9: Ch 1, sc dec, sc in each st across to last 2 sts, sc dec, turn. *(10, 8, 6)*

Rows 10–11: Ch 1, sc in each st across, turn.

Rows 12–14: Ch 1, 2 sc in first st, sc in each st across to last st, 2 sc in last st, turn. *(8, 10, 12)*

Row 15: Ch 1, sc in each st across, turn.

Rows 16–19: Ch 1, sc in first 4 sts, sc dec, sc in each st across, turn. *(8 sc at end of row 19)*

Row 20: Ch 1, sc in each st across. Fasten off.

Fold Ears in half at row 10. With tan yarn, sew ends of rows on one Ear together. Repeat on other Ear.

With tan yarn, sew Ears over rows 16–19 at back of Head Sides 3½" apart across top.

BODY SIDE (make 4)
Row 1: Starting at neck, with tan, ch 14, sc in second ch from hook, sc in each ch across, turn. *(13 sc made)*

Rows 2–4: Ch 1, sc in each st across, turn.

Rows 5–6: Ch 1, sc in first 6 sts, 2 sc in next st, sc in each st across, turn. *(14, 15)*

Rows 7–9: Ch 1, sc in first 7 sts, 2 sc in next st, sc in each st across, turn. *(16, 17, 18)*

Rows 10–18: Ch 1, sc in each st across, turn.

Rows 19–20: Ch 1, sc in first 8 sts, sc dec, sc in each st across, turn. *(17, 16)*

Rows 21–22: Ch 1, sc in first 7 sts, sc dec, sc in each st across, turn. *(15, 14)*

Rows 23–24: Ch 1, sc in first 6 sts, sc dec, sc in each st across, turn. *(13, 12)*

Rows 25–26: Ch 1, sc in first 5 sts, sc dec, sc in each st across, turn. *(11, 10)*

Rows 27–29: Ch 1, sc in each st across, turn.

Rows 30–31: Ch 1, sc in first 4 sts, sc dec, sc in each st across, turn. *(9, 8)*

Rows 32–33: Ch 1, sc in first 3 sts, sc dec, sc in each st across, turn. *(7, 6)*

Rows 34–35: Ch 1, sc in first 2 sts, sc dec, sc in each st across, turn. *(5, 4)*

Row 36: Ch 1, sc in first st, sc dec, sc in last st, turn. *(3)*

Row 37: Ch 1, sc in first st, sc dec, turn. *(2)*

Row 38: Ch 1, sc dec, fasten off. *(1)*

With tan yarn, sew matching ends of rows on Body Sides together, leaving neck opening unsewn.

ARM TOP SIDE (make 2)
Row 1: Starting at shoulder, with tan, ch 6, sc in second ch from hook, sc in each ch across, turn. *(5 sc made)*

Row 2: Ch 1, 2 sc in first st, sc in each st across with 2 sc in last st, turn. *(7)*

Row 3: Ch 1, sc in first 3 sts, 2 sc in next st, sc in each st across, turn. *(8)*

Rows 4–5: Ch 1, 2 sc in first st, sc in each st across with 2 sc in last st, turn. *(10, 12)*

Row 6: Ch 1, sc in first 6 sts, 2 sc in next st, sc in each st across, turn. *(13)*

Rows 7–10: Ch 1, sc in each st across, turn.

Rows 11–12: Ch 1, sc in first 7 sts, 2 sc in next st, sc in each st across, turn. *(14, 15)*

Rows 13–15: Ch 1, sc in each st across, turn.

Row 16: Ch 1, sc dec, sc in each st across, turn. *(14)*

Rows 17–18: Ch 1, sc in each st across, turn.

Row 19: Ch 1, sc in first 6 sts, sc dec, sc in each st across, turn. *(13)*

Rows 20–23: Ch 1, sc in each st across, turn.

Row 24: Ch 1, sc in each st across with 2 sc in last st, turn. *(14)*

Row 25: Ch 1, sc in each st across to last 2 sts, sc dec, turn. *(13)*

Rows 26–27: Repeat rows 24 and 25.

Rows 28–29: Ch 1, sc in each st across, turn.

Rows 30–31: Repeat rows 24 and 25.

Rows 32–35: Ch 1, sc dec, sc in each st across to last 2 sts, sc dec, turn. *(5 sts at end of row 35.)*

Row 36: Ch 1, sc in each st across. Fasten off.

ARM UNDERSIDE (make 2)

Rows 1–27: Repeat rows 1–27 of Arm Topside.

Row 28: Ch 1, sc in each st across, changing to brown in last st made *(see Stitch Guide)*, turn. Fasten off tan.

Row 29: For Paw, ch 1, sc in each st across, turn.

Row 30: Ch 1, sc in each st across with 2 sc in last st, turn. *(14)*

Row 31: Ch 1, sc in each st across to last 2 sts, sc dec, turn. *(13)*

Rows 32–35: Ch 1, sc dec, sc in each st across to last 2 sts, sc dec, turn. *(5 sts at end of row 35)*

Row 36: Ch 1, sc in each st across, fasten off.

LEG SIDE (make 4)

Row 1: Starting at bottom, with tan, ch 12, sc in second ch from hook, sc in each ch across, turn. *(11 sc made)*

Rows 2–4: Ch 1, 2 sc in first st, sc in each st across with 2 sc in last st, turn. *(13, 15, 17)*

Rows 5–8: Ch 1, sc in each st across, turn.

Row 9: Ch 1, 3-sc dec *(see Special Stitches)*, sc in each st across, turn. *(15)*

Row 10: Ch 1, sc in each st across, turn.

Row 11: Ch 1, sc dec, sc in each st across, turn. *(14)*

Row 12: Ch 1, sc in each st across, turn.

Row 13: Ch 1, 3-sc dec, sc in each st across, turn. *(12)*

Rows 14–15: Ch 1, sc in each st across, turn.

Rows 16–18: Ch 1, sc in first 6 sts, 2 sc in next st, sc in each st across, turn. *(13, 14, 15)*

Row 19: Ch 1, sc in each st across, turn.

Row 20: Ch 1, sc in first 7 sts, 2 sc in next st, sc in each st across, turn. *(16)*

Rows 21–22: Ch 1, sc in each st across, turn.

Row 23: Ch 1, sc in first 8 sts, 2 sc in next st, sc in each st across, turn. *(17)*

Rows 24–26: Ch 1, sc in each st across, turn.

Row 27: Ch 1, sc in first 8 sts, 2 sc in next st, sc in each st across, turn. *(18)*

Rows 28–29: Ch 2, sc in each st across, turn.

Rows 30–31: Ch 1, sc in first 8 sts, sc dec, sc in each st across, turn. *(17, 16)*

Row 32: Ch 1, sc dec, sc in each st across to last 2 sts, sc dec, turn. *(14)*

Row 33: Ch 1, sc in each st across, turn.

Row 34: Ch 1, sc dec, sc in each st across to last 2 sts, sc dec, turn. *(12)*

Rows 35–36: Ch 1, sc in each st across, turn.

Row 37: Ch 1, sc dec, sc in each st across to last 2 sts, sc dec, turn. *(10)*

Row 38: Ch 1, sc in each st across, turn.

Rows 39–40: Ch 1, sc dec, sc in each st across to last 2 sts, sc dec, turn. At end of last row, fasten off. *(8, 6)*

FOOT PAD (make 2)

Row 1: With brown, ch 7, sc in second ch from hook, sc in each ch across, turn. *(6 sc made)*

Row 2: Ch 1, sc in each st across, turn.

Row 3: Ch 1, 2 sc in first st, sc in each st across with 2 sc in last st, turn. *(8)*

Row 4: Ch 1, sc in each st across, turn.

Row 5: Ch 1, 2 sc in first st, sc in each st across with 2 sc in last st, turn. *(10)*

Rows 6–10: Ch 1, sc in each st across, turn.

Rows 11–13: Ch 1, sc dec, sc in each st across to last 2 sts, sc dec, turn. *(8, 6, 4)*

Row 14: Ch 1, sc dec 2 times, turn. *(2)*

Row 15: Ch 1, sc in next 2 sts. Fasten off.

ASSEMBLY

With matching yarn, sew matching ends of rows 1–36 and sts on one Arm Topside to one Arm Underside with Paw on bottom, leaving sts at shoulders unsewn. Reverse remaining Arm pieces and repeat.

For **Arm placement,** count four rows from shoulder on Arm Underside and six rows from neck edge on left side of Body Side, insert one locking stem from one doll joint through both thicknesses, place washer over stem and secure with lock washer. Repeat with other Arm.

With tan yarn, sew matching ends of rows 3–40 on two Leg Sides together, leaving sts on last row unsewn. Repeat with other Leg pieces.

For **Leg placement,** count down five rows from top on Leg and measure 2" from bottom of Body *(Leg placement will be directly below Arm),* insert one locking stem from one doll joint through both thicknesses, place washer over stem and secure with lock washer. Repeat with other Leg.

Stuff Body firmly, leaving neck open.

Stuff Arms. With tan yarn, sew opening at shoulder on Arm closed. Repeat on other Arm.

Stuff Legs. With brown yarn, sew opening at top of Leg closed. Repeat on other Leg.

With brown yarn, with center of row 1 on Foot Pad at one seam and center of row 15 at other end of seam, sew to bottom of Leg. Repeat with other Leg.

For **toes,** with brown yarn, using straight stitch *(see Stitch Guide),* embroider one stitch on top seam *(see foot illustration),* embroider stitches ½" apart. Repeat on other Leg.

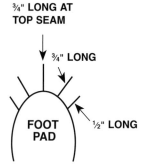

¾" LONG AT TOP SEAM

¾" LONG

FOOT PAD

½" LONG

continued on page 106

Old-Time Teddy

continued from page 105

With tan yarn, using a running stitch *(see illustration)*, gather neck edge on Body, pulling up to fit neck opening on Head, sew Head and Body together.

With tan yarn and sculpture needle, place a stitch through Arm Topside at joint, going through Body and out through other Arm at joint, going back through Body; pull tightly to make indentation in Arm. Secure end and fasten off.

With tan yarn and sculpture needle, place a stitch through one Leg at joint, going through Body and out through other Leg at joint, going back through Body; pull tightly to make an indentation in Leg. Secure end and fasten off.

Tie ribbon in bow around neck as desired. ❊

RUNNING STITCH

Rocking Horse

continued from page 101

Row 28: Repeat row 12. *(15)*

Row 29: Repeat row 4.

Rows 30–31: Repeat row 12. *(14, 13)*

Row 32: Ch 1, sc first 2 sts tog, sc in next 4 sts, sl st in next st leaving last 6 sts unworked; for **first piece, do not turn;** for **second piece, turn.**

Rnd 33: Working around outer edge, ch 1, sc in each st and in end of each row around, join with sl st in first sc. Fasten off.

Hold both pieces wrong sides together; matching sts, working through both thicknesses in **back lps** *(see Stitch Guide),* join brown with sl st in any st, sl st in each st around stuffing before closing, join with sl st in first sl st. Fasten off.

LEG SIDE (make 8)

Row 1: Starting at bottom, with brown, ch 6, sc in second ch from hook, sc in each ch across, turn. *(5 sc made)*

Row 2: Ch 1, sc in each st across, turn.

Row 3: Ch 1, sc first 2 sts tog, sc in each st across to last 2 sts, sc last 2 sts tog, turn. *(3)*

Rows 4–9: Repeat row 2.

Row 10: Ch 1, 2 sc in first st, sc in each st across to last st, 2 sc in last st, turn. *(5)*

Rows 11–12: Repeat rows 2 and 3, ending with 3 sts in last row.

Rows 13–14: Repeat row 2.

Rows 15–18: Repeat rows 10 and 2 alternately, ending with 7 sts in last row.

Rows 19–23: Repeat row 2.

Rows 24–25: Repeat row 3. At end of last row, **do not turn.** *(3)*

Rnd 26: Working around outer edge, ch 1, sc in end of each row and in each st around with 3 sc in each bottom corner, join with sl st in first sc. Fasten off.

For each Leg, hold two Side pieces wrong sides together; matching sts, working through both thicknesses in **back lps,** join brown with sl st in any st, sl st in each st around stuffing before closing, join with sl st in first st. Fasten off.

Sew rows 22–26 of two Legs over rows 4–8 on front end of each side of Body 1½" from joining seam. Sew rows 22–26 of other two Legs over rows 4–8 on back end of each side of Body 1" from joining seam.

EAR (make 2)

Note: Do not join rnds unless otherwise stated. Mark first st of each rnd.

Rnd 1: With brown, ch 2, 6 sc in second ch from hook. *(6 sc made)*

Rnds 2–3: Sc in each st around.

Rnd 4: (2 sc in next st, sc in next st) around. *(9)*

Rnd 5: Sc in each st around.

Rnd 6: (Sc next 2 sts tog) 4 times, sl st in last st. Fasten off.

Flatten rnd 6; sew over rows 31 and 32 on each side at back of head with ears pointing back slightly.

For **eyes,** with black, using satin stitch *(see Stitch Guide),* embroider over end of row 32 and rnd 33 in front of each ear ¾".

ROCKER SIDE (make 4)

Row 1: With red, ch 34, 2 sc in second ch from hook, sc in each ch across to last ch, 2 sc in last ch, turn. *(35 sc made)*

Rows 2–3: Ch 1, 2 sc in first st, sc in each st across to last st, 2 sc in last st, turn. *(37, 39)*

Row 4: For **first end,** ch 1, 2 sc in first st, sc in next st, sc next 2 sts tog leaving last 35 sts unworked, turn. *(4)*

Row 5: Ch 1, sc first 2 sts tog, sc in next st, 2 sc in last st, turn. *(4)*

Row 6: Ch 1, 2 sc in first st, sc in next st, sc next 2 sts tog, turn. *(4)*

Rows 7–13: Repeat rows 5 and 6 alternately. At end of last row, fasten off.

Row 4: For **second end** skip next 31 sts on row 3, join red with sl st in next st, ch 1, sc first 2 sts tog, sc in next st, 2 sc in last st, turn. *(13)*

Rows 5–13: Repeat rows 6 and 5 of first end alternately.

Rnd 14: Working around outer edge, ch 1, sc in each st and in end of each row around, join with sl st in first sc. Fasten off.

For each Rocker, hold two Side pieces wrong sides together; matching sts, working through both thicknesses in **back lps,** join red with sl st in any st, sl st in each st around stuffing firmly before closing, join with sl st in first sl st. Fasten off.

ROCKER BAR (make 2)

Rnd 1: With red, ch 10, sl st in first ch to form ring, sc in each ch around. *(10 sc made)*

Rnds 2–17: Sc in each st around. At end of last rnd, join with sl st in first sc. Fasten off. Stuff firmly.

Center one front Leg and one back Leg on top of one Rocker 6" apart, sew in place. Repeat with other Rocker.

Sew each end of one Bar to inside of Rockers between front Legs. Repeat with other Bar between back Legs.

MANE & TAIL

For each **mane fringe,** cut 2 strands off-white each 3" long; with both strands held together, fold in half, insert hook in st, pull fold through st, pull ends through fold, tighten. Work 16 fringe in joining seam along back of neck and head. Unravel fringe, brush lightly.

For **tail,** cut 10 strands off-white each 18" long; tie separate 14" strand of off-white around center of all strands held together leaving ends for sewing. Fold strands in half, sew to back end of Body on joining seam. Brush lightly.

BLANKET

Rnd 1: With blue, ch 15, sc in second ch from hook, sc in next 12 chs, 3 sc in last ch; working on opposite side of ch, sc in next 12 chs, 2 sc in last ch. *(30 sc made)*

Rnd 2: 2 sc in first st, sc in next 12 sts, 2 sc in each of next 3 sts, sc in next 12 sts, 2 sc in each of last 2 sts. *(36)*

Rnd 3: Sc in first st, 2 sc in next st, sc in next 12 sts, (2 sc in next st, sc in next st) 3 times, sc in next 13 sts, 2 sc in next st, sc in next st, 2 sc in last st, join with sl st in first sc. Fasten off. *(42)*

Rnd 4: Working this rnd in **back lps,** join red with sc in any st, ch 2, skip next st, (sc in next st, ch 2, skip next st) around, join with sl st in first sc. Fasten off.

Sew to Horse's back.

BRIDLE

For **nose band,** with blue, ch 18, sl st in first ch to form ring; ch 26, skip next 8 chs of nose band, sl st in next ch, turn; sl st in next 8 chs of ch-26; for **forehead band,** ch 10, skip next 10 chs of ch-26; sl st in next 8 chs; for **reins,** ch 70, sl st in st on opposite side of nose band. Fasten off.

Sew 1 jingle bell to each side of nose band at ends of reins. Place nose band on nose with 10 skipped chs of ch-26 behind Ears and with forehead band in front of ears. ✻

Yes, Virginia, There is a Santa Claus

I am 8 years old. Some of my little friends say there is no Santa Claus. Papa says, "If you see it in The Sun, it's so." Please tell me the truth, is there a Santa Claus? Virginia O'Hanlon

Virginia, your little friends are wrong. They have been affected by the skepticism of a skeptical age. They do not believe except they see. They think that nothing can be which is not comprehensible by their little minds. All minds, Virginia, whether they be men's or children's, are little. In this great universe of ours, man is a mere insect, an ant, in his intellect as compared with the boundless world about him, as measured by the intelligence capable of grasping the whole of truth and knowledge. Yes, Virginia, there is a Santa Claus. He exists as certainly as love and generosity and devotion exist, and you know that they abound and give to your life its highest beauty and joy. Alas! how dreary would be the world if there were not Santa Claus! It would be as dreary as if there were no Virginias. There would be no childlike faith then, no poetry, no romance to make tolerable this existence. We should have no enjoyment, except in sense and sight. The eternal light with which childhood fills the world would be extinguished. Not believe in Santa Claus! You might as well not believe in fairies. You might get your papa to hire men to watch in all the chimneys on Christmas eve to catch Santa Claus, but even if you did not see Santa Claus coming down, what would that prove? Nobody sees Santa Claus, but that is no sign that there is no Santa Claus. The most real things in the world are those that neither children nor men can see. Did you ever see fairies dancing on the lawn? Of course not, but that's no proof that there are not there. Nobody can conceive or imagine all the wonders there are unseen and unseeable in the world. You tear apart the baby's rattle and see what makes the noise inside, but there is a veil covering the unseen world which not the strongest man, nor even the united strength of all the strongest men that ever lived could tear apart. Only faith, poetry, love, romance, can push aside that curtain and view and picture the supernatural beauty and glory beyond. Is it all real? Ah, Virginia, in all this world there is nothing else real and abiding. No Santa Claus? Thank God he lives and lives forever. A thousand years from now, Virginia, nay, 10 times 10,000 years from now, he will continue to make glad the heart of childhood.

Francis P. Church, The New York Sun 1897

Designed by Michele Wilcox

Ice-Fishing Penguin

FINISHED SIZE: 3¾" tall.

MATERIALS:
- ❑ Sport yarn:
  - ½ oz. black
  - Small amount each white, green, orange, blue and off-white
- ❑ 4¾" twig
- ❑ 6" piece black crochet cotton
- ❑ Polyester fiberfill
- ❑ Tapestry needle
- ❑ D hook or hook needed to obtain gauge

GAUGE: 6 sc = 1"; 6 sc rows = 1".

BASIC STITCHES: Ch, sl st, sc, hdc, dc.

NOTE: Work in continuous rnds; do not join unless otherwise stated. Mark first st of each rnd.

BODY

Rnd 1: Starting at top of head, with black, ch 2, 6 sc in second ch from hook. *(6 sc made)*

Rnd 2: 2 sc in each st around. *(12)*

Rnd 3: Sc in each st around.

Rnd 4: (Sc in next st, 2 sc in next st) around. *(18)*

Rnds 5–7: Sc in each st around.

Rnd 8: (Sc in next st, sc next 2 sts tog) around. *(12)*

Rnd 9: (Sc in next st, 2 sc in next st) around. *(18)*

Rnd 10: (Sc in next 2 sts, 2 sc in next st) around. *(24)*

Rnds 11–20: Sc in each st around.

Rnd 21: (Sc in next 2 sts, sc next 2 sts tog) around. Stuff. *(18)*

Rnd 22: (Sc in next st, sc next 2 sts tog) around. *(12)*

Rnd 23: (Sc next 2 sts tog) around, join with sl st in first sc. *(6)*
Leaving 8" for sewing, fasten off. Sew opening closed.

BEAK
Rnd 1: With orange, ch 2, 6 sc in second ch from hook. *(6 sc made)*

Rnds 2–3: Sc in each st around. At end of last rnd, join with sl st in first sc. Fasten off.
Sew over rnds 4–6 of Body.
With blue, using French knot *(see Stitch Guide),* embroider eyes ⅝" apart between rnds 3–4 on Body.

FOOT *(make 2)*
For **toes,** with orange, (ch 4, sc in second ch from hook, sc in next 2 chs) 3 times, **do not turn,** ch 1, sc in end of next 3 toes. Fasten off.
Sew ½" apart on rnd 22 of Body.

TUMMY
Row 1: Starting at bottom, with white, ch 7, sc in second ch from hook, sc in each ch across, turn. *(6 sc made)*

Rows 2–3: Ch 1, 2 sc in first st, sc in each st across with 2 sc in last st, turn. *(8, 10)*

Rows 4–6: Ch 1, sc in each st across, turn.

Row 7: Ch 1, sc next 2 sts tog, sc in each st across to last 2 sts, sc last 2 sts tog, turn. *(8)*

Rows 8–11: Repeat rows 4 and 7 alternately. *(4 sc at end of row 11.)*

Rnd 12: Working around outer edge, ch 1, sc in each st and in end of each row around, join with sl st in first sc. Fasten off.
Sew Tummy over center front of rnds 10–20 on Body.

WING *(make 2)*
Rnds 1–2: With black, repeat rnds 1–2 of Body.

Rnds 3–6: Sc in each st around.

Row 7: Flatten last rnd; working through both thicknesses, sc in next 6 sts. Fasten off. *(6)*
Sew row 7 to rnd 10 on side of Body.

SCARF
Row 1: With green, ch 60, sc in

continued on page 110

continued from page 109

second ch from hook, sc in each ch across, turn. *(59 sc made)*

Rows 2–4: Ch 1, sc in each st across, turn. At end of last row, fasten off. Tie around neck.

FISH
Rnd 1: With off-white, ch 2, 6 sc in second ch from hook. *(6 sc made)*

Rnds 2–5: Sc in each st around.

Rnd 6: (Skip next st, sc in next st, sl st in next st) 2 times; for **tail fin,** (ch 4, sc in second ch from hook, hdc in next ch, dc in last ch, sl st in next st on rnd 5) 2 times. Fasten off.

Tie one end of crochet cotton to stick, tie other end to Fish. Place stick under left Wing. Tack Wing down.

Saucer Bear

FINISHED SIZE: 5" tall sitting

MATERIALS:
- ❏ Sport yarn:
    - ½ oz. beige
    - Small amount each blue, green and black
- ❏ ¾" × 14" red felt
- ❏ 4"-diameter saucer or basket
- ❏ Polyester fiberfill
- ❏ Craft glue
- ❏ D hook or hook needed to obtain gauge

GAUGE: 6 sc = 1"; 6 sc rows = 1".

BASIC STITCHES: Ch, sl st, sc.

NOTE: Work in continuous rnds; do not join unless otherwise stated. Mark first st of each rnd.

HEAD & BODY
Rnd 1: With beige, ch 2, 6 sc in second ch from hook. *(6 sc made)*

Rnd 2: 2 sc in each st around. *(12)*

Rnd 3: (Sc in next st, 2 sc in next st) around. *(18)*

Rnd 4: (Sc in next 2 sts, 2 sc in next st) around. *(24)*

Rnd 5: Sc in each st around.

Rnd 6: (Sc in next 3 sts, 2 sc in next st) around. *(30)*

Rnds 7–12: Sc in each st around.

Rnd 13: (Sc in next 3 sts, sc next 2 sts tog) around. *(24)*

Rnd 14: (Sc in next 2 sts, sc next 2 sts tog) around. *(18)*

Rnd 15: (Sc in next st, sc next 2 sts tog) around. *(12)*

Rnd 16: Sc in each st around, join with sl st in first sc. Fasten off.

Rnd 17: Join blue with sc in first st, sc in same st, 2 sc in each st around. *(24)*

Rnd 18: Sc in each st around.

Rnd 19: (Sc in next 3 sts, 2 sc in next st) around. *(30)*

Rnds 20–23: Sc in each st around. At end of last rnd, join as before. Fasten off.

Rnd 24: Join green with sc in first st, sc in each st around.

Rnds 25–26: Sc in each st around. At end of last rnd, join. Fasten off.

Rnd 27: Join blue with sc in first st, sc in each st around.

Rnd 28: Sc in each st around, join. Fasten off.

Rnd 29: Join beige with sc in first st, sc in each st around.

Rnds 30–32: Sc in each st around.

Rnds 33–35: Repeat rnds 13–15. Stuff.

Rnd 36: (Sc next 2 sts tog) around, join. Fasten off. Sew opening closed. *(6)*

MUZZLE
Rnd 1: With beige, ch 2, 6 sc in second ch from hook. *(6 sc made)*

Rnd 2: 2 sc in each st around. *(12)*

Rnds 3–4: Sc in each st around. At end of last rnd, join with sl st in first sc. Fasten off. Stuff. Sew over rnds 8–12 of Head.

EAR
Rnd 1: With beige, ch 2, 6 sc in second ch from hook. *(6 sc made)*

Rnd 2: 2 sc in each st around. *(12)*

Rnds 3–4: Sc in each st around. At end of last rnd, join with sl st in first sc.

Rnd 5: (Skip next st, sl st in next st) around, join with sl st in first st. Fasten off. Flatten rnd 5, sew over rnds 6–9 on each side of Head.

ARM
Rnd 1: With beige, ch 2, 6 sc in second ch from hook. *(6 sc made)*

Rnd 2: 2 sc in each st around. *(12)*

Rnds 3–4: Sc in each st around. At end of last rnd, join with sl st in first sc.

Rnd 5: Join blue with sc in first st, sc in each st around.

Rnds 6–10: Sc in each st around. At end of last rnd, join. Fasten off.

Rnd 11: Join green with sc in first st, sc in each st around, join. Fasten off.

Rnd 12: With blue, repeat rnd 11.

Rnd 13: Repeat rnd 11.

Rnd 14: Join blue with sc in first st, sc in each st around.

Rnds 15–16: Sc in each st around. At end of last rnd, join. Fasten off. Stuff. Flatten last rnd, sew to sides of Body.

LEG (make 2)
Rnd 1: With beige, ch 2, 6 sc in second ch from hook. *(6 sc made)*

Rnd 2: 2 sc in each st around. *(12)*

Rnd 3: (Sc in next st, 2 sc in next st) around. *(18)*

Rnd 4: 2 sc in each of next 6 sts, sc in last 12 sts. *(24)*

Rnds 5–6: Sc in each st around.

Rnd 7: (Sc next 2 sts tog) 6 times, sc in last 12 sts.

Rnds 8–16: Sc in each st around. At end of last rnd, join with sl st in first sc. Fasten off. Stuff. Flatten last rnd, sew to sides of Body in sitting position.

FINISHING

With black, using satin stitch *(see Stitch Guide)*, embroider eyes ⅞" apart over rnd 7 of Head and nose over center of rnd 1 of Muzzel; using Straight Stitch, embroider mouth.

For **scarf,** make ½" cut every ⅛" on each end of felt. Tie around neck. Glue Bear in basket.

Sled-Ride Goose

FINISHED SIZE: 4½" tall sitting.

MATERIALS:
- ❑ Sport yarn:
  - ½ oz. white
  - Small amount each red, blue, yellow, and black
- ❑ 4" or 5" wooden sled
- ❑ Red paint & paintbrush
- ❑ 10" twine
- ❑ Craft glue
- ❑ 1" piece cardboard
- ❑ Polyester fiberfill
- ❑ Tapestry needle
- ❑ D hook or hook needed to obtain gauge

GAUGE: 6 sc =1"; 6 sc rows = 1".

BASIC STITCHES: Ch, sl st, sc, hdc.

NOTE: Work in continuous rnds; do not join unless otherwise stated. Mark first st of each rnd.

GOOSE
Body
Rnd 1: Starting at top of head, with white, ch 2, 6 sc in second ch from hook. *(6 sc made)*
Rnd 2: 2 sc in each st around. *(12)*
Rnd 3: (Sc in next st, 2 sc in next st) around. *(18)*
Rnds 4–6: Sc in each st around.
Rnd 7: (Sc in next st, sc next 2 sts tog) around. Stuff. *(12)*
Rnds 8–13: Sc in each st around.
Rnd 14: (Sc in next st, 2 sc in next st) around. *(18)*
Rnd 15: (Sc in next 2 sts, 2 sc in next st) around. *(24)*
Rnds 16–20: Sc in each st around.
Rnd 21: Sc in first 9 sts, 2 sc in each of next 6 sts, sc in last 9 sts. *(30)*
Rnd 22: Sc in each st around.
Rnd 23: Sc in first 9 sts; for **tail,** skip next 12 sts; sc in last 9 sts. Stuff. *(18)*
Rnd 24: (Sc in next st, sc next 2 sts tog) around, join with sl st in first sc. Fasten off. *(12)*
Sew opening closed. Flatten tail, sew together.

Wing (make 2)
Row 1: With white, ch 9, sc in second ch from hook, sc in each ch across, turn. *(8 sc made)*
Row 2: Ch 1, sc in each st across leaving last st unworked, turn. *(7)*
Row 3: Ch 1, sc in each st across, turn.
Row 4: Repeat row 2. *(6)*
Row 5: Ch 1, sc in each st across; for **back of Wing,** working in ends of rows, (sc next 2 rows tog) 2 times. Fasten off.

Sew over rnds 15–18 on side of Body with row 1 at top.

BEAK
Rnd 1: With yellow, ch 2, 6 sc in second ch from hook. *(6 sc made)*
Rnd 2: (Sc in next st, 2 sc in next st) around. *(9)*
Rnds 3–5: Sc in each st around. At end of last rnd, join with sl st in first sc. Fasten off. Stuff.
Sew over rnds 4–5 of Head.

LEG (make 2)
Rnds 1–3: With yellow, repeat rnds 1–3 of Body.
Rnd 4: Working this rnd in **back lps,** (sc in next st, sc next 2 sts tog) around, join with sl st in first sc.
Rnd 5: (Sc next 2 sts tog) around. *(6)*
Rnds 6–9: Sc in each st around. At end of last rnd, fasten off.
Sew ½" apart over rnds 21–22 of Body.

HAT
Rnds 1–2: With blue, repeat rnds 1–2 of Beak.
Rnd 3: Sc in each st around.
Rnd 4: (Sc in next 2 sts, 2 sc in next st) around. *(12)*
Rnd 5: Sc in each st around.
Rnd 6: (Sc in next 3 sts, 2 sc in next st) around. *(15)*
Rnd 7: Sc in each st around.
Rnd 8: (Sc in next 4 sts, 2 sc in next st) around. *(18)*
Rnd 9: Sc in each st around.
Rnd 10: (Sc in next 5 sts, 2 sc in next st) around. *(21)*
Rnd 11: Sc in each st around.
Rnd 12: (Sc in next 6 sts, 2 sc in next st) around. *(24)*
Rnds 13–15: Sc in each st around.
Rnd 16: Working this rnd in **front lps,** sc in each st around.
Rnd 17: Sc in each st around, join with sl st in first sc. Fasten off.
Fold rnds 16–17 back and tack. Place on head. Sew rnds 1–7 to back of Head. Tack rnd 6 to rnd 15.

Pom-Pom
Wrap red around 1" cardboard 100 times; slide loops off cardboard, tie separate 6" strand red around center of all loops. Trim ends to ½". Sew to tip of Hat.

SCARF
Row 1: With red, ch 46, hdc in third ch from hook, hdc in each ch across, turn. Fasten off. *(44 hdc made)*
Row 2: Join blue with sc in first st, sc in each st across, turn. Fasten off.
Row 3: Join red with sl st in first st, ch 2, hdc in each st across. Fasten off. Tie around neck.

FINISHING
With black, using satin stitch *(see Stitch Guide)*, embroider eyes 1" apart over rnd 3 of Body.
Paint sled red. Let dry. Thread twine through holes on front of sled, tie knot in each end.
Glue Goose to sled.
Glue tip of each Wing over twine. ❄

Roly Poly People

Designed by Michele Wilcox

Santa

FINISHED SIZE: 8" high.

MATERIALS:
- ❑ Worsted yarn:
   - 3 oz. red
   - 1 oz. white
   - Small amounts each green, peach and black
- ❑ Three ⅝" buttons in assorted colors
- ❑ Polyester fiberfill
- ❑ Tapestry needle
- ❑ G hook or hook needed to obtain gauge

GAUGE: 4 sc = 1"; 4 sc rows = 1".

BASIC STITCHES: Ch, sl st, sc.

NOTES: Work in continuous rnds; do not join or turn unless otherwise stated. Mark first st of each rnd.

When **changing colors** *(see Stitch Guide)*, always change color in last st made and fasten off color not being used.

BODY
Rnd 1: Starting at bottom, with red, ch 2, 6 sc in second ch from hook. *(6 sc made)*
Rnd 2: 2 sc in each st around. *(12)*
Rnd 3: (Sc in next st, 2 sc in next st) around. *(18)*
Rnd 4: (Sc in next 2 sts, 2 sc in next st) around. *(24)*
Rnd 5: (Sc in next 3 sts, 2 sc in next st) around. *(30)*
Rnd 6: (Sc in next 4 sts, 2 sc in next st) around. *(36)*
Rnd 7: (Sc in next 5 sts, 2 sc in next st) around. *(42)*
Rnds 8–20: Sc in each st around.
Rnd 21: (Sc next 2 sts tog) around. *(21)*
Rnd 22: Sc in each st around changing to peach *(see Notes)*. Stuff Body.
Rnds 23–26: For **head**, sc in each st around changing to red at end of last rnd.

continued on page 114

Roly Poly People

continued from page 113

Rnds 27–31: For **hat,** sc in each st around.

Rnd 32: (Sc in next 5 sts, sc next 2 sts tog) around. *(18)*

Rnd 33: (Sc in next 4 sts, sc next 2 sts tog) around. Begin stuffing head. *(15)*

Rnd 34: (Sc in next 3 sts, sc next 2 sts tog) around. *(12)*

Rnd 35: (Sc in next 2 sts, sc next 2 sts tog) around. *(9)*

Rnd 36: (Sc in next st, sc next 2 sts tog) around. Finish stuffing. *(6)*

Rnd 37: (Sc next 2 sts tog) around, join with sl st in first sc. Leaving a long end of yarn, fasten off. *(3)*

Thread tapestry needle with end of yarn; weave through sts on last rnd and pull to close opening. Secure.

For **pom-pom,** wrap white around 2 fingers 40 times, slide loops off fingers, tie separate strand white tightly around center of all loops. Cut loops, trim to 2" ball. Sew to top of hat.

For **hanger,** with red, ch 25, sl st in first ch to form a ring. Sew ring to back of hat below pom-pom.

HAT TRIM

Row 1: With white, ch 24, sc in second ch from hook, sc in each ch across, turn. *(23 sc made)*

Row 2: Ch 1, sc in each st across. Fasten off.

Sew Hat Trim around rnds 28 and 29. Sew ends together.

BEARD

Row 1: With white, ch 13, sc in second ch from hook, sc in each ch across, turn. *(12 sc made)*

Row 2: Ch 5, sl st in next sc, (ch 5, sl st in next sc) across, turn.

Row 3: Ch 1, 6 sc in first ch-5 sp, sl st in next sl st, (6 sc in next ch-5 sp, sl st in next sl st) across. Fasten off.

Sew to rnds 23–27 as shown in photo.

ARM (make 2)

Rnd 1: With green, ch 2, 6 sc in second ch from hook. *(6 sc made)*

Rnd 2: 2 sc in each st around. *(12)*

Rnds 3–5: Sc in each st around changing to red at end of last rnd.

Rnds 6–15: Sc in each st around. At end of last rnd, join with sl st in first sc. Fasten off. Stuff.

For **Trim,** with white, ch 15, sc in second ch from hook, sc in each ch across. Fasten off. Sew around rnd 6 of Arm.

Flatten rnd 15 and sew Arms to Body.

FINISHING

1: With black, using French knots *(Stitch Guide),* embroider eyes as shown in photo.

2: With red, using fly stitch *(see illustrations),* embroider mouth as shown.

3: Sew three buttons down front of Body.

FLY STITCH

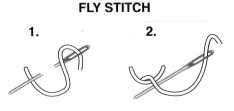

1.   2.

Snowman

FINISHED SIZE: 8" high.

MATERIALS:
- ❑ Worsted yarn:
  - 3 oz. white
  - 1 oz. black
  - 1 oz. green
  - Small amount red
- ❑ Three ½" blue buttons
- ❑ Polyester fiberfill
- ❑ Tapestry needle
- ❑ G hook or hook needed to obtain gauge

GAUGE: 4 sc = 1"; 4 sc rows = 1".

BASIC STITCHES: Ch, sl st, sc, hdc.

NOTES: Work in continuous rnds; do not join or turn unless otherwise stated. Mark first st of each rnd.

When **changing colors** *(see Stitch Guide),* always change color in last st made and fasten off color not being used.

BODY

Rnd 1: Starting at bottom of Body, with white, ch 2, 6 sc in second ch from hook. *(6 sc made)*

Rnd 2: 2 sc in each st around. *(12)*

Rnd 3: (Sc in next st, 2 sc in next st) around. *(18)*

Rnd 4: (Sc in next 2 sts, 2 sc in next st) around. *(24)*

Rnd 5: (Sc in next 3 sts, 2 sc in next st) around. *(30)*

Rnd 6: (Sc in next 4 sts, 2 sc in next st) around. *(36)*

Rnd 7: (Sc in next 5 sts, 2 sc in next st) around. *(42)*

Rnds 8–20: Sc in each st around.

Rnd 21: (Sc next 2 sts tog) around. *(21)*

Rnd 22: Sc in each st around. Stuff Body.

Rnds 23–30: For **head,** sc in each st around changing to black at end of last rnd.

Rnd 31: For **hat,** sc in each st around.

Rnd 32: Working in **front lps** *(see Stitch Guide),* (sl st, ch 2, hdc) in first st, 2 hdc in each st around, join with sl st in top of ch-2. Fasten off.

Rnd 33: Working in **back lps** of rnd 31, join red with sc in first st, sc in each st around.

Rnd 34: Sc in each st around changing to black.

Rnds 35–38: Sc in each st around. Stuff.

Rnd 39: Working in **back lps,** (sc next 2 sts tog) 10 times, sc in next st.

Rnd 40: (Sc next 2 sts tog) 5 times, sc in next st, join with sl st in first sc. Leaving a long end of yarn, fasten off.

Thread tapestry needle with end of yarn; weave through sts on last rnd and pull to close opening. Secure. Tack brim of hat up in front as shown in photo.

For **hanger,** with black, ch 25, sl st in first ch to form a ring. Sew ring to top of hat.

For **trim,** working in **remaining lps** of rnd 38, join black with sl st in first st, sl st in each st around, join with sl st in first st. Fasten off.

ARM (make 2)
Rnds 1–15: Using white throughout, work rnds 1–15 of Santa's Arm on page 114.

Flatten rnd 15 and sew Arms to Body.

SCARF
Row 1: With green, ch 6, sc in second ch from hook, sc in each ch across, turn. *(5 sc made)*

Rows 2–50: Working these rnds in **back lps,** ch 1, sc in each st across, turn. At end of last row, fasten off.

Tie Scarf around Snowman as shown in photo; tack in place.

FINISHING
Work steps 1–3 of Santa's Finishing on page 114.

Angel

FINISHED SIZE: 8" high.

MATERIALS:
❑ Worsted yarn:
    3 oz. teal
    1 oz. black
    1 oz. peach
    1 oz. gold
    Small amount red
❑ Three ⅝" star-shaped buttons
❑ 24" gold ¼" metallic ribbon
❑ Polyester fiberfill
❑ Tapestry needle
❑ G hook or hook needed to obtain gauge

GAUGE: 4 sc = 1"; 4 sc rows = 1".

BASIC STITCHES: Ch, sl st, sc, hdc, dc.

NOTES: Work in continuous rnds; do not join or turn unless otherwise stated. Mark first st of each rnd.

When **changing colors** *(see Stitch Guide),* always change color in last st made and fasten off color not being used.

BODY
Rnds 1–22: With teal, work rnds 1-22 of Santa Body on page 114 changing to peach at end of last rnd *(see Notes).* Stuff Body.

Rnds 23–31: For **head,** sc in each st around. Stuff.

Rnd 32: (Sc next 2 sts tog) 10 times, sc in next st.

Rnd 33: (Sc next 2 sts tog) 5 times, sc in next st, join with sl st in first sc. Leaving a long end of yarn, fasten off. *(6)*

Thread tapestry needle with end of yarn; weave through sts on last rnd and pull to close opening. Secure.

ARM (make 2)
Rnd 1: With peach, ch 2, 6 sc in second ch from hook. *(6 sc made)*

Rnd 2: 2 sc in each st around. *(12)*

Rnds 3–5: Sc in each st around changing to teal at end of last rnd.

Rnds 6–15: Sc in each st around. At end of last rnd, join with sl st in first sc. Leaving a long end of yarn, fasten off. Stuff.

Flatten rnd 15; sew to sides of Body.

WING (make 2)
Rnd 1: With gold, ch 6, sc in second ch from hook, sc in next ch, hdc in next 2 chs, 6 dc in last ch; working in remaining lps on opposite side of ch, hdc in next 2 chs, sc in next ch, 2 sc in next ch. *(15 sts made)*

Rnd 2: 2 sc in first st, sc in next st, 2 hdc in each of next 2 sts, 2 dc in each of next 6 sts, 2 hdc in each of next 2 sts, 2 sc in next st, sc in next st, 2 sc in next st.

Rnd 3: (Sc in next st, ch 3, skip next st) around, join with sl st in first sc. Fasten off.

Sew Wings to back of Body.

FINISHING
1: For **hair,** with tapestry needle and two strands black, leaving an area unworked for face, embroider turkey work *(see illustrations)* around head.

2: For **halo,** with gold, ch 22, sl st in first ch to form ring, sl st in each ch around. Fasten off. Tack to back of head.

3: For **hanger,** with teal, ch 22, sl st in first ch to form ring. Fasten off. Tack to back of head below halo.

4: Tie ribbon in a bow around neck.

5: Work steps 1–3 of Santa's Finishing on page 114. ❄

TURKEY STITCH

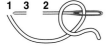 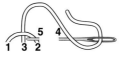 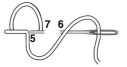

Jingles the Clown

Designed by Karen Saul

FINISHED SIZE: Approximately 27" tall.

MATERIALS:
- ❑ Worsted yarn:
    - 21 oz. variegated
    - 3½ oz. each white, green and red
    - Small amount black
- ❑ 3½ yds. red, green and gold 1" ribbon
- ❑ Polyester fiberfill
- ❑ Five 25mm jingle bells
- ❑ Tapestry needle
- ❑ I hook or hook needed to obtain gauge

GAUGE: 5 sc = 2"; 6 sc rows - 2"; 2 dc rows = 1½".

BASIC STITCHES: Ch, sl st, sc, dc.

BODY SIDE (make 2)
Row 1: Starting at bottom, with variegated, ch 51, sc in second ch from hook, sc in each ch across, turn. *(50 sc made)*

Rows 2–44: Ch 1, sc in each st across, turn. At end of last row, fasten off.

Match and sew ends of rows 16–44 on one end of Body Side to ends of rows 16–44 on one end of other Body Side, for seam. Repeat on other end of Body Sides leaving top and bottom open.

For **Leg**, match and sew ends of rows 1–15 on one Body Side together. Repeat on other Body Side.

LEG TRIM
Rnd 1: Working on opposite side of starting ch on row 1 of one Body Side, join variegated with sc in first ch, sc in each ch around, join with sl st in first sc. *(50 sc made)*

Rnd 2: Ch 1, sc first 2 sts tog, (sc next 2 sts tog) around, join. *(25)*

Rnd 3: For **Ruffle**, working in **front lps** *(see Stitch Guide),* (ch 3, 4 dc) in first st, 5 dc in each st around, join with sl st in top of ch-3. Fasten off. Repeat on other Leg.

SHOE (make 1 red, 1 green)
Rnd 1: Starting at bottom, ch 25, 2 dc in third ch from hook, dc in next 21 chs, 3 dc in last ch; working on opposite side of starting ch, dc in next 21 chs leaving last ch unworked, join with sl st in top of ch-3. *(48 dc made)*

Rnd 2: (Ch 3, dc) in first st, 3 dc in next st, 2 dc in next st, dc in next 21 sts, 2 dc in next st, 3 dc in next st, 2 dc in next st, dc in last 21 sts, join with sl st in top of ch-3. *(56 dc)*

Rnd 3: For **Side**, working this rnd only in **back lps**, ch 3, dc in each st around, join.

Rnd 4: Working in **back lps,** ch 3, dc in each st around, join.

Rnd 5: Ch 1, sc first 2 sts tog, (sc next 2 sts tog) around, join with sl st in first sc. Fasten off, leaving 6" for sewing. *(28 sc)*

Fold in half lengthwise *(see illustration)*; for **Top of Shoe,** match and sew 14 sts together leaving remaining sts unsewn. Lightly stuff.

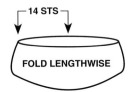

Easing to fit, sew **back lps** on rnd 2 of Leg Trim to remaining sts on Top of Shoe.

Sew one jingle bell to Top of Shoe.

NECK TRIM
Rnd 1: Join variegated with sc in first st on row 44 of one Body Side, sc in each st around Body Sides with 2 sc in each seam, join with sl st in first sc. *(104 sc made)*

Rnd 2: Ch 1, sc first 2 sts tog, (sc next 2 sts tog) around, join. *(52)*

Rnd 3: Ch 1, sc in each st around, join.

Rnd 4: Ch 1, sc first 2 sts tog, (sc next 2 sts tog) around, join. *(26)*

Rnd 5: Ch 1, sc in each st around, join.

Rnd 6: Ch 1, sc in first st, (sc next 2 sts tog) 2 times, sc in next st, (sc next 2 sts tog) 7 times, sc in next st, (sc next 2 sts tog) 2 times, sc in last st, join. *(15)*

Rnd 7: For **Ruffle,** working this rnd only in **front lps,** (ch 3, 4 dc) in first st, 5 dc in each st around, join with sl st in top of ch-3. *(75 dc)*

Rnd 8: Working in **both lps,** (ch 3, 4 dc) in first st, 5 dc in each st around, join. Fasten off. Stuff Body until it feels like a soft pillow.

HEAD
Rnd 1: Starting at bottom, with white, ch 4, sl st in first ch to form ring, ch 3, 10 dc in ring, join with sl st in top of ch-3. *(11 dc made)*

Rnd 2: (Ch 3, dc) in first st, 2 dc in each st around, join. *(22 dc)*

Rnd 3: Working this rnd only in **back lps,** (ch 3, 2 dc) in first st, dc in next st, (2 dc in next st, dc in next st) 10 times, join. *(34 dc)*

continued on page 118

Jingles the Clown

continued from page 116

Rnd 4: Working in **both lps,** ch 3, (2 dc in next st, dc in next st) 16 times, 2 dc in last st, join. *(51 dc)*

Rnds 5–9: Ch 3, dc in each st around, join.

Rnd 10: (Ch 3, dc) in first st, (dc next 2 sts tog, dc in next st) 16 times, dc last 2 sts tog, join. *(35 dc)*

Rnd 11: Ch 3, (dc next 2 sts tog) around, join. Lightly stuff. *(18 dc)*

Rnd 12: Ch 3, (dc next 2 sts tog) 8 times, dc in last st, join. *(10 dc)*

Rnd 13: Ch 1, sc first 2 sts tog, (sc next 2 sts tog) around, join with sl st in first sc. Fasten off. Sew opening closed. *(5 sc)*

Easing to fit, sew **front lps** on rnd 2 of Head to **back lps** on rnd 6 of Neck Trim.

HAT

Rnd 1: With variegated, ch 4, sl st in first ch to form ring, ch 3, 12 dc in ring, join with sl st in top of ch-3. *(13 dc made)*

Rnd 2: (Ch 3, dc) in first st, 2 dc in each st around, join. *(27 dc)*

Rnd 3: (Ch 3, 2 dc) in first st, (dc in next st, 2 dc in each of next 2 sts) 8 times, dc in next st, 2 dc in last st, join. *(46 dc)*

Rnd 4: Ch 3, (dc in next st, 2 dc in each of next 3 sts) 5 times, dc in next st, (dc in next st, 2 dc in each of next 3 sts) 6 times, join. *(79 dc)*

Rnds 5–6: (Ch 3, dc) in first st, dc in each st around, join. *(80, 81)*

Rnd 7: Ch 3, dc next 2 sts tog, (dc in next st, dc next 2 sts tog) around, join. *(54 dc)*

Rnds 8–9: Ch 3, dc in each st around, join.

Rnd 10: For **Ruffle,** working in **front lps,** (ch 3, 2 dc) in first st, 3 dc in each st around, join. Fasten off.

Lightly stuff Hat; sew Hat over rnds 6–12 on Head with joining on same side as joining on Head. Sew one jingle bell to center of rnd 1 on top of Hat.

NOSE

Rnd 1: With red, ch 4, sl st in first ch to form ring, ch 1, 10 sc in ring, join with sl st in first sc. *(10 sc made)*

Rnds 2–3: Ch 1, sc in each st around, join. Stuff firmly.

Rnd 4: Ch 1, sc first 2 sts tog, (sc next 2 sts tog) around, join. Fasten off, leaving 6" end for sewing.

Sew Nose to center of rnd 8 on Head.

FACIAL FEATURES

With black, using straight stitches, embroider eyes over rnds 8 and 9 on Head 2½" apart with Nose between *(see facial illustration).*

With red, using satin stitch, embroider mouth over rnd 6 on Head below Nose.

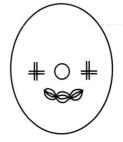

ARM

Rnd 1: With variegated, ch 4, sl st in first ch to form ring, ch 3, 14 dc in ring, join with sl st in top of ch-3. *(15 dc made)*

Rnd 2: (Ch 3, dc) in first st, (dc in next st, 2 dc in next st) around, join. *(24 dc)*

Rnd 3: Ch 3, 2 dc in next st, (dc in next st, 2 dc in next st) around, join. *(36 dc)*

Rnd 4: Ch 3, dc in next st, (2 dc in next st, dc in next st) around, join. *(53 dc)*

Rnds 5–14: Ch 3, dc in each st around, join.

Rnds 15–16: Ch 3, (dc next 2 sts tog) around, join. *(27 dc, 14 dc)*

Rnd 17: For **Ruffle,** working in **front lps,** (ch 3, 2 dc) in first st, 3 dc in each st around, join. Fasten off.

Lightly stuff. Sew opening on rnd 16 closed.

HAND *(make 2)*

Rnd 1: With white, ch 6, dc in third ch from hook, dc in next 2 chs, 3 dc in last ch; working on opposite side of starting ch, dc in next 2 chs, 3 dc in last ch, join with sl st in first ch of ch-6. *(12 dc made)*

Rnd 2: (Ch 3, dc) in first st, dc in each st around, join with sl st in top of ch-3. *(13 dc)*

Rnd 3: Ch 3, (dc in next 4 sts, 2 dc in each of next 2 sts) 2 times, join. *(17 dc)*

Rnd 4: Ch 3, (dc in next 6 sts, 2 dc in each of next 2 sts) 2 times, join. *(21 dc)*

Rnd 5: Ch 3, dc in each st around, join.

Rnd 6: Ch 3, (dc next 2 sts tog) around, join. Leaving 6" for sewing, fasten off. Stuff. *(11 dc)*

Flatten last rnd, sew to rnd 16 on inside of Arm. Sew one jingle bell to rnd 4 on Hand.

Sew rnd 1 of Arm to rnds 5 and 6 on Neck Trim 4" apart. ❋

Skirts, Stockings & More

Silver Bells

City sidewalks, busy sidewalks, dressed in holiday style. In the air there's a feeling of Christmas. Children laughing, people passing, meeting smile after smile and on ev'ry street corner you'll hear. Silver bells, silver bells, it's Christmas time in the city. Ring-a-ling, hear them sing. Soon it will be Christmas day.

Beautiful Bells

Designed by Ann Emery Smith

FINISHED SIZE: Tree Skirt is 18" long without Bells. Stocking is 16½" long.

MATERIALS:
- ❏ 22 oz. white baby pompadour yarn
- ❏ 10 oz. red acrylic sport yarn
- ❏ Tapestry needle
- ❏ E hook or hook needed to obtain gauge

GAUGE: On **Skirt**, 5 sts = 1", 4 post st rows = 2"; on **Stocking,** 5 hdc = 1", 3 hdc rows = 1".

BASIC STITCHES: Ch, sl st, sc, hdc, dc, tr.

TREE SKIRT
Panel (make 5)
Row 1: Beginning at top edge, with white, ch 83, skip first 3 chs, dc next 2 chs tog, *dc in next 5 chs, (2 dc, ch 1, 2 dc) in next ch, dc in next 5 chs, dc next 5 chs tog; repeat from * 3 more times, dc in next 5 chs, (2 dc, ch 1, 2 dc) in next ch, dc in next 5 chs, dc last 3 chs tog, turn. *(Ch-3 at beginning of row is **not** worked into or counted as a st—81 sts and chs made.)*

NOTES: Back *of row 1 is right side of work.*

*For **dc back post (bp)** or **dc front post (fp)**, yo, insert hook around post of st (see Stitch Guide), yo, pull through st, complete as dc.*

*For **post st decrease (dec)**, *yo, insert hook around front or back of next st as indicated, yo, pull lp through, yo, pull through 2 lps on hook; repeat from * number of times stated for decrease.*

Row 2: Ch 3, skip first st, **2-st bp dec** (see Notes), *fp around next 5 sts, (2 dc, ch 1, 2 dc) in next ch sp, fp around next 5 sts, 5-st bp dec; repeat from * 3 more times, fp around next 5 sts, (2 dc, ch 1, 2 dc) in next ch sp, fp around next 5 sts, 3-st bp dec, turn.

Row 3: Ch 3, skip first dec, 2-st fp dec, *bp around next 5 sts, (2 dc, ch 1, 2 dc) in next ch sp, bp around next 5 sts, 5-st fp dec; repeat from * 3 more times, bp around next 5 sts, (2 dc, ch 1, 2 dc) in next ch sp, bp around next 5 sts, 3-st fp dec, turn.

Row 4: Ch 3, skip first dec, 2-st bp dec, *fp around next 5 sts, (2 dc, ch 1, 2 dc) in next ch sp, fp

continued on page 122

Beautiful Bells

continued from page 121

around next 5 sts, 5-st bp dec; repeat from * 3 more times, fp around next 5 sts, (2 dc, ch 1, 2 dc) in next ch sp, fp around next 5 sts, 3-st bp dec, turn.

Row 5: Ch 3, skip first dec, 2-st fp dec, *bp around next 5 sts, (3 dc, ch 1, 3 dc) in next ch sp, bp around next 5 sts, 5-st fp dec; repeat from * 3 more times, bp around next 5 sts, (3 dc, ch 1, 3 dc) in next ch sp, bp around next 5 sts, 3-st fp dec, turn. *(91 sts and chs)*

Row 6: Ch 3, skip first dec, 2-st bp dec, *fp around next 6 sts, (2 dc, ch 1, 2 dc) in next ch sp, fp around next 6 sts, 5-st bp dec; repeat from * 3 more times, fp around next 6 sts, (2 dc, ch 1, 2 dc) in next ch sp, fp around next 6 sts, 3-st bp dec, turn.

Row 7: Ch 3, skip first dec, 2-st fp dec, *bp around next 6 sts, (2 dc, ch 1, 2 dc) in next ch sp, bp around next 6 sts, 5-st fp dec; repeat from * 3 more times, bp around next 6 sts, (2 dc, ch 1, 2 dc) in next ch sp, bp around next 6 sts, 3-st fp dec, turn.

Rows 8–13: Repeat rows 6 and 7 alternately. At end of last row, fasten off.

Row 14: Join red with sl st in first st, repeat row 6.

Row 15: Repeat row 7. Fasten off red.

Row 16: Join white with sl st in first st, ch 3, skip first dec, 2-st bp dec, *fp around next 6 sts, (2 dc, ch 1, 2 dc) in next ch sp, fp around next 6 sts, 5-st bp dec; repeat from * 3 more times, fp around next 6 sts, (2 dc, ch 1, 2 dc) in next ch sp, fp around next 6 sts, 3-st bp dec, turn.

Row 17: Ch 3, skip first dec, 2-st fp dec, *bp around next 6 sts, (3 dc, ch 1, 3 dc) in next ch sp, bp around next 6 sts, 5-st fp dec; repeat from * 3 more times, bp around next 6 sts, (3 dc, ch 1, 3 dc) in next ch sp, bp around next 6 sts, 3-st fp dec, turn. *(101 sts and chs)*

Row 18: Ch 3, skip first dec, 2-st bp dec, *fp around next 7 sts, (2 dc, ch 1, 2 dc) in next ch sp, fp around next 7 sts, 5-st bp dec; repeat from * 3 more times, fp around next 7 sts, (2 dc, ch 1, 2 dc) in next ch sp, fp around next 7 sts, 3-st bp dec, turn.

Row 19: Ch 3, skip first dec, 2-st fp dec, *bp around next 7 sts, (2 dc, ch 1, 2 dc) in next ch sp, bp around next 7 sts, 5-st fp dec; repeat from * 3 more times, bp around next 7 sts, (2 dc, ch 1, 2 dc) in next ch sp, bp around next 7 sts, 3-st fp dec, turn.

Rows 20–21: Repeat rows 18 and 19.

Row 22: Repeat row 18.

Row 23: Ch 3, skip first dec, 2-st fp dec, *bp around next 7 sts, (3 dc, ch 1, 3 dc) in next ch sp, bp around next 7 sts, 5-st fp dec; repeat from * 3 more times, bp around next 7 sts, (3 dc, ch 1, 3 dc) in next ch sp, bp around next 7 sts, 3-st fp dec, turn. *(111 sts and chs)*

Row 24: Ch 3, skip first dec, 2-st bp dec, *fp around next 8 sts, (2 dc, ch 1, 2 dc) in next ch sp, fp around next 8 sts, 5-st bp dec; repeat from * 3 more times, fp around next 8 sts, (2 dc, ch 1, 2 dc) in next ch sp, fp around next 8 sts, 3-st bp dec, turn.

Row 25: Ch 3, skip first dec, 2-st fp dec, *bp around next 8 sts, (2 dc, ch 1, 2 dc) in next ch sp, bp around next 8 sts, 5-st fp dec; repeat from * 3 more times, bp around next 8 sts, (2 dc, ch 1, 2 dc) in next ch sp, bp around next 8 sts, 3-st fp dec, turn.

Rows 26–28: Repeat rows 24 and 25 alternately, ending with row 24.

Row 29: Ch 3, skip first dec, 2-st fp dec, *bp around next 8 sts, (3 dc, ch 1, 3 dc) in next ch sp, bp around next 8 sts, 5-st fp dec; repeat from * 3 more times, bp around next 8 sts, (3 dc, ch 1, 3 dc) in next ch sp, bp around next 8 sts, 3-st fp dec. Fasten off. *(121 sts and chs)*

With same side of all Panels facing you, using white yarn, sew ends of rows on Panels together *(see Tree Skirt Assembly illustration)*.

Bottom Edging

With right side of row 29 on Panels facing you, working in tops of sts across all Panels, join red with sc in top of first ch-3 on first Panel, (sc in each st across to next ch-1 sp, ch 3, skip ch-1 sp) across to last 11 sts on last Panel, sc in each st across. Fasten off. *(25 ch-3 sps)*

First Bell

Rnd 1: Skip first ch sp on Bottom Edging, join white with sl st in next ch sp, (ch 3, 6 dc) in same ch sp as joining, join with sl st in top of first ch-3. *(7 dc made)*

Rnd 2: (Ch 3, dc) in first st, 2 dc in each st around, join. *(14)*

Rnd 3: Ch 4, skip next st, (dc in next st, ch 1, skip next st) around, join with sl st in third ch of ch-4. *(7 dc)*

Rnd 4: Ch 1, sc in first st, ch 3, skip next ch sp, (sc in next st, ch 3, skip next ch sp) around, join with sl st in first sc. Fasten off.

Next Bell (make 11)

Rnd 1: Skip next ch sp on Bottom Edging, join white with sl st in next ch sp, (ch 3, 6 dc) in same ch sp as joining, join with sl st in top of first ch-3. *(7 dc made)*

Rnds 2–4: Repeat rnds 2–4 of First Bell.

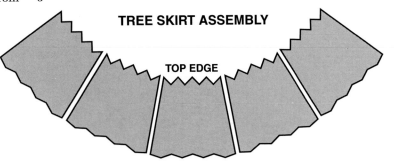

TREE SKIRT ASSEMBLY

TOP EDGE

Ribbon (make 12)

With red, ch 32, 2 dc in fourth ch from hook, 2 dc in each of next 8 chs, hdc in next ch, sc in next 9 chs, hdc in next ch, 2 dc in each of last 9 chs. Fasten off.

Tie center of one Ribbon around top of each Bell on Bottom Edging.

Top Border

Row 1: With right side of row 1 facing you, working on opposite side of starting chs on Panels, join red with sc in first ch on first Panel, sc in each ch across all Panels, turn.

Row 2: Ch 1, sc in first st, (ch 1, sc in st at center of next point) across with last sc in last st, turn.

Row 3: Ch 1, sc in first st, (2 sc in next ch-1 sp, sc in next st) across, turn.

Row 4: Ch 1, sc in each st across, turn.

Row 5: Ch 1, sl st in each st across. Fasten off.

STOCKING

Cuff

Rows 1–3: Work same as rows 1–3 of Tree Skirt Panel. At end of last row, fasten off.

Row 4: With wrong side of row 3 facing you, join red with sl st in first st, ch 3, 2-st bp dec, *fp around next 5 sts, (3 dc, ch 1, 3 dc) in next ch sp, fp around next 5 sts, 5-st bp dec; repeat from * 3 more times, fp around next 5 sts, (3 dc, ch 1, 3 dc) in next ch sp, fp around next 5 sts, 3-st bp dec, turn. *(91 sts and chs)*

Row 5: Ch 3, skip first dec, 2-st fp dec, *bp around next 6 sts, (2 dc, ch 1, 2 dc) in next ch sp, bp around next 6 sts, 5-st fp dec; repeat from * 3 more times, bp around next 6 sts, (2 dc, ch 1, 2 dc) in next ch sp, bp around next 6 sts, 3-st fp dec, **do not turn.**

Row 6: Ch 1, sc in first st on row 5, (sc in each st across to next ch sp, ch 1, skip ch sp) 5 times, sc in each st across. Leaving end for sewing, fasten off. Sew ends of rows 4–6 together.

Leg

Row 1: Working on opposite side of starting ch on row 1 of Cuff, join white with sc in first ch, sc in next ch, (*hdc in next 2 chs, dc in next 2 chs, tr in next 5 chs, dc in next 2 chs, hdc in next 2 chs*, sc in next 3 chs) 4 times; repeat between first and second *, sc in last ch, turn. *(80 sts made)*

Row 2: Working this row in **front lps** *(see Stitch Guide),* ch 3, dc in next 5 sts, dc next 3 sts tog, (dc in next 13 sts, dc next 3 sts tog) 4 times, dc in next 5 sts, dc last 2 sts tog, turn. *(Ch-3 at beginning of row is worked into and counted as first dc—69 dc made.)*

Row 3: Ch 3, dc in each st across, turn.

Row 4: Ch 3, dc in next 2 sts, (dc next 2 sts tog, dc in next 9 sts) 6 times, turn. *(63)*

Row 5: Ch 3, dc in each st across, turn.

Row 6: Ch 3, (dc in next 8 sts, dc next 2 sts tog) 6 times, dc in last 2 sts, turn. *(57)*

Rows 7–28: Ch 2 *(counts as first hdc),* hdc in each st across, turn. At end of last row, fasten off.

With white, sew ends of remaining rows together on Cuff and Leg.

Foot

Row 1: For **Heel,** with right side of last row on Leg facing you, join white with sc in 44th st on last row, sc in last 13 sts, sc in first 14 sts leaving remaining 29 sts unworked across instep, turn. *(28 sc made)*

Row 2: Ch 1, sc in first 17 sts leaving last 11 sts unworked, turn. *(17)*

Row 3: Ch 1, sc in first 6 sts leaving last 11 sts unworked, turn. *(6)*

Rows 4–25: Ch 1, sc in each st across, sc in next unworked st on previous row, turn. At end of last row, fasten off. *(28 sc)*

Row 26: Skip first 14 sts on row 25, join white with sl st in next st, ch 2, hdc in each st across, hdc in same st on last row of Leg as last st of row 25, hdc in each unworked st across last row of Leg, hdc in next worked st, hdc in first 14 skipped sts on row 25, turn. *(59 hdc)*

Rows 27–37: Ch 2, hdc in each st across, turn.

Rnd 38: Working in rnds, for **Toe,** ch 1, sc in first 4 sts, (sc next 2 sts tog, sc in next 9 sts) 5 times, join with sl st in first sc, **do not turn.** *(54 sc)*

Rnd 39: Ch 1, sc in each st around, join.

Rnd 40: Ch 1, sc in first 7 sts, sc next 2 sts tog, (sc in next 7 sts, sc next 2 sts tog) 5 times, join. *(48)*

Rnd 41: Ch 1, sc in each st around, join.

Rnd 42: Ch 1, sc in first 6 sts, sc next 2 sts tog, (sc in next 6 sts, sc next 2 sts tog) 5 times, join. *(42)*

Rnd 43: Ch 1, sc in each st around, join.

Rnd 44: Ch 1, sc in first 5 sts, sc next 2 sts tog, (sc in next 5 sts, sc next 2 sts tog) 5 times, join. *(36)*

Rnd 45: Ch 1, sc in each st around, join.

Rnd 46: Ch 1, sc in first 4 sts, sc next 2 sts tog, (sc in next 4 sts, sc next 2 sts tog) 5 times, join. *(30)*

Rnd 47: Ch 1, sc in each st around, join.

Rnd 48: Ch 1, sc first 2 sts tog, (sc next 2 sts tog) around, join. *(15)*

Rnd 49: Ch 1, sc in each st around, join. Leaving a 10" strand, fasten off.

Weave 10" strand through tops of sts on last rnd, pull tight to close opening and secure.

With white, sew ends of rows 26–37 together.

Top Edging

Rnd 1: Fold Cuff down over top of Leg; working in **remaining lps** on row 1 of Leg, join white with sc in first ch, sc in next 5 chs, (sc next 2 chs tog, sc in next ch) 23 times, sc in last 5 chs, join with sl st in first sc, turn.

Rnd 2: Ch 1, sc in each st around, join.

Rnd 3: Ch 1, sl st in each st around to last st; for **Loops,** (sl st, ch 20, sl st, ch 20, sl st, ch 28 for **Hanger,** sl st, ch 20, sl st, ch 20, sl st) in last st, join with sl st in first sl st. Fasten off.

Bells & Ribbons

Make six Bells same as First Bell in Tree Skirt Bottom Edging, placing one Bell in each ch-sp on rnd 6 of Cuff and one Bell in center of ch-28 Hanger on last rnd of Top Edging.

Make six Ribbons same as for Tree Skirt. Tie center of one Ribbon around top of each Bell on Cuff and Hanger. ✻

Country Stockings

Designed by Carolyn Christmas

Basic Instructions

STOCKING ASSEMBLY

1: To prevent cording from fraying, tape ends securely or stitch over and around ends. Tuck end of cording into Stocking about 1" at top edge of foot side of Stocking. With sewing needle and matching thread, sew end of cord securely to inside seam of Stocking. Sew cord around outside bottom edges of Stocking using small even stitches. When you reach the opposite top edge secure sewing thread and cut thread. **Do not cut cording.**

2: Allowing cording to hang loose, place crocheted Lace over top edge of Stocking, matching beginning chs of Stocking, sew together. If desired, tack bottom edge of Lace to Stocking.

3: Continue to sew cording around top edge; form loop at top edge of heel side. Sew end of cording securely to inside seam of Stocking.

OPTIONAL LINING

1: Using one Stocking Side as pattern, trace outline onto desired fabric (½ yd.) Cut one and one reversed.

2: Allowing ¼" on all sides for seam, sew together leaving top edge open. **Do not** turn right side out. Press.

3: After crocheted Stocking is completed, place Lining inside; turn top edge under and sew to top edge of Stocking with matching thread and sewing needle.

Small Striped

FINISHED SIZE: 5½" long excluding hanger.

MATERIALS:
- ❑ Worsted yarn:
    - ¼ oz. green
    - ¼ oz. gold
- ❑ 50 yds. ecru size 10 crochet cotton thread
- ❑ 24" cream poly cording
- ❑ Sewing thread to match cording
- ❑ Sewing and tapestry needles
- ❑ No. 7 steel hook and H hook or hooks needed to obtain gauges

GAUGES: H hook and yarn, 7 sc = 2", 4 sc rows = 1"; **No. 7 hook and size 10 thread,** 9 sc = 1"; 3 sc rows = ⅜".

BASIC STITCHES: Ch, sl st, sc, dc, tr.

SPECIAL STITCH: For **treble crochet cluster (tr cluster),** yo 2 times, insert hook in st, yo, pull through, (yo, pull through 2 lps on hook) 2 times, leaving last lps on hook; *yo 2 times, insert hook in same st, yo, pull through, (yo, pull through 2 lps on hook) 2 times, leaving last lps on hook; repeat from * number of times needed for number of tr in cluster; yo, pull through all lps on hook.

STOCKING FIRST SIDE

Row 1: With green and H hook, ch 9, sc in second ch from hook, sc in each ch across, turn. *(8 sc made)*

Row 2: Ch 1, sc in each st across changing to gold in last st made *(see Stitch Guide),* turn.

Row 3: Ch 1, sc in each st across, turn.

Row 4: Ch 1, sc in each st across changing to green in last st made, turn.

Row 5: Ch 1, sc in each st across, turn.

Row 6: Ch 1, sc in each st across changing to gold in last st made, turn.

Rows 7–9: Repeat rows 3–5.

Row 10: Ch 1, 2 sc in first st, sc in each st across changing to gold in last st made, turn. *(9 sc)*

Row 11: Ch 1, 2 sc in first st, sc in each st across, turn. *(10 sc)*

Row 12: Ch 1, 2 sc in first st, sc in each st across changing to green in last st made, turn. *(11 sc).*

Row 13: Ch 1, sc in each st across to last st, 2 sc in last st, turn. *(12 sc)*

Row 14: Ch 1, 2 sc in first st, sc in each st across changing to gold in last st made, turn. *(13 sc)*

Row 15: Ch 1, skip first st, sc in each st across to last st, 2 sc in last st, turn.

Row 16: Ch 1, sc in first 9 sts changing to green in last st made leaving remaining sts unworked, turn. *(9 sc)*

Row 17: Ch 1, skip first st, sc in each st across, turn. *(8 sc)*

Row 18: Ch 1, sc in each st across to last 2 sts, sc last 2 sts tog changing to gold in last st made, turn. *(7 sc)*

Row 19: Ch 1, skip first st, sc next 2 sts tog, sc in next 2 sts, sc last 2 sts tog. Fasten off.

STOCKING SECOND SIDE

Row 1: With green, ch 9, sc in second ch from hook, sc in each ch across, turn. *(8 sc made)*

Rows 2–9: Ch 1, sc in each st across, turn.

Rows 10–12: Ch 1, 2 sc in first st, sc in each st across, turn. *(11 sts at end of row 12)*

Row 13: Ch 1, sc in each st across to last st, 2 sc in last st, turn. *(12 sc)*

continued on page 126

Country Stockings

continued from page 124

Row 14: Ch 1, 2 sc in first st, sc in each st across, turn. *(13 sc)*

Row 15: Ch 1, skip first st, sc in each st across to last st, 2 sc in last st, turn.

Row 16: Ch 1, sc in first 9 sts leaving remaining sts unworked, turn. *(9 sc)*

Row 17: Ch 1, skip first st, sc in each st across, turn. *(8 sc)*

Row 18: Ch 1, sc in each st across to last 2 sts, sc last 2 sts tog, turn. *(7 sc)*

Row 19: Ch 1, skip first st, sc next 2 sts tog, sc in next 2 sts, sc last 2 sts tog, **do not turn.** Fasten off.

LACE

Rnd 1: With size 10 crochet cotton and No. 7 hook, ch 44; being careful not to twist chain, sl st in first ch to form ring, ch 1, sc in first ch, sc in each ch around, join with sl st in first sc. *(44 sc made)*

Rnds 2–3: Ch 1, sc in each st around, join.

Rnd 4: Ch 1, sc in first st, ch 3, skip next 3 sts, (sc in next st, ch 3, skip next 3 sts) around, join with sl st in first sc.

Rnd 5: Sl st in first ch sp, ch 3, 2-tr cluster *(see Special Stitch)* in same ch sp, ch 2, 3 tr cluster in same ch sp, (3-tr cluster, ch 2, 3-tr cluster) in each ch sp around, join with sl st in top of first cluster.

Rnd 6: Sl st in first ch sp, ch 1, (sc, ch 3, sl st in third ch from hook, sc, ch 2) in each ch sp around, join. Fasten off.

ASSEMBLY

1: With green and H hook, working through both thicknesses in end of each row and holding hook on top of work with yarn underneath, sl st Sides wrong sides together forming decorative chain around edge and leaving top edge open.

2: Work Basic Instructions on page 124.

Crazy Quilt

FINISHED SIZE: 15" long excluding hanger.

MATERIALS:
- ❏ Worsted yarn:
  - 2 oz. periwinkle
  - ½ oz. gold
  - ½ oz. green
  - ½ oz. burgundy
  - ½ oz. purple
  - ½ oz. black
- ❏ 100 yds. cream size 10 crochet cotton thread
- ❏ 1¾ yds. black poly cording
- ❏ Sewing thread to match cording
- ❏ Sewing and tapestry needles
- ❏ No. 7 steel hook and H hook or hooks needed to obtain gauges

GAUGES: H hook and yarn, 7 sc = 2", 4 sc rows = 1";
No. 7 hook and size 10 crochet thread, 9 sc = 1"; 3 sc rows = ⅜".

BASIC STITCHES: Ch, sl st, sc, hdc, dc, tr.

SPECIAL STITCHES: For **increase**, 2 sc in st.
For **decrease**, sc next 2 sts tog or leave number of stitches indicated according to graph unworked.

STOCKING FIRST SIDE

Row 1: With burgundy and H hook, ch 23, sc in second ch from hook, sc in each ch across, turn. *(22 sc made)*

Rows 2–57: Ch 1, sc in each st across changing colors *(see Stitch Guide)*, increasing and decreasing in the ends of the rows *(see Special Stitches)* according to graph on page 127, turn. At end of last row, fasten off.

Using fly stitch, French knot, feather stitch, chain stitch and buttonhole stitch *(see illustrations on page 127)*, embroider Stocking Side as desired using photo as guide.

SECOND STOCKING SIDE

Row 1: With periwinkle and H hook, ch 23, sc in second ch from hook, sc in each ch across, turn. *(22 sc made)*

Rows 2–57: Using periwinkle throughout, ch 1, sc in each st across increasing and decreasing in ends of rows according to graph, turn. At end of last row, fasten off.

LACE

Rnd 1: With size 10 crochet cotton and No. 7 hook, ch 100; being careful not to twist chain, sl st in first ch to form ring, ch 3 *(counts as first dc)*, dc in each ch around, join with sl st in top of ch-3. *(100 dc made)*

Rnds 2–5: Ch 3, dc in each st around, join.

Rnd 6: Ch 1, sc in first st, ch 3, sc in next st, ch 3, skip next 3 sts, (sc in next st, ch 3, sc in next st, ch 3, skip next 3 sts) around, join with sl st in first sc. *(40 ch sps)*

Rnd 7: Sl st in first ch sp, (sc, hdc, dc, 5 tr, dc, hdc, sc) in same ch sp, sc in next ch sp, *(sc, hdc, 5 tr, dc, hdc, sc) in next ch sp, sc in next ch sp; repeat from * around, join.

Rnd 8: Sl st in next 4 sts, (ch 1, sc in next st, ch 3, sl st in third ch from hook, sc) in next st, ch 3, *(sc, ch 3, sl st in third ch from hook, sc) in center st of next tr-group, ch 3; repeat from * around, join. Fasten off.

ASSEMBLY

1: With periwinkle and H hook, working through both thicknesses in ends of each row and holding hook on top of work with yarn underneath, sl st Sides wrong sides together forming decorative chain around edge and leaving top edge open.

2: Work Basic Instructions on page 124.

Harlequin Stocking pattern on page 135

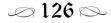

BUTTONHOLE STITCH

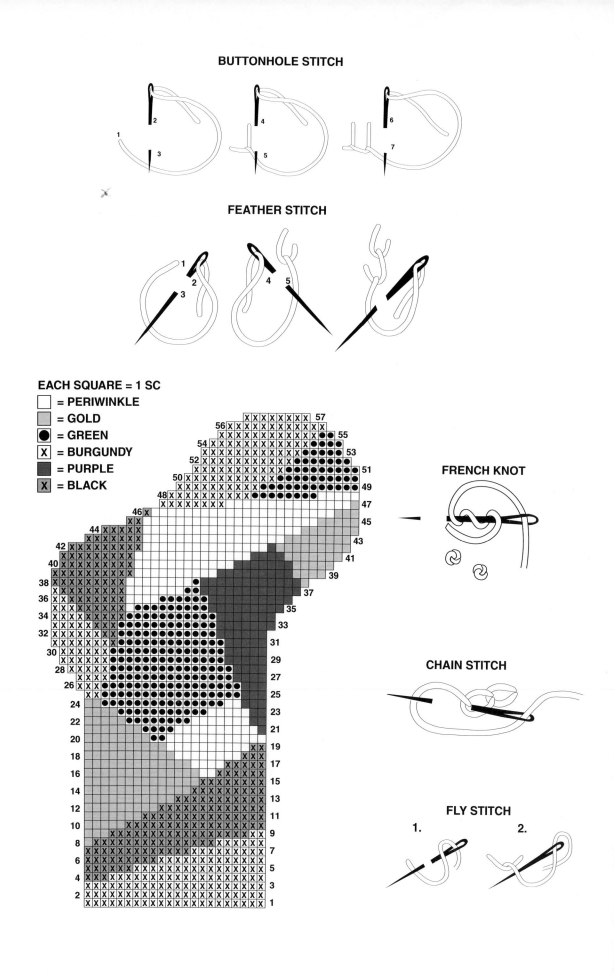

FEATHER STITCH

EACH SQUARE = 1 SC

☐ = PERIWINKLE
▨ = GOLD
● = GREEN
☒ = BURGUNDY
■ = PURPLE
▨ = BLACK

FRENCH KNOT

CHAIN STITCH

FLY STITCH

1.   2.

Pineapple Tree Skirt & Topper

An Original by Annie

Basic Instructions

STIFFENING & BLOCKING

For blocking thread crochet pieces with water, dampen finished piece and arrange and shape on a padded surface. Pin in place with rustproof stainless steel pins; allow to dry completely, then remove pins.

If crochet pieces need more stiffening and shaping, fabric stiffener or starching solution may be used. Shaped pieces such as the Angel may be blocked using Styrofoam® balls or cones covered with plastic wrap.

BASIC MATERIALS:

❑ Clear drying craft glue
❑ Fabric stiffener
❑ White sewing thread and needle
❑ Tapestry needle
❑ No. 7 steel hook

BASIC STITCHES: Ch, sl st, sc, dc, tr.

Angel Tree Topper

FINISHED SIZE: 13½" tall.

MATERIALS:

❑ 240 yds. white size 10 crochet cotton thread
❑ 28" length marabou trim
❑ 2¼" porcelain doll head and hands
❑ 7"-span feather wings
❑ Horn charm
❑ 12" plastic doll cone
❑ 1⅝" plastic ring
❑ 12" white ¼" satin ribbon

GAUGE: 6 dc = 1"; 4 dc rows = 1".

ANGEL
Dress

Rnd 1: Starting at neckline, ch 32, sl st in first ch to form ring, ch 3, dc in same ch, dc in next ch, (2 dc in next ch, dc in next ch) around, join with sl st in top of ch-3. *(48 dc made)*

Rnd 2: Ch 3, dc in next st, 2 dc in next st, (dc in next 2 sts, 2 dc in next st) around, join. *(64 dc)*

Rnd 3: Ch 3, dc in next 2 sts, 2 dc in next st, (dc in next 3 sts, 2 dc in next st) around, join. *(80 dc)*

Rnd 4: Ch 3, dc in each st around, join.

Rnd 5: Ch 3, dc in next 7 sts; for **sleeve opening,** skip next 24 sts; dc in next 16 sts; for **sleeve opening,** skip next 24 sts; dc in last 8 sts, join. *(32 dc)*

Rnd 6: Ch 3, dc in each st around, join.

Rnd 7: Ch 3, dc in next 7 sts, ch 6 *(base of pineapple made),* (dc in next 8 sts, ch 6) around, join, **turn.**

Rnd 8: Sl st in first ch-6 sp, ch 3, 10 dc in same ch sp, skip next 2 sts, dc in next 4 sts, skip next 2 sts, (11 dc in next ch-6 sp, skip next 2 sts, dc in next 4 sts, skip next 2 sts) 3 times, join, **turn.**

Rnd 9: Sl st in next 2 sts, ch 3, dc in next st, skip next st, dc in next st, (ch 1, dc in next st) 10 times, skip next st, *dc in next 2 sts, skip next st, dc in next st, (ch 1, dc in next st) 10 times, skip next st; repeat from * 2 more times, join, **do not turn.**

Rnd 10: Ch 3, dc in next st, (ch 3, sc in next ch-1 sp) 10 times, ch 3, *dc in next 2 sts, (ch 3, sc in next ch-1 sp) 10 times, ch 3; repeat from * 2 more times, join.

Rnd 11: (Ch 3, dc) in first st, 2 dc in next st, ch 3, skip next ch-3 sp, (sc in next ch-3 sp, ch 3) 9 times, *2 dc in each of next 2 sts, ch 3, skip next ch-3 sp, (sc in next ch-3 sp, ch 3) 9 times; repeat from * 2 more times, join.

Rnd 12: Ch 3, dc in next 3 sts, ch 3, skip next ch-3 sp, (sc in next ch-3 sp, ch 3) 8 times, *dc in next 4 sts, ch 3, skip next ch-3 sp, (sc in next ch-3 sp, ch 3) 8 times; repeat from * 2 more times, join.

Rnd 13: Ch 3, dc in next 3 sts, ch 3, skip next ch-3 sp, (sc in next ch-3 sp, ch 3) 7 times, *dc in next 4 sts, ch 3, skip next ch-3 sp, (sc in next ch-3 sp, ch 3) 7 times; repeat from * 2 more times, join.

Rnd 14: Ch 3, dc in next 3 sts, ch 3, skip next ch-3 sp, (sc in next ch-3 sp, ch 3) 6 times, *dc in next 4 sts, ch 3, skip next ch-3 sp, (sc in next ch-3 sp, ch 3) 6 times; repeat from * 2 more times, join.

Rnd 15: Ch 3, dc in next 3 sts, ch 3, skip next ch-3 sp, (sc in next ch-3 sp, ch 3) 5 times, *dc in next 4 sts, ch 3, skip next ch-3 sp, (sc in next ch-3 sp, ch 3) 5 times; repeat from * 2 more times, join.

Rnd 16: (Ch 3, dc) in first st, dc in next 2 sts, 2 dc in next st, ch 3, skip next ch-3 sp, (sc in next ch-3 sp,

continued on page 130

Pineapple Tree Skirt & Topper

continued from page 129

ch 3) 4 times, *2 dc in next st, dc in next 2 sts, 2 dc in next st, ch 3, skip next ch-3 sp, (sc in next ch-3 sp, ch 3) 4 times; repeat from * 2 more times, join.

Rnd 17: (Ch 3, dc) in first st, dc in next 4 sts, 2 dc in next st, ch 3, skip next ch-3 sp, (sc in next ch-3 sp, ch 3) 3 times, *2 dc in next st, dc in next 4 sts, 2 dc in next st, ch 3, skip next ch-3 sp, (sc in next ch-3 sp, ch 3) 3 times; repeat from * 2 more times, join.

Rnd 18: (Ch 3, dc) in first st, dc in next 6 sts, 2 dc in next st, ch 3, skip next ch-3 sp, (sc in next ch-3 sp, ch 3) 2 times, *2 dc in next st, dc in next 6 sts, 2 dc in next st, ch 3, skip next ch-3 sp, (sc in next ch-3 sp, ch 3) 2 times; repeat from * 2 more times, join.

Rnd 19: Ch 3, dc in next 4 sts, ch 4, dc in next 5 sts, ch 3, skip next ch-3 sp, sc in next ch-3 sp, ch 3, *dc in next 5 sts, ch 4, dc in next 5 sts, ch 3, skip next ch-3 sp, sc in next ch-3 sp, ch 3; repeat from * 2 more times, join.

Rnd 20: Ch 3, dc in next 3 sts, ch 1, skip next st, 8 dc in next ch-4 sp, ch 1, skip next st, dc in next 4 sts, ch 4, skip next 2 ch-3 sps, *dc in next 4 sts, ch 1, skip next st, 8 dc in next ch-4 sp, ch 1, dc in next 4 sts, ch 4, skip next 2 ch-3 sps; repeat from * 2 more times, join.

Rnd 21: Ch 3, dc in next 3 sts, [*ch 2, dc in next st, (ch 1, dc in next st) 7 times, ch 2, dc in next 4 sts, ch 1, 8 dc in next ch-4 sp, ch 1], dc in next 4 sts; repeat from * 2 more times; repeat between [ ], join.

Rnd 22: Ch 3, dc in next 3 sts, [*ch 2, sc in next ch-1 sp, (ch 3, sc in next ch-3 sp) 6 times, ch 2, dc in next 4 sts, ch 2, dc in next st, (ch 1, dc in next st) 7 times, ch 2], dc in next 4 sts; repeat from * 2 more times; repeat between [ ], join.

Rnd 23: Ch 3, dc in next 3 sts, [*ch 3, (sc in next ch-3 sp, ch 3) 6 times, dc in next 4 sts, ch 2, (sc in next ch-3 sp, ch 3) 6 times, sc in next ch-3 sp, ch 2], dc in next 4 sts; repeat from * 2 more times; repeat between [ ], join.

Rnd 24: Ch 3, dc in next 3 sts, [*ch 3, skip next ch-3 sp, (sc in next ch-3 sp, ch 3) 5 times, dc in next 4 sts, ch 3, skip next ch-2 sp, (sc in next ch-3 sp, ch 3) 6 times], dc in next 4 sts; repeat from * 2 more times; repeat between [ ], join.

Rnd 25: Ch 3, dc in next 3 sts, [*ch 3, skip next ch-3 sp, (sc in next ch-3 sp, ch 3) 4 times, dc in next 4 sts, ch 3, skip next ch-3 sp, (sc in next ch-3 sp, ch 3) 5 times], dc in next 4 sts; repeat from * 2 more times; repeat between [ ], join.

Rnd 26: (Ch 3, dc) in first st, dc in next 2 sts, 2 dc in next st, *[ch 3, skip next ch-3 sp, (sc in next ch-3 sp, ch 3) 3 times, 2 dc in next st, dc in next 2 sts, 2 dc in next st, ch 3, skip next ch-3 sp, (sc in next ch-3 sp, ch 3) 4 times], 2 dc in next st, dc in next 2 sts, dc in next st; repeat from * 2 more times; repeat between [ ], join.

Rnd 27: (Ch 3, dc) in first st, dc in next 4 sts, 2 dc in next st, [*ch 3, skip next ch-3 sp, (sc in next ch-3 sp, ch 3) 2 times, 2 dc in next st, dc in next 4 sts, 2 dc in next st, ch 3, skip next ch-3 sp, (sc in next ch-3 sp, ch 3) 3 times], 2 dc in next st, dc in next 4 sts, 2 dc in next st; repeat from * 2 more times; repeat between [ ], join.

Rnd 28: (Ch 3, dc) in first st, dc in next 6 sts, 2 dc in next st, [*ch 3, skip next ch-3 sp, sc in next ch-3 sp, ch 3, 2 dc in next st, dc in next 6 sts, 2 dc in next st, ch 3, skip next ch-3 sp, (sc in next ch-3 sp, ch 3) 2 times], 2 dc in next st, dc in next 6 sts, 2 dc in next st; repeat from * 2 more times; repeat between [ ], join.

Rnd 29: (Ch 3, dc) in first st, dc in next 2 sts, ch 5, skip next 4 sts, dc in next 2 sts, 2 dc in next st, [*skip next 2 ch-3 sps, 2 dc in next st, dc in next 2 sts, ch 5, skip next 4 sts, dc in next 2 sts, 2 dc in next st, ch 3, skip next ch-3 sp, sc in next ch-3 sp, ch 3], 2 dc in next st; repeat from * 2 more times; repeat between [ ], join.

Rnd 30: Ch 3, dc in next 3 sts, ch 1, 8 dc in next ch-5 sp, ch 1, (dc in next 8 sts, ch 1, 8 dc in next ch-5 sp, ch 1) 7 times, dc in last 4 sts, join.

Rnd 31: Ch 3, dc in next 3 sts, ch 2, dc in next st, (ch 1, dc in next st) 7 times, ch 2, *dc in next 8 sts, ch 2, dc in next st, (ch 1, dc in next st) 7 times, ch 2; repeat from * 6 more times, dc in last 4 sts, join.

Rnd 32: Ch 3, dc in next 3 sts, ch 3, (sc in next ch-1 sp, ch 3) 7 times, *dc in next 8 sts, ch 3, (sc in next ch-1 sp, ch 3) 7 times; repeat from * 6 more times, dc in last 4 sts, join.

Rnd 33: Ch 3, dc in next 3 sts, ch 3, skip next ch-3 sp, (sc in next ch-3 sp, ch 3) 6 times, *dc in next 8 sts, ch 3, skip next ch-3 sp, (sc in next ch-3 sp, ch 3) 6 times; repeat from * 6 more times, dc in last 4 sts, join.

Rnd 34: Ch 3, dc in next 3 sts, ch 3, skip next ch-3 sp, (sc in next ch-3 sp, ch 3) 5 times, *dc in next 4 sts, ch 2, dc in next 4 sts, ch 3, skip next ch-3 sp, (sc in next ch-3 sp, ch 3) 5 times; repeat from * 6 more times, dc in last 4 sts, ch 2, join.

Rnd 35: Ch 3, dc in next 3 sts, ch 3, skip next ch-3 sp, (sc in next ch-3 sp, ch 3) 4 times, *dc in next 4 sts, ch 2, dc in next 4 sts, ch 3, skip next ch-3 sp, (sc in next ch-3 sp, ch 3) 4 times; repeat from * 6 more times, dc in last 4 sts, ch 2, join.

Rnd 36: Ch 3, dc in next 3 sts, ch 3, skip next ch-3 sp, (sc in next ch-3 sp, ch 3) 3 times, *dc in next 4 sts, ch 3, dc in next 4 sts, ch 3, skip next ch-3 sp, (sc in next ch-3 sp, ch 3) 4 times; repeat from * 6 more times, dc in last 4 sts, ch 3, join.

Rnd 37: Ch 3, dc in next 3 sts, ch 3, skip next ch-3 sp, (sc in next ch-3 sp, ch 3) 2 times, *dc in next 4 sts, ch 3, sc in next ch-3 sp, ch 3, dc in next 4 sts, ch 3, skip next ch-3 sp, (sc in next ch-3 sp, ch 3) 2 times; repeat from * 6 more times, dc in last 4 sts, ch 3, sc in last ch-3 sp, ch 3, join.

Rnd 38: Ch 3, dc in next 3 sts, ch 3, skip next ch-3 sp, sc in next ch-3 sp, ch 3, *dc in next 4 sts, ch 3, (sc in next ch-3 sp, ch 3) 2 times, dc in next 4 sts, ch 3, skip next ch-3 sp, sc in next ch-3 sp, ch 3; repeat from * 6 more times, dc in next 4 sts, ch 3, (sc in next ch-3 sp, ch 3) 2 times, join.

Rnd 39: Ch 3, dc in next 3 sts, skip next 2 ch-3 sps, *dc in next 4 sts, ch 3, (sc in next ch-3 sp, ch 3) 3 times, dc in next 4 sts, skip next 2 ch-3 sps; repeat from * 6 more times, dc in next 4 sts, ch 3, (sc in next ch-3 sp, ch 3) 3 times, join.

Rnd 40: Ch 1, sc in first st, [*ch 3, sc in next sp between 4-dc groups, ch 3, skip next 3 sts, sc in next st, ch 3, (sc in next ch-3 sp, ch 3) 4 times], sc in next st; repeat from * 6 more times; repeat between [ ], join with dc in first sc.

Rnd 41: Ch 1, (sc, ch 1) in each st and (sc, ch 1) 3 times in each ch-3 sp around, join with sl st in first sc. Fasten off.

EDGING

Join with sc in any st on neckline, ch 1, (sc, ch 1) in each st around, join with sl st in first sc. Fasten off.

With sewing needle and thread, sew marabou to last rnd of Skirt.

SLEEVES

Rnd 1: Join with sl st in first st on sleeve opening, ch 3, evenly space 24 dc around, join with sl st in top of ch-3. *(25 dc made)*

Rnds 2–4: Ch 3, dc in each st around, join.

Rnd 5: Ch 1, sc in first st, ch 1, (sc in next st, ch 1) around, join with sl st in first sc. Fasten off.

Repeat on other sleeve opening.

ARMS

Row 1: Ch 45, sc in second ch from hook, sc in each ch across, turn. *(44 sc made)*

Rows 2–10: Ch 1, sc in each st across, turn. At end of last row, fasten off.

Sew rows 1 and 10 together.

EDGING

Working in ends of rows, join with sc in end of row 1, ch 1, (sc in end of next row, ch 1) around, join with sl st in first sc. Fasten off.

Repeat on opposite end of Arm.

HALO

Working around plastic ring, sc around ring *(see illustration)* until ring is evenly covered, join with sl st in first sc. Fasten off.

ASSEMBLY

1: Place top of plastic cone inside doll head. Glue bottom edge of doll head to area where it touches the cone. Place Dress on doll.

2: Glue one hand to inside at each end of Arm; with thumbs pointing inward, weave through Sleeves. Glue horn charm to hands.

3: Cut 6" piece satin ribbon; wrap piece around doll's waist overlapping ends, tack on back to secure. Tie remaining piece in bow and sew or glue to center front of neckline.

4: Glue Wings to back of doll.

5: Glue Halo to back of doll's head as shown in photo.

Tree Skirt

FINISHED SIZE: 64" diameter.

MATERIALS:
- ❏ 1,750 yds. white size 10 crochet cotton thread
- ❏ 8 pieces ½"-long × ¼"-wide Velcro®

GAUGE: Rows 1–6 = 2".

SPECIAL STITCHES: For **shell**, (2 dc, ch 2, 2 dc) in ch sp of next shell or next ch sp.

To **join with dc,** place slip knot on hook, yo, insert hook in st, yo, pull lp through st, (yo, pull through 2 lps on hook) 2 times.

WEDGE (make 6)

Row 1: Ch 6, sl st in first ch to form ring, (ch 3—*counts as first dc,* dc, ch 2, 2 dc) in ring, ch 2, (2 dc, ch 2, 2 dc) in ring, turn. *(8 dc, 3 ch-2 sps made)*

Row 2: Ch 6, (**shell**—*see Special Stitches,* ch 2) 2 times, shell, turn. *(3 shells)*

Rows 3–4: Ch 6, (shell, ch 4) 2 times, shell, turn.

Row 5: Ch 6, (shell, ch 5) 2 times, shell, turn.

Row 6: Ch 6, shell, ch 5, (dc, ch 2) 5 times in next shell, dc in same shell, ch 5, shell, turn.

Row 7: Ch 6, shell, ch 3, shell in next ch-2 sp, (ch 3, skip next ch sp, shell in next ch sp) 2 times, ch 3, shell, turn.

Row 8: Ch 6, *shell, ch 4, (shell, ch 2, 2 dc) in next shell, ch 4; repeat from *, shell, turn.

Row 9: Ch 6, *shell, ch 4, shell in each of next 2 ch-2 sps, ch 4; repeat from *, shell, turn.

Row 10: Ch 6, shell, ch 4, shell, ch 2, (dc, ch 5, dc) in next shell, ch 2, shell, ch 2, (dc, ch 5, dc) in next shell, ch 2, shell, ch 4, shell, turn.

Row 11: Ch 6, shell, ch 4, (shell, 20 dc in next ch-5 sp) 2 times, shell, ch 4, shell, turn.

Row 12: Ch 6, shell, ch 4, sc in next shell, dc in next st, (ch 1, dc in next st) 19 times, shell, dc in next st, (ch 1, dc in next st) 19 times, sc in next shell, ch 4, shell, turn.

Row 13: Ch 6, shell, ch 4, sc in next ch-1 sp, (ch 3, sc in next ch-1 sp) 18 times, shell, sc in next ch-1 sp, (ch 3, sc in next ch-1 sp) 18 times, ch 4, shell, turn.

Row 14: Ch 6, shell, ch 4, sc in next ch-3 sp, (ch 3, sc in next ch-3 sp) 17 times, shell, sc in next ch-3 sp, (ch 3, sc in next ch-3 sp) 17 times, ch 4, shell, turn.

Row 15: Ch 6, shell, ch 4, sc in next ch-3 sp, (ch 3, sc in next ch-3 sp) 16 times, ch 1, shell, ch 1, sc in

continued on page 132

Pineapple Tree Skirt & Topper

continued from page 131

next ch-3 sp, (ch 3, sc in next ch-3 sp) 16 times, ch 4, shell, turn.

Row 16: Ch 6, shell, ch 4, sc in next ch-3 sp, (ch 3, sc in next ch-3 sp) 15 times, ch 1, shell, ch 1, sc in next ch-3 sp, (ch 3, sc in next ch-3 sp) 15 times, ch 4, shell, turn.

Row 17: Ch 6, shell, ch 4, sc in next ch-3 sp, (ch 3, sc in next ch-3 sp) 14 times, ch 2, (2 dc, ch 2, dc, ch 2, dc, ch 2, 2 dc) in next shell, ch 2, sc in next ch-3 sp, (ch 3, sc in next ch-3 sp) 14 times, ch 4, shell, turn.

Row 18: Ch 6, (shell, ch 2, 2 dc) in first shell, ch 4, sc in next ch-3 sp, (ch 3, sc in next ch-3 sp) 13 times, ch 3, shell in next ch-2 sp, (dc, ch 2, dc) in next ch-2 sp, shell in next ch-2 sp, ch 3, sc in next ch-3 sp, (ch 3, sc in next ch-3 sp) 13 times, ch 4, (shell, ch 2, 2 dc) in last shell, turn.

Row 19: Ch 6, shell in each of next 2 ch-2 sps, ch 4, sc in next ch-3 sp, (ch 3, sc in next ch-3 sp) 12 times, ch 3, shell in each of next 3 ch-2 sps, ch 3, sc in next ch-3 sp, (ch 3, sc in next ch-3 sp) 12 times, ch 4, shell in each of last 2 ch-2 sps, turn.

Row 20: Ch 6, shell in each of next 2 shells, ch 4, sc in next ch-3 sp, (ch 3, sc in next ch-3 sp) 11 times, ch 3, shell in each of next 3 shells, ch 3, sc in next ch-3 sp, (ch 3, sc in next ch-3 sp) 11 times, ch 4, shell in each of last 2 shells, turn.

Row 21: Ch 6, shell in each of next 2 shells, ch 4, (sc in next ch-3 sp, ch 3) 11 times, (shell, ch 2) 2 times, shell, (ch 3, sc in next ch-3 sp) 11 times, ch 4, shell in each of last 2 shells, turn.

Row 22: Ch 6, shell in each of next 2 shells, ch 4, (sc in next ch-3 sp, ch 3) 10 times, (shell, ch 1) 2 times, shell, ch 3, skip next ch-3 sp, sc in next ch-3 sp, (ch 3, sc in next ch-3 sp) 9 times, ch 4, shell in each of last 2 shells, turn.

Row 23: Ch 6, shell, ch 1, shell, ch 4, sc in next ch-3 sp, (ch 3, sc in next ch-3 sp) 8 times, ch 4, (shell, ch 3) 2 times, shell, ch 4, sc in next ch-3 sp, (ch 3, sc in next ch-3 sp) 8 times, ch 4, shell, ch 1, shell, turn.

Row 24: Ch 6, shell, ch 2, shell, ch 4, sc in next ch-3 sp, (ch 3, sc in next ch-3 sp) 7 times, ch 4, (shell, ch 2, 2 dc) in next shell, ch 4, shell, ch 4, (2 dc, ch 2, shell) in next shell, ch 4, sc in next ch-3 sp, (ch 3, sc in next ch-3 sp) 7 times, ch 4, shell, ch 2, shell, turn.

Row 25: Ch 6, (shell, ch 4) 2 times, sc in next ch-3 sp, (ch 3, sc in next ch-3 sp) 6 times, ch 4, shell, shell in next ch-2 sp, ch 4, shell, ch 4, shell in next ch-2 sp, shell, ch 4, sc in next ch-3 sp, (ch 3, sc in next ch-3 sp) 6 times, (ch 4, shell) 2 times, turn.

Row 26: Ch 6, (shell, ch 4) 2 times, sc in next ch-3 sp, (ch 3, sc in next ch-3 sp) 5 times, ch 4, shell, ch 2, (shell, ch 4) 2 times, shell, ch 2, shell, ch 4, sc in next ch-3 sp, (ch 3, sc in next ch-3 sp) 5 times, (ch 4, shell) 2 times, turn.

Row 27: Ch 6, (shell, ch 4) 2 times, sc in next ch-3 sp, (ch 3, sc in next ch-3 sp) 4 times, ch 4, (shell, ch 4) 5 times, sc in next ch-3 sp, (ch 3, sc in next ch-3 sp) 4 times, (ch 4, shell) 2 times, turn.

Row 28: Ch 6, shell, ch 4, (shell, ch 2, 2 dc) in next shell, ch 4, sc in next ch-3 sp, (ch 3, sc in next ch-3 sp) 3 times, ch 4, (shell, ch 4) 5 times, sc in next ch-3 sp, (ch 3, sc in next ch-3 sp) 3 times, ch 4, (2 dc, ch 2, shell) in next shell, ch 4, shell, turn.

Row 29: Ch 6, shell, ch 4, shell in each of next 2 ch-2 sps, ch 4, sc in next ch-3 sp, (ch 3, sc in next ch-3 sp) 2 times, ch 4, shell, ch 4, (2 dc, ch 5, 2 dc) in next shell, ch 4, shell, ch 4, (2 dc, ch 5, 2 dc) in next shell, ch 4, shell, ch 4, sc in next ch-3 sp, (ch 3, sc in next ch-3 sp) 2 times, ch 4, shell in each of next 2 ch-2 sps, ch 4, shell, turn.

Row 30: Ch 6, shell, ch 4, shell in each of next 2 shells, ch 4, sc in next ch-3 sp, ch 3, sc in next ch-3 sp, (ch 4, shell, ch 4, 20 dc in next ch-5 sp) 2 times, ch 4, shell, ch 4, sc in next ch-3 sp, ch 3, sc in next ch-3 sp, ch 4, shell in each of next 2 shells, ch 4, shell, turn.

Row 31: Ch 6, (shell, ch 4) 3 times, sc in next ch-3 sp, ch 4, shell, (ch 1, dc in next dc) 20 times, ch 1, shell, (ch 1, dc in next dc) 20 times, ch 1, shell, ch 4, sc in next ch-3 sp, ch 4, (shell, ch 4) 2 times, shell, turn.

Row 32: Ch 6, (shell, ch 4) 2 times, shell in each of next 2 shells, ch 1, skip next ch-1 sp, sc in next ch-1 sp, (ch 3, sc in next ch-1 sp) 18 times, ch 1, skip next ch-1 sp, shell, ch 1, skip next ch-1 sp, sc in next ch-1 sp, (ch 3, sc in next ch-1 sp) 18 times, ch 1, skip next ch-1 sp, shell in each of next 2 shells, (ch 4, shell) 2 times, turn.

Row 33: Ch 6, (shell, ch 4) 2 times, 2 dc in next shell, ch 2, 2 dc in next shell, ch 1, sc in next ch-3 sp, (ch 3, sc in next ch-3 sp) 17 times, ch 1, shell, ch 1, sc in next ch-3 sp, (ch 3, sc in next ch-3 sp) 17 times, ch 1, 2 dc in next shell, ch 2, 2 dc in next shell, (ch 4, shell) 2 times, turn.

Row 34: Ch 6, (shell, ch 4) 2 times, shell in next ch-2 sp, ch 1, sc in next ch-3 sp, (ch 3, sc in next ch-3 sp) 16 times, ch 1, shell, ch 1, sc in next ch-3 sp, (ch 3, sc in next ch-3 sp) 16 times, ch 1, shell in next ch-2 sp, (ch 4, shell) 2 times, turn.

Row 35: Ch 6, (shell, ch 4) 2 times, shell, ch 1, sc in next ch-3 sp, (ch 3, sc in next ch-3 sp) 15 times, ch 1, shell, ch 1, sc in next ch-3 sp, (ch 3, sc in next ch-3 sp) 15 times, ch 1, shell, (ch 4, shell) 2 times, turn.

Row 36: Ch 6, (shell, ch 4) 2 times, shell, ch 2, sc in next ch-3 sp, (ch 3, sc in next ch-3 sp) 14 times, ch 2, shell, ch 2, sc in next ch-3 sp, (ch 3, sc in next ch-3 sp) 14 times, ch 2, (shell, ch 4) 2 times, shell, turn.

Row 37: Ch 6, (shell, ch 4) 2 times, shell, ch 3, sc in next ch-3 sp, (ch 3, sc in next ch-3 sp) 13 times, ch 3, shell, ch 3, sc in next ch-3 sp, (ch 3, sc in next ch-3 sp) 13 times, ch 3, (shell, ch 4) 2 times, shell, turn.

Row 38: Ch 6, shell, ch 4, (2 dc, ch 5, 2 dc) in next shell, ch 4, shell, ch 4, skip next ch-3 sp, sc in

132

next ch-3 sp, (ch 3, sc in next ch-3 sp) 12 times, ch 4, shell, ch 4, sc in next ch-3 sp, (ch 3, sc in next ch-3 sp) 12 times, ch 4, skip next ch-3 sp, shell, ch 4, (2 dc, ch 5, 2 dc) in next shell, ch 4, shell, turn.

Row 39: Ch 6, shell, ch 2, 20 dc in next ch-5 sp, ch 4, shell, ch 4, sc in next ch-3 sp, (ch 3, sc in next ch-3 sp) 11 times, ch 4, shell, ch 4, sc in next ch-3 sp, (ch 3, sc in next ch-3 sp) 11 times, ch 4, shell, ch 4, 20 dc in next ch-5 sp, ch 2, shell, turn.

Row 40: Ch 6, shell, ch 4, dc in next dc, (ch 1, dc in next dc) 19 times, ch 2, shell, ch 4, sc in next ch-3 sp, (ch 3, sc in next ch-3 sp) 10 times, ch 4, shell, ch 4, sc in next ch-3 sp, (ch 3, sc in next ch-3 sp) 10 times, ch 4, shell, ch 2, dc in next dc, (ch 1, dc in next dc) 19 times, ch 4, shell, turn.

Row 41: Ch 6, shell, ch 4, sc in next ch-1 sp, (ch 3, sc in next ch-1 sp) 18 times, ch 4, shell, ch 4, sc in next ch-3 sp, (ch 3, sc in next ch-3 sp) 9 times, ch 4, shell, ch 4, sc in next ch-3 sp, (ch 3, sc in next ch-3 sp) 9 times, ch 4, shell, ch 4, sc in next ch-1 sp, (ch 3, sc in next ch-1 sp) 18 times, ch 4, shell, turn.

Row 42: Ch 6, shell, ch 4, sc in next ch-3 sp, (ch 3, sc in next ch-3 sp) 17 times, ch 4, shell, ch 4, sc in next ch-3 sp, (ch 3, sc in next ch-3 sp) 8 times, ch 4, shell, ch 4, sc in next ch-3 sp, (ch 3, sc in next ch-3 sp) 8 times, ch 4, shell, ch 4, sc in next ch-3 sp, (ch 3, sc in next ch-3 sp) 17 times, ch 4, shell, turn.

Row 43: Ch 6, shell, ch 4, sc in next ch-3 sp, (ch 3, sc in next ch-3 sp) 16 times, ch 4, shell, ch 4, sc in next ch-3 sp, (ch 3, sc in next ch-3 sp) 7 times, ch 4, shell, ch 4, sc in next ch-3 sp, (ch 3, sc in next ch-3 sp) 7 times, ch 4, shell, ch 4, sc in next ch-3 sp, (ch 3, sc in next ch-3 sp) 16 times, ch 4, shell, turn.

Row 44: Ch 6, shell, ch 4, sc in next ch-3 sp, (ch 3, sc in next ch-3 sp) 15 times, ch 4, shell, ch 4, sc in next ch-3 sp, (ch 3, sc in next ch-3 sp) 6 times, ch 4, shell, ch 4, sc in next ch-3 sp, (ch 3, sc in next ch-3 sp) 6 times, ch 4, shell, ch 4, sc in next ch-3 sp, (ch 3, sc in next ch-3 sp) 15 times, ch 4, shell, turn.

Row 45: Ch 6, shell, ch 4, sc in next ch-3 sp, (ch 3, sc in next ch-3 sp) 14 times, ch 4, shell, ch 4, sc in next ch-3 sp, (ch 3, sc in next ch-3 sp) 5 times, ch 4, (2 dc, ch 2) 3 times in next shell, 2 dc in same shell, ch 4, sc in next ch-3 sp, (ch 3, sc in next ch-3 sp) 5 times, ch 4, shell, ch 4, sc in next ch-3 sp, (ch 3, sc in next ch-3 sp) 14 times, ch 4, shell, turn.

Row 46: Ch 6, shell, ch 4, sc in next ch-3 sp, (ch 3, sc in next ch-3 sp) 13 times, ch 4, shell, ch 4, sc in next ch-3 sp, (ch 3, sc in next ch-3 sp) 4 times, ch 4, shell in next ch-2 sp, (dc, ch 2, dc) in next ch sp, shell in next ch-2 sp, ch 4, sc in next ch-3 sp, (ch 3, sc in next ch-3 sp) 4 times, ch 4, shell, ch 4, sc in next ch-3 sp, (ch 3, sc in next ch-3 sp) 13 times, ch 4, shell, turn.

Row 47: Ch 6, shell, ch 4, sc in next ch-3 sp, (ch 3, sc in next ch-3 sp) 12 times, ch 4, shell, ch 4, sc in next ch-3 sp, (ch 3, sc in next ch-3 sp) 3 times, ch 4, shell, ch 2, shell in next ch-2 sp, ch 2, shell, ch 4, sc in next ch-3 sp, (ch 3, sc in next ch-3 sp) 3 times, ch 4, shell, ch 4, sc in next ch-3 sp, (ch 3, sc in next ch-3 sp) 12 times, ch 4, shell, turn.

Row 48: Ch 6, shell, ch 4, sc in next ch-3 sp, (ch 3, sc in next ch-3 sp) 11 times, ch 4, shell, ch 4, sc in next ch-3 sp, (ch 3, sc in next ch-3 sp) 2 times, (ch 4, shell) 3 times, ch 4, sc in next ch-3 sp, (ch 3, sc in next ch-2 sp) 2 times, ch 4, shell, ch 4, sc in next ch-3 sp, (ch 3, sc in next ch-3 sp) 11 times, ch 4, shell, turn.

Row 49: Ch 6, shell, ch 4, sc in next ch-3 sp, (ch 3, sc in next ch-3 sp) 10 times, ch 4, (shell, ch 2, 2 dc) in next shell, ch 4, sc in next ch-3 sp, ch 3, sc in next ch-3 sp, ch 4, (shell, ch 2, 2 dc) in next shell, ch 4, shell, ch 4, (shell, ch 2, 2 dc) in next shell, ch 4, sc in next ch-3 sp, ch 3, sc in next ch-3 sp, ch 4, (shell, ch 2, 2 dc) in next shell, ch 4, sc in next ch-3 sp, (ch 3, sc in next ch-3 sp) 10 times, ch 4, shell, turn.

Row 50: Ch 6, (shell, ch 2, 2 dc) in first shell, ch 4, sc in next ch-3 sp, (ch 3, sc in next ch-3 sp) 9 times, ch 4, shell in each of next 2 ch-2 sps, ch 4, sc in next ch-3 sp, ch 4, shell in each of next 2 ch-2 sps, ch 4, shell, ch 4, shell in each of next 2 ch-2 sps, ch 4, sc in next ch-3 sp, ch 4, shell in each of next 2 ch-2 sps, ch 4, sc in next ch-3 sp, (ch 3, sc in next ch-3 sp) 9 times, ch 4, (shell, ch 2, dc) in last shell, turn.

Row 51: Ch 6, shell, ch 4, shell in next ch-2 sp, ch 4, sc in next ch-3 sp, (ch 3, sc in next ch-3 sp) 8 times, ch 4, shell, ch 4, 2 dc in each of next 2 shells, ch 4, (shell, ch 4) 3 times, 2 dc in each of next 2 shells, ch 4, shell, ch 4, sc in next ch-3 sp, (ch 3, sc in next ch-3 sp) 8 times, (ch 4, shell) 2 times, turn.

Row 52: Ch 6, (shell, ch 4) 2 times, sc in next ch-3 sp, (ch 3, sc in next ch-3 sp) 7 times, ch 4, shell, ch 4, shell in sp between next 2 dc-groups, ch 4, (2 dc, ch 5, 2 dc) in next shell, ch 4, shell, ch 4, (2 dc, ch 5, 2 dc) in next shell, ch 4, shell in sp between next 2 dc-groups, ch 4, shell, ch 4, sc in next ch-3 sp, (ch 3, sc in next ch-3 sp) 7 times, (ch 4, shell) 2 times, turn.

Row 53: Ch 6, (shell, ch 4) 2 times, sc in next ch-3 sp, (ch 3, sc in next ch-3 sp) 6 times, (ch 4, shell) 2 times, ch 2, 20 dc in next ch-5 sp, ch 2, shell, ch 2, 20 dc in next ch-5 sp, ch 2, (shell, ch 4) 2 times, sc in next ch-3 sp, (ch 3, sc in next ch-3 sp) 6 times, (ch 4, shell) 2 times, turn.

Row 54: Ch 6, shell, ch 4, (shell, ch 2, 2 dc) in next shell, ch 4, sc in next ch-3 sp, (ch 3, sc in next ch-3 sp) 5 times, (ch 4, shell) 2 times, ch 2, (dc in next dc, ch 1) 19 times, dc in next dc, ch 2, shell, ch 2, (dc in next dc, ch 1) 19 times, dc in next dc, ch 2, (shell, ch 4) 2 times, sc in next ch-3 sp, (ch 3, sc in next ch-3 sp) 5 times, (2 dc, ch 2, shell) in next shell, ch 4, shell, turn.

Row 55: Ch 6, shell, ch 4, shell in next ch-2 sp, ch 4, shell, ch 4, sc in next ch-3 sp, (ch 3, sc in next ch-3 sp) 4 times, (ch 4, shell) 2 times, ch 2, sc in next ch-1 sp, (ch 3, sc in next ch-1 sp) 18 times, ch 2, shell, ch 2, sc in next ch-1 sp, (ch 3, sc in next ch-1 sp) 18 times, ch 2, (shell, ch 4) 2 times, sc in next ch-3 sp, (ch 3, sc in next ch-3 sp) 4 times, ch 4, shell in next ch-2 sp, (ch 4, shell) 2 times, turn.

Row 56: Ch 6, (shell, ch 4) 3 times, sc in next ch-3 sp, (ch 3, sc in next ch-3 sp) 3 times, (ch 4, shell) 2 times, ch 2, sc in next ch-3 sp, (ch 3, sc in next ch-3 sp) 17 times, ch 2, shell, ch 2, sc in next ch-3

continued on page 134

Pineapple Tree Skirt & Topper

continued from page 133

sp, (ch 3, sc in next ch-3 sp) 17 times, ch 2, (shell, ch 4) 2 times, ch 4, sc in next ch-3 sp, (ch 3, sc in next ch-3 sp) 3 times, (ch 4, shell) 3 times, turn.

Row 57: Ch 6, (shell, ch 4) 3 times, sc in next ch-3 sp, (ch 3, sc in next ch-3 sp) 2 times, (ch 4, shell) 2 times, ch 2, sc in next ch-3 sp, (ch 3, sc in next ch-3 sp) 16 times, ch 2, shell, ch 2, sc in next ch-3 sp, (ch 3, sc in next ch-3 sp) 16 times, ch 2, (shell, ch 4) 2 times, sc in next ch-3 sp, (ch 3, sc in next ch-3 sp) 2 times, (ch 4, shell) 3 times, turn.

Row 58: Ch 6, sc in last st of first shell, (ch 4, shell) 2 times, ch 4, sc in next ch-3 sp, ch 3, sc in next ch-3 sp, (ch 4, shell) 2 times, ch 2, sc in next ch-3 sp, (ch 3, sc in next ch-3 sp) 15 times, ch 2, shell, ch 2, sc in next ch-3 sp, (ch 3, sc in next ch-3 sp) 15 times, ch 2, (shell, ch 4) 2 times, sc in next ch-3 sp, ch 3, sc in next ch-3 sp, (ch 4, shell) 2 times, tr in last st of last shell, turn.

Row 59: Ch 6, (shell, ch 4) 2 times, sc in next ch-3 sp, ch 4, (shell, ch 4) 2 times, sc in next ch-3 sp, (ch 3, sc in next ch-3 sp) 14 times, ch 4, shell, ch 4, sc in next ch-3 sp, (ch 3, sc in next ch-3 sp) 14 times, ch 4, (shell, ch 4) 2 times, sc in next ch-3 sp, (ch 4, shell) 2 times, turn.

Row 60: Ch 6, sc in last st of first shell, ch 4, shell in each of next 2 shells, ch 4, shell, ch 4, sc in next ch-3 sp, (ch 3, sc in next ch-3 sp) 13 times, ch 4, shell, ch 4, sc in next ch-3 sp, (ch 3, sc in next ch-3 sp) 13 times, ch 4, shell, ch 4, shell in each of next 2 shells, tr in last st of last shell, turn.

Row 61: Ch 6, shell in each of first 2 shells, ch 4, shell, ch 4, sc in next ch-3 sp, (ch 3, sc in next ch-3 sp) 12 times, ch 4, shell, ch 4, sc in next ch-3 sp, (ch 3, sc in next ch-3 sp) 12 times, ch 4, shell, ch 4, shell in each of last 2 shells, turn.

Row 62: Ch 6, shell in each of first 2 shells, ch 4, shell, ch 4, sc in next ch-3 sp, (ch 3, sc in next ch-3 sp) 11 times, ch 4, (shell, ch 2, 2 dc) in next shell, ch 4, sc in next ch-3 sp, (ch 3, sc in next ch-3 sp) 11 times, (ch 4, shell) 2 times, shell, turn.

Row 63: Ch 6, skip first shell, (shell, ch 4) 2 times, sc in next ch-3 sp, (ch 3, sc in next ch-3 sp) 10 times, ch 4, shell in each of next 2 ch-2 sps, ch 4, sc in next ch-3 sp, (ch 3, sc in next ch-3 sp) 10 times, (ch 4, shell) 2 times leaving remaining shell unworked, turn.

Row 64: Ch 6, (shell, ch 4) 2 times, sc in next ch-3 sp, (ch 3, sc in next ch-3 sp) 9 times, ch 4, (shell, ch 4) 2 times, sc in next ch-3 sp, (ch 3, sc in next ch-3 sp) 9 times, (ch 4, shell) 2 times, turn.

Row 65: Ch 6, (shell, ch 4) 2 times, sc in next ch-3 sp, (ch 3, sc in next ch-3 sp) 8 times, ch 4, (shell, ch 4) 2 times, sc in next ch-3 sp, (ch 3, sc in next ch-3 sp) 8 times, (ch 4, shell) 2 times, turn.

Row 66: Ch 6, skip first shell, shell, ch 4, sc in next ch-3 sp, (ch 3, sc in next ch-3 sp) 7 times, ch 4, shell, ch 4, shell in next ch-4 sp, ch 4, shell, ch 4, sc in next ch-3 sp, (ch 3, sc in next ch-3 sp) 7 times, ch 4, shell leaving remaining shell unworked, turn.

Row 67: Ch 6, shell, ch 4, sc in next ch-3 sp, (ch 3, sc in next ch-3 sp) 6 times, (ch 4, shell) 3 times, ch 4, sc in next ch-3 sp, (ch 3, sc in next ch-3 sp) 6 times, ch 4, shell, turn.

Row 68: Ch 6, shell, ch 4, sc in next ch-3 sp, (ch 3, sc in next ch-3 sp) 5 times, ch 4, (shell, ch 2, 2 dc) in next shell, ch 4, shell, ch 4, (2 dc, ch 2, 2 dc, ch 2, 2 dc) in next shell, ch 4, sc in next ch-3 sp, (ch 3, sc in next ch-3 sp) 5 times, ch 4, shell, turn.

Row 69: Ch 6, shell, ch 4, sc in next ch-3 sp, (ch 3, sc in next ch-3 sp) 4 times, (ch 4, shell) in each of next 2 ch-2 sps, ch 4, shell, ch 4, (shell, ch 4) in each of next 2 ch-2 sps, sc in next ch-3 sp, (ch 3, sc in next ch-3 sp) 4 times, ch 4, shell, turn.

Row 70: Ch 6, shell, ch 4, sc in next ch-3 sp, (ch 3, sc in next ch-3 sp) 3 times, ch 4, (shell, ch 4) 5 times, sc in next ch-3 sp, (ch 3, sc in next ch-3 sp) 3 times, ch 4, shell, turn.

Row 71: Ch 6, shell, ch 4, sc in next ch-3 sp, (ch 3, sc in next ch-3 sp) 2 times, ch 4, (shell, ch 4) 5 times, sc in next ch-3 sp, (ch 3, sc in next ch-3 sp) 2 times, ch 4, shell, turn.

Row 72: Ch 6, shell, ch 4, sc in next ch-3 sp, ch 3, sc in next ch-3 sp, ch 4, (shell, ch 4) 3 times, sc in next ch-3 sp, ch 3, sc in next ch-3 sp, ch 4, shell, turn.

Row 73: Ch 6, shell, ch 4, sc in next ch-3 sp, ch 4, (shell, ch 4) 5 times, sc in next ch-3 sp, ch 4, shell, turn.

Row 74: Ch 6, shell in each of first 2 shells, (ch 4, shell) 5 times, ch 4, shell in each of last 2 shells, turn.

Row 75: (Ch 5, sl st in third ch from hook, ch 3, sc in first st of next shell, ch 5, sl st in third ch from hook, ch 3, sc in last st of same shell) 5 times, ch 5, sl st in third ch from hook, ch 3, sc in last st of last shell. Fasten off.

Row 76: Working in ch-6 sps on side and bottom edges, join with sc in ch-6 at end of row 58, (ch 6, sc in next ch-6 sp) 28 times, ch 5, sc in ring of row 1, ch 5, sc in next ch-6 sp, (ch 6, sc in next ch-6 sp) 27 times. Fasten off. *(57 ch sps)*

JOINING

Holding two Wedges wrong sides together and working back and forth between the two, matching sts and ch sps, **join with dc** *(see Special Stitches)* in first sc on side edge of Wedge held in front, dc in sc on back Wedge, (*ch 1, dc next 2 ch sps of both Wedges tog, ch 1, dc in next sc on front Wedge*, ch 1, dc in next sc on back Wedge) 26 times; repeat between first and second *, ch 3, sl st in sc on back Wedge, shell in top of last dc made, sl st in base of last dc. Fasten off.

Repeat Joining 4 more times.

On **remaining edges,** join with sl st in bottom corner, hdc in each st and 4 hdc in each ch sp down edge to top. Fasten off.

Sew 8 Velcro pieces evenly spaced on opened edges for Skirt closure. ❄

Country Stocking

photo on page page 127

Harlequin

FINISHED SIZE: 15" long excluding hanger.

MATERIALS:
- ❑ Worsted yarn:
  - 2 oz. gold
  - 2 oz. black
- ❑ 100 yds. cream size 10 crochet cotton thread
- ❑ 1¾ yds. black poly cording
- ❑ Sewing thread to match cording
- ❑ Sewing and tapestry needles
- ❑ No. 7 steel hook and H hook or hooks needed to obtain gauges

GAUGES: H hook and worsted yarn, 7 sc = 2", 4 sc rows = 1"; **No. 7 hook and size 10 thread,** 9 sc = 1"; 3 sc rows = ⅜".

BASIC STITCHES: Ch, sl st, sc, dc, tr.

SPECIAL STITCHES: For **increase,** 2 sc in st.
For **decrease,** sc next 2 sts tog or leave number of stitches indicated according to graph unworked.

STOCKING SIDE (make 2)
Row 1: With gold and H hook, ch 20, sc in second ch from hook, sc in each ch across changing colors *(see Stitch Guide)* according to graph, turn. *(19 sc made)*

Rows 2–57: Ch 1, sc in each st across increasing and decreasing in the ends of the rows *(see Special Stitches)* and changing colors according to graph. At end of last row, fasten off.

LACE BAND
Rnd 1: With size 10 crochet cotton and No. 7 hook, ch 105; being careful not to twist chain, sl st in first ch to form ring, ch 3 *(counts as first dc),* dc in each ch around, join with sl st in top of ch-3. *(105 dc made)*

Rnds 2–5: Ch 3, dc in each st around, join.

Rnd 6: Ch 1, sc in first st, ch 4, skip next 4 sts, (sc in next st, ch 4, skip next 4 sts) around, join with sl st in first sc.

Rnd 7: Sl st in first ch sp, ch 1, (sc, ch 5, sl st in third ch from hook —*first picot made,* ch 8, sl st in third ch from hook—*picot made,* ch 2, sc) in same ch sp, *[sc in next sc, (sc, ch 3, sl st in third ch from hook—*picot made,* sc) in next ch sp, sc in next sc *(mark stitch),* (sc, ch 3, sl st in third ch from hook, sc) in next ch sp], sc in next sc, (sc, ch 5, sl st in third ch from hook, ch 8, sl st in third ch from hook, ch 2, sc) in next ch sp; repeat from * 5 more times; repeat between [ ], sc in first st over sl st, join. Fasten off.

Rnd 8: Join with sl st in any large loop after first picot, ch 5, tr in same loop, (ch 1, tr) 5 times in same loop, *ch 4, sc in next marked sc, ch 4, (tr, ch 1) 6 times in sp between picots on next large

loop, tr in same loop; repeat from * 5 more times, ch 4, sc in next marked sc, ch 4, join with sl st in fourth ch of ch-5.

Rnd 9: Sl st in first ch-1 sp, ch 1, sc in same sp, *(ch 3, sl st in third ch from hook, sc in next ch sp) 5 times, sc in next ch-4 sp, ch 3, sl st in third ch from hook, sc in next ch-4 sp; repeat from * around, join. Fasten off.

ASSEMBLY
1: With black and H hook, working through both thicknesses in end of each row and holding hook on top of work with yarn underneath, sl st Sides together forming decorative chain around edge and leaving top edge open.

2: Work Basic Instructions on page 124. ❄

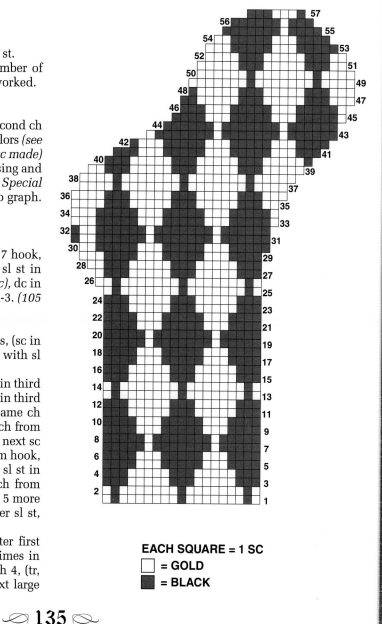

EACH SQUARE = 1 SC
☐ = GOLD
■ = BLACK

FINISHED SIZE: Tree Skirt is 26" long without Looped Fringe. Stocking is 18" long.

MATERIALS:
- ❏ Worsted yarn:
  - 28 oz. black
  - 12 oz. green
  - 7 oz. brown
  - 7 oz. red
  - 7 oz. orange
  - 4 oz. off-white
- ❏ 12" square piece of cardboard
- ❏ Bobby pins for markers
- ❏ Tapestry needle
- ❏ F, H and I hooks or hooks needed to obtain gauges

GAUGES: **H hook,** 7 sts = 2"; 7 sc rows = 2".
I hook, 3 sts = 1", 3 sc rows = 1", 3 dc rows = 2".

BASIC STITCHES: Ch, sl st, sc, dc.

NOTES: When **changing colors** *(see Stitch Guide),* drop last color to wrong side of work, pick up again when needed. Do not carry dropped color across work; use separate ball of yarn for each section of color. Always change to next color in last st made. Fasten off each color when no longer needed.

When working into marked st, remove marker, work st, mark st just made.

TREE SKIRT
Panel (make 5)

Row 1: With I hook and black, ch 88, sc in second ch from hook, sc in each ch across, turn. *(87 sc made)*

Row 2: Ch 1, sc first 2 sts tog, sc in next 7 sts, **mark** last sc made, sc in next 70 sts, **mark** last sc made, sc in next 6 sts, sc last 2 sts tog, turn. *(85)*

Row 3: Ch 1, sc in each st across to first marker, sc in marked st *(see Note),* (work according to corresponding row of Tree Skirt Graph on page 138—see Note for color change information) 3 times, sc in marked st, sc in each st across, turn.

Row 4: Ch 1, sc first 2 sts tog, sc in each st across to first marker, sc in marked st, (work according to corresponding row of Tree Skirt Graph) 3 times, sc in marked st, sc in each st across to last 2 sts, sc last 2 sts tog, turn. *(83)*

Rows 5–16: Repeat rows 3 and 4 alternately. At end of last row, remove markers. *(71 sts)*

Row 17: Ch 1, sc in first st, (work according to row 17 of Tree Skirt Graph) 3 times, sc in last st, turn.

Mark 8th, 18th, 31st, 41st, 54th and 64th sts on row 17.

Row 18: Ch 1, sc first 2 sts tog, (sc in each st across to next marker, sc in marked st, work according to corresponding row of Tree Skirt Graph, sc in next marked st) 3 times, sc in each st across to last 2 sts, sc last 2 sts tog, turn. *(69)*

Row 19: Ch 1, sc in first st, (sc in each st across to

continued on page 138

Gingerbread Men

Designed by Ann Emery Smith

Gingerbread Men

continued from page 136

next marker, sc in marked st, work according to corresponding row of Tree Skirt Graph, sc in next marked st) 3 times, sc in each st across, turn.

Rows 20–23: Repeat rows 18 and 19 alternately. At end of last row, remove markers. *(65 sc)*

Rows 24–43: Ch 3 *(counts as first dc)*, dc next 2 sts tog, dc in each st across to last 3 sts, dc next 2 sts tog, dc in last st, turn. *(25 dc at end of last row)*

Row 44: Ch 3, dc in each st across. Fasten off.

Holding yarn behind work and working around entire outer edge of one gingerbread boy *(see Tree Skirt Graph)*, join off-white with sl st in any st, sl st around edge of boy, join with sl st in first sl st. Fasten off. Repeat on each boy.

With off-white, work three French knots *(see Stitch Guide)* on each Boy according to Tree Skirt Graph.

With black, sew ends of rows on Panels together *(see Tree Skirt Assembly illustration)*.

For **Drawstring,** with off-white, ch to measure 88". Fasten off. Fold in half; tie overhand knot *(see illustration)* 2" from fold; hold ends together and tie overhand knot 2" from other end forming a double strand with a knot at each end.

Weave Drawstring through sts of last row on all Panels.

Bottom Border

Row 1: With right side of assembled Panels facing you, working across all Panels on opposite side of starting ch on row 1, with I hook, join green with sl st in first ch on first Panel, ch 3 *(counts as first dc)*, dc in each ch across all Panels, **do not turn.** Fasten off. *(435 dc made)*

*NOTE: For rows 2–9, hold right side of work facing you; **do not turn.***

Row 2: Join red with sl st in top of ch-3, ch 3, dc in next 2 sts changing to orange, (dc in next 5 sts, ch 1, dc in next 5 sts changing to red, dc in next 3 sts, ch 1, dc in next 3 sts changing to orange) across to last 16 sts, dc in next 5 sts, ch 1, dc in next 5 sts changing to red, dc in next 3 sts, ch 1, dc in last 3 sts. Fasten off. *(435 dc, 54 ch-1 sps)*

Rows 3–4: Join orange with sl st in top of ch-3, ch 3, dc in next 2 sts changing to green, (dc in next 5 sts, ch 1, dc in next 5 sts changing to orange, dc in next 3 sts, ch 1, dc in next 3 sts changing to green) across to last 16 sts, dc in next 5 sts, ch 1, dc in next 5 sts changing to orange, dc in next 3 sts, ch 1, dc in last 3 sts. Fasten off.

Row 5: Join red with sc in top of ch-3, (sc in each st across to next ch sp, ch 1, skip ch sp) across to last 3 sts, sc in last 3 sts. Fasten off.

Rows 6–7: Join orange with sl st in top of ch-3, ch 3, dc in next 2 sts changing to green, (dc in next 5 sts, ch 2, dc in next 5 sts changing to orange, dc in next 3 sts, ch 2, dc in next 3 sts changing to green) across to last 16 sts, dc in next 5 sts, ch 2, dc in next 5 sts changing to orange, dc in next 3 sts, ch 2, dc in last 3 sts. Fasten off.

Row 8: Join red with sl st in top of ch-3, ch 3, dc in next 2 sts changing to orange, (dc in next 5 sts, ch 2, dc in next 5 sts changing to red, dc in next 3 sts, ch 2, dc in next 3 sts changing to orange) across to last 16 sts, dc in next 5 sts, ch 2, dc in next 5 sts changing to red, dc in next 3 sts, ch 2, dc in last 3 sts. Fasten off.

Row 9: Join green with sl st in top of ch-3, ch 3, (dc in each st across to next ch sp, ch 2, skip ch sp) across to last 3 sts, dc in last 3 sts. Fasten off.

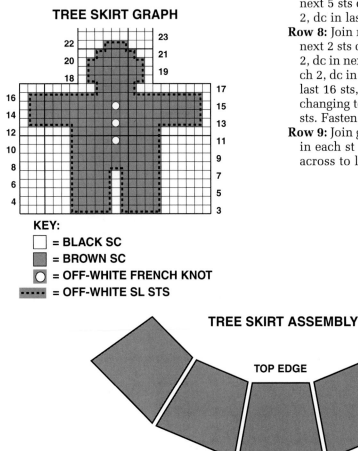

TREE SKIRT GRAPH

KEY:
☐ = BLACK SC
▨ = BROWN SC
◯ = OFF-WHITE FRENCH KNOT
▪▪▪▪ = OFF-WHITE SL STS

OVERHAND KNOT

TREE SKIRT ASSEMBLY

TOP EDGE

Knotted Trim (make 27 red, 27 green)

For each Knotted Trim, wrap yarn four times around 12" cardboard; slip wraps off cardboard. Tie an overhand knot 1½" from one end.

With ends of loops on right side of work and knotted end on row 2, weave red Knotted Trim through first column of ch sps over rows 2–9 on Bottom Border and tie loose ends in overhand knot at center of ch-sp on row 9; weave green Knotted Trim through next column of ch sps and tie loose ends in same manner; alternating red and green Knotted Trim, continue across all columns of ch sps across Bottom Border. (If desired, cut and trim loops.)

Place Skirt around tree, pull drawstring tight and tie in bow.

STOCKING
Cuff

Row 1: With H hook and green, ch 43, sc in second ch from hook, sc in each ch across, **do not turn.** Fasten off. *(42 sc made)*

Row 2: Join red with sc in first st, sc in next st, ch 1, skip next st, sc in next 2 sts changing to orange, (sc in next 4 sts, ch 1, skip next st, sc in next 4 sts changing to red, sc in next 2 sts, ch 1, skip next st, sc in next 2 sts changing to orange) 2 times, sc in next 4 sts, ch 1, skip next st, sc in last 4 sts, turn.

Row 3: Ch 1, sc in first 4 sts, ch 1, skip next ch sp, sc in next 4 sts changing to red, (sc in next 2 sts, ch 1, skip next ch sp, sc in next 2 sts changing to orange, sc in next 4 sts, ch 1, skip next ch sp, sc in next 4 sts changing to red) 2 times, sc in next 2 sts, ch 1, skip next ch sp, sc in last 2 sts, turn. Fasten off both colors.

Row 4: Join orange with sc in first st, sc in next st, ch 1, skip next ch sp, sc in next 2 sts changing to green, (sc in next 4 sts, ch 1, skip next ch sp, sc in next 4 sts changing to orange, sc in next 2 sts, ch 1, skip next ch sp, sc in next 2 sts changing to green) 2 times, sc in next 4 sts, ch 1, skip next ch sp, sc in last 4 sts, turn.

Row 5: Ch 1, sc in first 4 sts, ch 1, skip next ch sp, sc in next 4 sts changing to orange, (sc in next 2 sts, ch 1, skip next ch sp, sc in next 2 sts changing to green, sc in next 4 sts, ch 1, skip next ch sp, sc in next 4 sts changing to orange) 2 times, sc in next 2 sts, ch 1, skip next ch sp, sc in last 2 sts, turn.

Row 6: Ch 1, sc in first 2 sts, ch 1, skip next ch sp, sc in next 2 sts changing to green, (sc in next 4 sts, ch 1, skip next ch sp, sc in next 4 sts changing to orange, sc in next 2 sts, ch 1, skip next ch sp, sc in next 2 sts changing to green) 2 times, sc in next 4 sts, ch 1, skip next ch sp, sc in last 4 sts, turn.

Row 7: Ch 1, sc in first 4 sts, ch 1, skip next ch sp, sc in next 4 sts changing to orange, (sc in next 2 sts, ch 1, skip next ch sp, sc in next 2 sts changing to green, sc in next 4 sts, ch 1, skip next ch sp, sc in next 4 sts changing to orange) 2 times, sc in next 2 sts, ch 1, skip next ch sp, sc in last 2 sts, turn. Fasten off both colors.

Row 8: Join red with sc in first st, (sc in each st across to next ch sp, ch 1, skip ch sp) across to last 4 sts, sc in last 4 sts. Fasten off.

Row 9: Join orange with sc in first st, sc in next st, ch 1, skip next ch sp, sc in next 2 sts changing to green, (sc in next 4 sts, ch 1, skip next ch sp, sc in next 4 sts changing to orange, sc in next 2 sts, ch 1, skip next ch sp, sc in next 2 sts changing to green) 2 times, sc in next 4 sts, ch 1, skip next ch sp, sc in last 4 sts, turn.

Row 10: Ch 1, sc in first 4 sts, ch 1, skip next ch sp, sc in next 4 sts changing to orange, (sc in next 2 sts, ch 1, skip next ch sp, sc in next 2 sts changing to green, sc in next 4 sts, ch 1, skip next ch sp, sc in next 4 sts changing to orange) 2 times, sc in next 2 sts, ch 1, skip next ch sp, sc in last 2 sts, turn.

Row 11: Ch 1, sc in first 2 sts, ch 1, skip next ch sp, sc in next 2 sts changing to green, (sc in next 4 sts, ch 1, skip next ch sp, sc in next 4 sts changing to orange, sc in next 2 sts, ch 1, skip next ch sp, sc in next 2 sts changing to green) 2 times, sc in next 4 sts, ch 1, skip next ch sp, sc in last 4 sts, turn.

Row 12: Ch 1, sc in first 4 sts, ch 1, skip next ch sp, sc in next 4 sts changing to orange, (sc in next 2 sts, ch 1, skip next ch sp, sc in next 2 sts changing to green, sc in next 4 sts, ch 1, skip next ch sp, sc in next 4 sts changing to orange) 2 times, sc in next 2 sts, ch 1, skip next ch sp, sc in last 2 sts, turn. Fasten off both colors.

Row 13: Join red with sc in first st, sc in next st, ch 1, skip next st, sc in next 2 sts changing to orange, (sc in next 4 sts, ch 1, skip next st, sc in next 4 sts changing to red, sc in next 2 sts, ch 1, skip next st, sc in next 2 sts changing to orange) 2 times, sc in next 4 sts, ch 1, skip next st, sc in last 4 sts, turn.

Row 14: Ch 1, sc in first 4 sts, ch 1, skip next ch sp, sc in next 4 sts changing to red, (sc in next 2 sts, ch 1, skip next ch sp, sc in next 2 sts changing to orange, sc in next 4 sts, ch 1, skip next ch sp, sc in next 4 sts changing to red) 2 times, sc in next 2 sts, ch 1, skip next ch sp, sc in last 2 sts, turn. Fasten off both colors.

Row 15: Join green with sc in first st, sc in each st and in each ch sp across. Fasten off.

STOCKING GRAPH

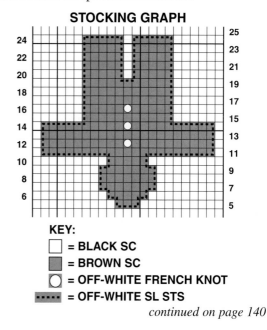

KEY:
☐ = BLACK SC
▨ = BROWN SC
◯ = OFF-WHITE FRENCH KNOT
▪▪▪ = OFF-WHITE SL STS

continued on page 140

Gingerbread Men

continued from page 139

Leg

Row 1: Working this row in **back lps** *(see Stitch Guide),* with H hook, join black with sc in first st, sc in each st across, turn. *(42 sc made)*

Rows 2–3: Ch 1, sc in each st across, turn.

Row 4: Ch 1, sc in first 3 sts, **mark** last sc made, sc in next 24 sts, **mark** last sc made, sc in last 15 sts, turn.

Rows 5–24: Ch 1, sc in each st across to first marker, sc in marked st, work according to corresponding row of Stocking Graph, sc in marked st, sc in each st across, turn.

Rows 25–26: Ch 1, sc in each st across, turn. At end of last row, fasten off.

Holding yarn behind work and working around entire outer edge of gingerbread boy *(see Stocking Graph),* join off-white with sl st in any st, sl st around edge of boy, join with sl st in first sl st. Fasten off.

With off-white, work three French knots on boy according to Stocking Graph.

With matching colors, sew ends of rows 1–26 together.

Foot

Row 1: For **Heel,** with right side of last row on Leg facing you, skip first 32 sts; with H hook, join red with sc in next st, sc in last 9 sts, sc in first 10 sts leaving remaining 22 sts unworked across instep, turn. *(20 sc made)*

Row 2: Ch 1, sc in first 13 sts leaving last 7 sts unworked, turn. *(13)*

Row 3: Ch 1, sc in first 6 sts leaving last 7 sts unworked, turn. *(6)*

Rows 4–17: Ch 1, sc in each st across, sc in next unworked st on previous row, turn. At end of last row, fasten off. *(20 sc)*

Rnd 18: Working in rnds, with right side of row 17 facing you, skip first 10 sts, join black with sc in next st, sc in last 9 sts, skip next unworked st on last row of Leg, sc in next 20 sts, skip next st, sc in first 10 skipped sts on row 17, join with sl st in first sc, **turn.** *(40)*

Rnds 19–35: Ch 1, sc in each st around, join, **turn.** At end of last rnd, fasten off.

Rnd 36: For **Toe,** join red with sc in first st, sc in next 7 sts, (sc next 2 sts tog, sc in next 6 sts) 4 times, join with sl st in first sc, **do not turn.** *(36)*

Rnd 37: Ch 1, sc in first 4 sts, sc next 2 sts tog, (sc in next 4 sts, sc next 2 sts tog) 5 times, join. *(30)*

Rnd 38: Ch 1, sc in each st around, join.

Rnd 39: Ch 1, sc in first 3 sts, sc next 2 sts tog, (sc in next 3 sts, sc next 2 sts tog) 5 times, join. *(24)*

Rnd 40: Ch 1, sc in each st around, join.

Rnd 41: Ch 1, sc in first 2 sts, sc next 2 sts tog, (sc in next 2 sts, sc next 2 sts tog) 5 times, join. *(18)*

Rnd 42: Ch 1, sc in each st around, join.

Rnd 43: Ch 1, sc first 2 sts tog, (sc next 2 sts tog) around, join. Leaving a 10" strand, fasten off.

Weave 10" strand through tops of sts on last rnd, pull tight to close opening and secure. *(9)*

Knotted Trim (make 3 red, 3 green)

Wrap yarn four times around 12" cardboard; slide wraps off cardboard. Tie an overhand knot 1½" from one end.

With knotted end on outside, weave red Knotted Trim through first column of ch sps on Cuff, beginning on outside of row 14 and ending on inside of row 2; fold unknotted end of wraps to inside and tack in place.

In same manner, weave green Knotted Trim through next column of ch sps.

Alternating red and green Knotted Trims, continue across all columns of ch sps on Cuff. *(If desired, cut and trim loops at knotted end as shown in photo.)*

Cookie Side (make 2)

Row 1: With F hook and brown, ch 14, sc in second ch from hook, sc in each ch across, turn. *(13 sc made)*

Row 2: Ch 1, sc in each st across, turn.

Row 3: Ch 1, sl st in first 3 sts, ch 1, sc in next 7 sts leaving last 3 sts unworked, turn. *(7 sc)*

Rows 4–5: Ch 1, sc in each st across, turn.

Row 6: For first **Leg,** ch 1, sc in first 3 sts leaving last 4 sts unworked, turn. *(3)*

Row 7: Ch 1, sc in each st across, turn.

Row 8: Ch 1, sc in each st across. Fasten off.

Row 6: For second **Leg,** skip next unworked st on row 5, join brown with sc in next st, sc in last 2 sts, turn. *(3)*

Row 7: Ch 1, sc in each st across, turn.

Row 8: Ch 1, sc in each st across. Fasten off.

Row 9: For **Head,** working on opposite side of starting ch on row 1, skip first 5 chs, join brown with sc in next ch, sc in next 2 chs leaving remaining chs unworked, turn. *(3)*

Row 10: Ch 1, 2 sc in first st, sc in next st, 2 sc in last st, turn. *(5)*

Row 11: Ch 1, sc in each st across, turn.

Row 12: Ch 1, sc first 2 sts tog, sc in next st, sc last 2 sts tog. Fasten off.

For **Front,** work off-white French knots at center of row 1 and row 3 on one Cookie Side.

Matching edges, hold Sides together with Front toward you; working through both thicknesses, join off-white with sl st in center of last row on Head; spacing sts so edge lays flat, sl st together around all edges, join with sl st in first sl st; for **Hanger,** ch 12, join with sl st in joining sl st. Fasten off.

Cuff Edging

With right side of row 1 facing you, working on opposite side of starting ch on row 1 of Cuff, with H hook, join black with sl st in first ch; for **Loops,** (ch 15, sl st, ch 15, sl st) in same ch as joining sl st, ch 1, drop lp from hook, insert hook in ch-12 Hanger at top of Cookie, return dropped lp to hook and pull lp through Hanger, ch 1, (sl st, ch 15, sl st, ch 15, sl st) in next ch, sl st in each ch around, sl st in first 2 chs *(below Loops).* Fasten off. ❈

Ornamental Elegance

It's Beginning to Look a Lot Like Christmas

It's beginning to look a lot like Christmas ev'rywhere you go; take a look in the five-and-ten, glistening once again with candy canes and silver lanes aglow. It's beginning to look a lot like Christmas, toys in ev'ry store.

Metallic Ornaments

Designed by Carol Allen

General Instructions

Each pattern contains written instructions for the crochet piece only. After working the first few rounds, lay piece over metallic ball to check that it will lay smoothly.

To attach crochet piece to metallic ball, use pearl head straight pins inserted through the piece and into the ball in desired arrangement.

Decorate each metallic ball as desired *(see photo)* using ribbon roses, lace, strung beads and ribbon. Decorative straight pins or craft glue can be used to secure.

For **hanger**, form loop with metallic thread and sew or glue ends to center of crochet piece.

Ornament No. 1

FINISHED SIZE: Cover fits 3" metallic ball.

MATERIALS:
❑ 15 yds. white size 30 crochet cotton thread
❑ No. 11 steel hook

BASIC STITCHES: Ch, sl st, sc, dc.

ORNAMENT COVER
Rnd 1: Ch 16, sl st in first ch to form ring, ch 1, 24 sc in ring, join with sl st in first sc. *(24 sc made)*
Rnd 2: Working in **back lps** *(see Stitch Guide)*, ch 1, sc in same st, ch 3, skip next sc, (sc in next sc, ch 3) around, join with sl st in first ch of first ch sp. *(12 ch sps)*
Rnd 3: Sl st in second ch of first ch sp; working in **back lps**, ch 4, (sc in second ch of next ch sp, ch 4) around, join. *(12 ch sps)*
Rnd 4: Ch 1, (2 sc, ch 3, 2 sc) in each ch sp around, join with sl st in first sc.
Rnd 5: Sl st in next st, sl st in next ch sp, (ch 3, 2 dc, ch 3, 3 dc) in same sp, ch 1, *(3 dc, ch 3, 3 dc) in next ch sp, ch 1; repeat from * around, join with sl st in top of ch-3.
Rnd 6: Sl st in next 2 sts, sl st in next ch sp, (ch 3, 2 dc, ch 3, 3 dc) in same sp, ch 3, skip next 3 sts, sc in next ch, ch 3, skip next 3 sts, *(3 dc, ch 3, 3 dc) in next ch sp, ch 3, skip next 3 sts, sc in next ch, ch 3, skip next 3 sts; repeat from * around, join with sl st in top of first ch-3.
Rnd 7: Sl st in next 2 sts, sl st in next ch sp, ch 1, 3 sc in same sp, ch 7, (skip next 2 ch sps, 3 sc in next ch sp, ch 7) around, join with sl st in first sc.
Rnd 8: Sl st in next sc, ch 1, sc in same st, ch 5, (3 sc in fourth ch of next ch sp, ch 5, sc in center st

of next 3-sc group, ch 5) around, join with sl st in first sc.
Rnd 9: Sl st in next 5 chs and next 2 sc, ch 13, (sc in center sc of next 3-sc group, ch 13) around, join.
Rnd 10: Sl st in next 7 chs, ch 1, 3 sc in same st, ch 15, (3 sc in seventh ch of next ch sp, ch 15) around, join. Fasten off.
Finish according to General Instructions.

Ornament No. 2

FINISHED SIZE: Cover fits 3" metallic ball.

MATERIALS:
❑ 15 yds. white size 30 crochet cotton thread
❑ No.11 steel hook

BASIC STITCHES: Ch, sl st, sc, hdc, dc, tr.

ORNAMENT COVER
Rnd 1: Ch 20, sl st in first ch to form ring, ch 3 *(counts as first dc)*, 35 dc in ring, join with sl st in top of ch-3. *(36 dc made)*
Rnd 2: Ch 6, dc in first st, ch 1, skip next 2 dc, *(dc, ch 3, dc) in next dc, ch 1, skip next 2 dc; repeat from * around, join with sl st in third ch of ch-6. *(12 ch sps)*
Rnd 3: Sl st in first ch sp, ch 6, dc in same sp as sl st, ch 1, *(dc, ch 3, dc) in next ch sp, ch 1; repeat from * around, join with sl st in third ch of ch-6.
Rnd 4: (Sl st, ch 1, sc, hdc, dc, tr, dc, hdc, sc) in first ch sp, sc in next ch sp, *(sc, hdc, dc, tr, dc, hdc, sc) in next ch sp, sc in next ch sp; repeat from * around, join with sl st in first sc.
Rnd 5: Working in **back lps** *(see Stitch Guide)*, ch 1, sc in first st, ch 11, (skip next 7 sts, sc in next sc, ch 11) around, join.
Rnd 6: Sl st in next 6 chs, ch 6, dc in same ch, ch 5, *(dc, ch 5, dc) in sixth ch of next ch, ch 5; repeat from * around, join with sl st in third ch of ch-6.
Rnd 7: Sl st in next ch sp, ch 1, (sc, hdc, dc, tr, dc, hdc, sc) in same sp, ch 3, 3 sc in next ch sp, ch 3, *(sc, hdc, dc, tr, dc, hdc, sc) in next ch sp, ch 3, 3 sc in next ch sp, ch 3; repeat from * around, join with sl st in first sc.
Rnd 8: Sl st in next 9 sts, ch 1, sc in same st as last sl st, ch 13, (sc in center sc of next 3-sc group, ch 13) around, join with sl st in first sc.
Rnd 9: Ch 1, sc in first st, ch 15, (sc in next sc, ch 15) around, join. Fasten off.
Finish according to General Instructions.

continued on page 150

Wee Winter Trinkets

Designed by Beth Mueller

Angel

FINISHED SIZE: Approximately 2¼" tall.

MATERIALS:
- ❏ Size 10 crochet cotton thread:
    - 50 yds. white
    - 24 yds. each ecru and yellow
- ❏ 6" piece gold metallic thread
- ❏ Small amount dk. pink embroidery floss
- ❏ 2 black ½" half-round shank buttons
- ❏ 2 blue 2mm seed beads
- ❏ 2mm lt. pink seed bead
- ❏ 5½" of 1"-wide white gathered lace
- ❏ 7" of ⅛"-wide lt. blue ribbon
- ❏ 2¼" of 1/16" gold cord
- ❏ 2" × 3" piece of light flesh color felt
- ❏ 1" Styrofoam® ball
- ❏ 1½" Styrofoam® ball
- ❏ Light flesh color acrylic paint
- ❏ Small round bristle paintbrush
- ❏ Hot glue or craft glue
- ❏ Pencil
- ❏ Clear acrylic spray
- ❏ Pink powder blush
- ❏ Embroidery needle
- ❏ No. 7 steel hook or hook needed to obtain gauge

GAUGE: 7 hdc = 1"; 6 hdc rows = 1".

BASIC STITCHES: Ch, sl st, hdc.

STYROFOAM BODY ASSEMBLY
Using 1½" ball as Body and 1" ball as Head, cut ⅛" from one end on each Styrofoam ball. Glue cut ends together. Set aside to be used later.

BODY
Rnd 1: Starting at bottom, with white crochet cotton, ch 5, sl st in first ch to form ring, ch 2, 10 hdc in ring, join with sl st in top of ch-2. *(Ch-2 counts as first hdc—11 hdc made. Joining is back of Body.)*

Rnd 2: Ch 2, (hdc in next st, 2 hdc in next st) around, join. *(16)*

Rnd 3: Ch 2, (hdc in next 2 sts, 2 hdc in next st) around, join. *(21)*

Rnd 4: Ch 2, (hdc in next 3 sts, 2 hdc in next st) around, join. *(26)*

Rnd 5: Ch 2, (hdc in next 4 sts, 2 hdc in next st) around, join. *(31)*

Rnd 6: Ch 2, (hdc in next 5 sts, 2 hdc in next st) around, join. *(36)*

Rnds 7–9: Ch 2, hdc in each st around, join. Insert Styrofoam Body inside crochet Body.

Rnd 10: Ch 2, (hdc in next 5 sts, hdc next 2 sts tog) around, join. *(31)*

Rnd 11: Ch 2, (hdc in next 4 sts, hdc next 2 sts tog) around, join. Fasten off. *(26)*

Rnd 12: For **Neck**, join ecru crochet cotton with sc in first st, sc in each st around, join with sl st in first sc.

Rnd 13: For **Head**, ch 2, (hdc in next 2 sts, 2 hdc in next st) 8 times, hdc in last st, join with sl st in top of ch-2. *(34 hdc)*

Rnd 14: Ch 2, hdc in each st around, join.

Rnd 15: Ch 2, (hdc in next 2 sts, hdc next 2 sts tog) 8 times, hdc in last st, join. *(26)*

Rnd 16: Ch 2, (hdc in next 2 sts, hdc next 2 sts tog) 6 times, hdc in last st, join. *(20)*

Rnd 17: Ch 2, (hdc in next st, hdc next 2 sts tog) 6 times, hdc in last st, join. Leaving 8" for sewing, fasten off. *(14)*

With embroidery needle and 8" end, sew opening closed.

HAIR
1: Wrap yellow crochet cotton around pencil 35 times, slide loops off pencil, insert a separate piece of yellow crochet cotton through center of all loops and tie loops together.

2: Glue one Hair piece in front to lay even with bottom of rnd 17 on Head for bangs; glue one Hair Piece on each side of bangs over rnds 14-16 of Head; glue one Hair Piece behind bangs, glue two Hair Pieces over rnds 14 and 15 at back of Head.

3: For **halo**, glue ends on cord together to form a ring. Glue to top of Head.

FINISHING
1: For **eyes**, glue two blue seed beads to front of rnd 15 on Head ⅛" apart.

2: For **nose**, glue lt. pink seed bead centered below eyes at top of rnd 14 on Head.

continued on page 146

continued from page 144

3: For **mouth,** separate floss into individual strands; with embroidery needle and one strand of floss, embroider straight stitches *(see Stitch Guide)* over rnds 13 and 14 on front of Head *(see illustration).*

EYES

CHEEKS

4: For **cheeks,** brush pink blush on Head at each side of mouth.

5: Tie ribbon in bow; glue to center front at Neck.

6: For **skirt,** glue gathered edge of lace to top of rnd 9 on Body with ends meeting at back.

7: For **arms,** paint buttons with flesh color, painting several times if needed to cover black color. Let dry. Spray with clear acrylic sealer spray. Let dry. Push shank of buttons into Styrofoam ball and glue over rnds 9-11 on each side of Body ¼" apart.

8: From felt, cut wings according to pattern piece. Glue to back of Body over rnds 10 and 11.

9: For **hanger,** thread embroidery needle with 6" piece of metallic thread, run through center top of Head; tie ends together.

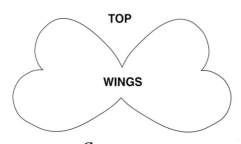

TOP

WINGS

Snowman

FINISHED SIZE: Approximately 2¾" tall.

MATERIALS:
- ❑ Size 10 crochet cotton thread:
    - 50 yds. white
    - 25 yds. black
- ❑ 6" piece gold metallic thread
- ❑ 5 black 3mm round beads
- ❑ ³⁄₁₆" red button
- ❑ 5½" long by ¼" wide strip of green felt
- ❑ 2½" of ⅛"-wide red ribbon
- ❑ 1" Styrofoam® ball
- ❑ 1½" Styrofoam® ball
- ❑ Small amount of polyester fiberfill
- ❑ Hot glue or craft glue
- ❑ Pink powder blush
- ❑ Embroidery needle
- ❑ No. 7 steel hook or hook needed to obtain gauge

GAUGE: 7 hdc = 1"; 6 hdc rows = 1".

BASIC STITCHES: Ch, sl st, sc, hdc.

STYROFOAM BODY ASSEMBLY
Using 1½" ball as Body and 1" ball as Head, cut ⅛" from one end on each Styrofoam ball. Glue cut ends together. Set aside to be used later.

BODY
Rnd 1: Starting at bottom, with white crochet cotton, ch 5, sl st in first ch to form ring, ch 2, 10 hdc in ring, join with sl st in top of ch-2. *(Ch-2 counts as first hdc—11 hdc made. Joining is back of Body.)*

Rnd 2: Ch 2, (hdc in next st, 2 hdc in next st) around, join. *(16)*

Rnd 3: Ch 2, (hdc in next 2 sts, 2 hdc in next st) around, join. *(21)*

Rnd 4: Ch 2, (hdc in next 3 sts, 2 hdc in next st) around, join. *(26)*

Rnd 5: Ch 2, (hdc in next 4 sts, 2 hdc in next st) around, join. *(31)*

Rnd 6: Ch 2, (hdc in next 5 sts, 2 hdc in next st) around, join. *(36)*

Rnds 7–9: Ch 2, hdc in each st around, join. Insert Styrofoam body inside crochet Body.

Rnd 10: Ch 2, (hdc in next 5 sts, hdc next 2 sts tog) around, join. *(31)*

Rnd 11: Ch 2, (hdc in next 4 sts, hdc next 2 sts tog) around, join. *(26)*

Rnd 12: For **Neck,** ch 1, sc in first st, sc in each st around, join with sl st in first sc.

Rnd 13: For **Head,** ch 2, (hdc in next 2 sts, 2 hdc in next st) 8 times, hdc in last st, join with sl st in top of ch-2. *(34 hdc)*

Rnd 14: Ch 2, hdc in each st around, join.

Rnd 15: Ch 2, (hdc in next 2 sts, hdc next 2 sts tog) 8 times, hdc in last st, join. *(26)*

Rnd 16: Ch 2, (hdc in next 2 sts, hdc next 2 sts tog) 6 times, hdc in last st, join. *(20)*

Rnd 17: Ch 2, (hdc in next st, hdc next 2 sts tog) 6 times, hdc in last st, join. Leaving 8" for sewing, fasten off. *(14)*

With embroidery needle and 8" end, sew opening closed.

HAT
Rnd 1: Starting at top, with black crochet cotton, ch 2, 5 sc in second ch from hook, join with sl st in first sc. *(Joining is back of Hat—5 sc made)*

Rnd 2: Ch 1, 2 sc in each st around, join. *(10)*

Rnd 3: Ch 1, sc in first st, (2 sc in next st, sc in next st) 4 times, 2 sc in last st, join. *(15)*

Rnd 4: Working this rnd in **back lps** only *(see Stitch Guide),* ch 1, sc in each st around, join.

Rnds 5–7: Ch 1, sc in each st around, join.

Rnd 8: Working this rnd in **back lps** only, ch 1, 2 sc in each st around, join. *(30)*

Rnd 9: Ch 1, sc in first st, (2 sc in next st, sc in next st) 14 times, 2 sc in last st, join. Fasten off. *(45)*

Glue ribbon around rnds 5–7 on Hat with ends at back.

FINISHING

1: For **eyes**, glue two black beads to front of rnd 15 on Head ¼" apart.

2: For **nose**, glue button centered below eyes between rnds 14–15.

3: For **mouth**, with embroidery needle and black, embroider straight stitches *(see Stitch Guide)* over rnds 14 and 15 on Head *(see illustration)*.

4: For **cheeks**, brush pink blush on Head at each side of mouth.

5: For **scarf**, cut two ¼" slits at each end on felt *(see illustration)* for fringe. Wrap scarf around Neck overlapping ends *(see photo)*.

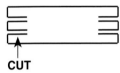

6: Glue Hat to top of Head at an angle with small amount of fiberfill inside.

7: Glue three beads evenly spaced down center front of Body on rnds 7–10.

8: For **hanger**, thread embroidery needle with 6" piece of metallic thread, run through any st on Hat; tie ends together.

Elf

FINISHED SIZE: Approximately 3" tall.

MATERIALS:
- ❏ Size 10 crochet cotton thread:
  - 25 yds. each green, red and ecru
  - 15 yds. brown
- ❏ 6" piece gold metallic thread
- ❏ Small amount dk. pink embroidery floss
- ❏ 4 round ½" wood plugs
- ❏ 2 white 2mm seed beads
- ❏ 2mm lt. pink seed bead
- ❏ 10" of ⅛"-wide green ribbon
- ❏ ¼" miniature jingle bell
- ❏ 1" Styrofoam® ball
- ❏ 1½" Styrofoam® ball
- ❏ Pink powder blush
- ❏ Small amount of polyester fiberfill
- ❏ Green, light flesh color and black acrylic paints
- ❏ Small round bristle paintbrush
- ❏ Hot glue or craft glue
- ❏ Pencil
- ❏ Clear acrylic sealer spray
- ❏ Embroidery needle
- ❏ No. 7 steel hook or hook needed to obtain gauge

GAUGE: 7 hdc = 1"; 6 hdc rows = 1".

BASIC STITCHES: Ch, sl st, sc, hdc, dc.

STYROFOAM BODY ASSEMBLY

Using 1½" ball as Body and 1" ball as Head, cut ⅛" from one end on each Styrofoam ball. Glue cut ends together. Set aside to be used later.

BODY

Rnd 1: Starting at bottom of pants, with green crochet cotton, ch 5, sl st in first ch to form ring, ch 2, 10 hdc in ring, join with sl st in top of ch-2. *(Ch-2 counts as first hdc—11 hdc made. Joining is back of Body.)*

Rnd 2: Ch 2, (hdc in next st, 2 hdc in next st) around, join. *(16)*

Rnd 3: Ch 2, (hdc in next 2 sts, 2 hdc in next st) around, join. *(21)*

Rnd 4: Ch 2, (hdc in next 3 sts, 2 hdc in next st) around, join. *(26)*

Rnd 5: Ch 2, (hdc in next 4 sts, 2 hdc in next st) around, join. *(31)*

Rnd 6: Ch 2, (hdc in next 5 sts, 2 hdc in next st) around, join. *(36)*

Rnd 7: Ch 2, hdc in each st around, join. Fasten off.

Rnd 8: For **shirt**, join red crochet cotton with sl st in first st, ch 2, hdc in each st around, join.

Rnd 9: Ch 2, hdc in each st around, join. Insert Styrofoam Body inside crochet Body.

Rnd 10: Ch 2, (hdc in next 5 sts, hdc next 2 sts tog) around, join. *(31)*

Rnd 11: Ch 2, (hdc in next 4 sts, hdc next 2 sts tog) around, join. Fasten off. *(26)*

Rnd 12: For **Neck**, join ecru crochet cotton with sc in first st, sc in each st around, join with sl st in first sc.

Rnd 13: For **Head**, ch 2, (hdc in next 2 sts, 2 hdc in next st) 8 times, hdc in last st, join with sl st in top of ch-2. *(34 hdc)*

Rnd 14: Ch 2, hdc in each st around, join.

Rnd 15: Ch 2, (hdc in next 2 sts, hdc next 2 sts tog) 8 times, hdc in last st, join. *(26)*

Rnd 16: Ch 2, (hdc in next 2 sts, hdc next 2 sts tog) 6 times, hdc in last st, join. *(20)*

Rnd 17: Ch 2, (hdc in next st, hdc next 2 sts tog) 6 times, hdc in last st, join. Leaving 8" for sewing, fasten off. *(14)*

With embroidery needle and 8" end, sew opening closed.

HAT

Rnd 1: Starting at bottom, with green crochet cotton, ch 28, sl st in first ch to form ring, ch 3, dc in each ch around, join with sl st in top of ch-3. *(Ch-3 counts as first dc—28 dc made. Joining is back of Hat.)*

Rnd 2: Working this rnd in **back lps** *(see Stitch Guide)*, ch 3, dc in each st around, join.

Rnds 3–4: Ch 3, (dc next 2 sts tog, dc in next st) around, join. *(19, 13)*

Rnd 5: Ch 3, dc in each st around, join. Fasten off leaving 8" for sewing.

With embroidery needle and 8" end, sew opening closed. Sew jingle bell to top of Hat.

continued on page 148

Wee Winter Trinkets

continued from page 147

EAR (make 2)

With ecru crochet cotton, ch 7, yo, insert hook in fourth ch from hook, yo, pull through ch, yo, pull through 2 lps on hook, (yo, insert hook in next ch, yo, pull through ch, yo, pull through 2 lps on hook) 3 times, yo, pull through all 5 lps on hook. Fasten off.

With embroidery needle and ecru crochet cotton, sew bottom of Ears over rnds 13 and 14 on each side of Head 1½" apart.

FINISHING

1: For **eyes**, glue white beads to front of rnd 15 on Head ¼" apart. Paint a black dot on each eye.

2: For **nose**, glue lt. pink bead centered below eyes at top of rnd 14 on Head.

3: For **mouth**, separate embroidery floss into one strand; with embroidery needle and one strand of floss, embroider straight stitches *(see Stitch Guide)* over rnd 14 on front of Head *(see illustration).*

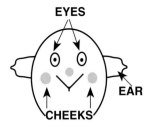

EYES

EAR

CHEEKS

4: For **cheeks**, brush pink blush on Head at each side of mouth.

5: For **arms**, paint two wooden plugs with flesh color paint. Let dry. Spray with clear acrylic sealer spray. Let dry. Glue arms over rnds 9–11 on each side of Body 1½" apart.

6: For **legs**, paint remaining two wooden plugs with green paint. Let dry. Spray with clear acrylic sealer spray. Let dry. Glue legs over rnds 3–6 on front of Body ½" apart.

7: Tie ribbon in bow around Neck at front.

8: For **Hair Piece**, wrap brown crochet cotton around a pencil 35 times, slide loops off pencil, insert a separate piece of brown crochet cotton through center of all loops and tie loops together.

9: Glue Hair Piece to top of Head over rnd 17.

10: Stuff inside of Hat lightly. Glue bottom of Hat over back of Head and over Hair Piece leaving ¼" of hair showing.

11: For **hanger**, thread embroidery needle with 6" piece of metallic thread, run through st at center front of Hat, tie ends together.

Poinsettia

FINISHED SIZE: Approximately 1½" tall.

MATERIALS:
❑ Size 10 crochet cotton thread:

25 yds. white/gold metallic
5 yds. red
❑ 6" piece gold metallic thread
❑ 7 yellow 2mm seed beads
❑ 1½" square green felt
❑ 1½" Styrofoam® ball
❑ Hot glue or craft glue
❑ Tracing paper
❑ Pinking shears
❑ Embroidery needle
❑ No. 7 steel hook or hook needed to obtain gauge

GAUGE: 7 hdc = 1"; 6 hdc rows = 1".

BASIC STITCHES: Ch, sl st, sc, hdc, dtr.

SPECIAL STITCHES: For **double treble cluster (dtr cl)**, *yo 3 times, insert hook in ring, yo, pull through ring, (yo, pull through 2 lps on hook) 3 times; repeat from *, yo, pull through all 3 lps on hook.
For **picot**, ch 3, sl st in third ch from hook.

BALL

Rnd 1: Starting at bottom, with white/gold metallic, ch 5, sl st in first ch to form ring, ch 2, 10 hdc in ring, join with sl st in top of ch-2. *(Ch-2 counts as first hdc—11 hdc made. Joining is back of Ball.)*

Rnd 2: Ch 2, (hdc in next st, 2 hdc in next st) around, join. *(16)*

Rnd 3: Ch 2, (hdc in next 2 sts, 2 hdc in next st) around, join. *(21)*

Rnd 4: Ch 2, (hdc in next 3 sts, 2 hdc in next st) around, join. *(26)*

Rnd 5: Ch 2, (hdc in next 4 sts, 2 hdc in next st) around, join. *(31)*

Rnd 6: Ch 2, (hdc in next 5 sts, 2 hdc in next st) around, join. *(36)*

Rnds 7-9: Ch 2, hdc in each st around, join. Insert Styrofoam ball inside crochet Ball.

Rnd 10: Ch 2, (hdc in next 5 sts, hdc next 2 sts tog) around, join. *(31)*

Rnd 11: Ch 2, (hdc in next 4 sts, hdc next 2 sts tog) around, join. *(26)*

Rnd 12: Ch 2, (hdc in next 3 sts, hdc next 2 sts tog) around, join. *(21)*

Rnd 13: Ch 2, (hdc in next 2 sts, hdc next 2 sts tog) around, join. Leaving 8" for sewing, fasten off. *(16 hdc)*

With embroidery needle and 8" end, sew opening closed.

POINSETTIA

With red crochet cotton, ch 5, sl st in first ch to form ring, ch 1, sc in ring; for **point**, (ch 5; **dtr cl**—*see Special Stitches*, picot—*see Special Stitches*, ch 5, sl st) 5 times in ring. Fasten off.

FINISHING

1: Trace leaf from tracing paper according to pattern piece; place pattern piece on felt and cut out using pinking shears.

LEAF
(cut 1 felt)

2: Glue leaf centered to front of Ball over rnds 4–11.

3: Center and glue Poinsettia over leaf so each point on leaf is between each point on Poinsettia. Glue seed beads to center of Poinsettia.

4: For **hanger,** thread embroidery needle with 6" piece of metallic thread, run through center top of Ball; tie ends together.

Snowflake

FINISHED SIZE: 1½" tall.

MATERIALS:
- ❑ Size 10 crochet cotton thread:
  - 25 yds. dk. blue
  - 15 yds. white
- ❑ 6" piece gold metallic thread
- ❑ 6 white 2mm seed beads
- ❑ 1½" Styrofoam® ball
- ❑ Hot glue or craft glue
- ❑ Embroidery needle
- ❑ No. 7 steel hook or hook needed to obtain gauge

GAUGE: 7 hdc = 1"; 6 hdc rows = 1".

BASIC STITCHES: Ch, sl st, sc, hdc, dc.

BALL
Rnd 1: Starting at bottom, with dk. blue crochet cotton, ch 5, sl st in first ch to form ring, ch 2, 10 hdc in ring, join with sl st in top of ch-2. *(Ch-2 counts as first hdc—11 hdc made. Joining is back of Ball.)*

Rnd 2: Ch 2, (hdc in next st, 2 hdc in next st) around, join. *(16)*

Rnd 3: Ch 2, (hdc in next 2 sts, 2 hdc in next st) around, join. *(21)*

Rnd 4: Ch 2, (hdc in next 3 sts, 2 hdc in next st) around, join. *(26)*

Rnd 5: Ch 2, (hdc in next 4 sts, 2 hdc in next st) around, join. *(31)*

Rnd 6: Ch 2, (hdc in next 5 sts, 2 hdc in next st) around, join. *(36)*

Rnds 7-9: Ch 2, hdc in each st around, join. Insert Styrofoam ball inside crochet Ball.

Rnd 10: Ch 2, (hdc in next 5 sts, hdc next 2 sts tog) around, join. *(31)*

Rnd 11: Ch 2, (hdc in next 4 sts, hdc next 2 sts tog) around, join. *(26)*

Rnd 12: Ch 2, (hdc in next 3 sts, hdc next 2 sts tog) around, join. *(21)*

Rnd 13: Ch 2, (hdc in next 2 sts, hdc next 2 sts tog) around, join. Leaving 8" for sewing, fasten off. *(16 hdc)*

With embroidery needle and 8" end, sew opening closed.

SNOWFLAKE
Rnd 1: With white crochet cotton, ch 7, sl st in first ch to form ring, ch 1, sc in ring, (ch 4, sc in ring) 11 times, ch 1, join with dc in first sc *(last ch sp made). (12 ch sps)*

Rnd 2: Ch 1, sc in last ch sp made, *ch 5; for **picot, sl st in third ch of ch-5;** ch 2, skip next ch sp, (sc, ch 2, sc) in next ch sp; repeat from * 4 more times, ch 5, picot, ch 2, skip last ch sp, (sc, ch 1) in same ch sp where first sc was made, join with sl st in first sc. Fasten off. *(6 picots made) (Snowflake should measure approximately 1¾" across.)*

FINISHING
1: Glue wrong side of Snowflake centered on front of Ball. Center and glue one seed bead between each picot.

2: For **hanger,** thread embroidery needle with 6" piece of metallic thread, run through center top of Ball; tie ends together.

Striped

FINISHED SIZE: 1½" tall.

MATERIALS:
- ❑ Size 10 crochet cotton thread:
  - 15 yds. each green, red and white
- ❑ 6" piece gold metallic thread
- ❑ 12" of ⅜"-wide doubled-loop trim
- ❑ 20 gold 4mm beads
- ❑ 20 rust-proof straight pins
- ❑ 1½" Styrofoam® ball
- ❑ Hot glue or craft glue
- ❑ Embroidery needle
- ❑ No. 7 steel hook or hook needed to obtain gauge

GAUGE: 7 hdc = 1"; 6 hdc rows = 1".

BASIC STITCHES: Ch, sl st, hdc.

BALL
Rnd 1: Starting at bottom, with green crochet cotton, ch 5, sl st in first ch to form ring, ch 2, 10 hdc in ring, join with sl st in top of ch-2. *(Ch-2 counts as first hdc—11 hdc made. Joining is back of Ball.)*

Rnd 2: Ch 2, (hdc in next st, 2 hdc in next st) around, join. Fasten off. *(16)*

Rnd 3: Join red crochet cotton with (sl st, ch 2) in first st, (hdc in next 2 sts, 2 hdc in next st) around, join. *(21)*

Rnd 4: Ch 2, (hdc in next 3 sts, 2 hdc in next st) around, join. Fasten off. *(26)*

Rnd 5: Join white crochet cotton with sl st in first st, ch 2, (hdc in next 4 sts, 2 hdc in next st) around, join. *(31)*

Rnd 6: Ch 2, (hdc in next 5 sts, 2 hdc in next st) around, join. Fasten off. *(36)*

continued on page 150

Wee Winter Trinkets

continued from page 149

Rnd 7: Join green crochet cotton with sl st in first st, ch 2, hdc in each st around, join.

Rnd 8: Ch 2, hdc in each st around, join. Fasten off.

Rnd 9: Join red with sl st in first st, ch 2, hdc in each st around, join. Insert Styrofoam ball inside crochet Ball.

Rnd 10: Ch 2, (hdc in next 5 sts, hdc next 2 sts tog) around, join. Fasten off. *(31)*

Rnd 11: Join white crochet cotton with sl st in first st, ch 2, (hdc in next 4 sts, hdc next 2 sts tog) around, join. *(26)*

Rnd 12: Ch 2, (hdc in next 3 sts, hdc next 2 sts tog) around, join. *(21)*

Rnd 13: Join green crochet cotton with sl st in first st, ch 2, (hdc in next 2 sts, hdc next 2 sts tog) around, join. Leaving 8" for sewing, fasten off. *(16 hdc)*

With embroidery needle and 8" end, sew opening closed.

FINISHING

1: Starting at back of Ball, glue trim over rnds 5 and 6 cutting off excess. Starting at back of Ball, glue remainder of trim over rnds 8 and 9; cut off excess. Insert one straight pin inside each bead; evenly space ten straight pins with beads inserted into Ball around each trim.

2: For **hanger,** thread embroidery needle with 6" piece of metallic thread, run through center top of Ball; tie ends together. ❋

Metallic Ornaments

continued from page 143

Ornament No. 3

FINISHED SIZE: Cover fits 3" metallic ball.

MATERIALS:
- ❏ 15 yds. white size 30 crochet cotton thread
- ❏ No. 11 steel hook

BASIC STITCHES: Ch, sl st, sc, dc, tr.

ORNAMENT COVER

Rnd 1: Ch 24, join with sl st in first ch to form ring, ch 3 *(counts as first dc)*, 49 dc in ring, join with sl st in top of ch-3. *(50 dc made)*

Rnd 2: Working in **back lps** *(see Stitch Guide),* ch 1, sc in each st around, join with sl st in first sc. *(50 sc)*

Rnd 3: Working in **back lps,** ch 7, tr in first st, ch 4, skip next 4 sts, sc in next sc, ch 4, skip next 4 sts, *(tr, ch 3, tr) in next st, ch 4, skip next 4 sts, sc in next st, ch 4, skip next 4 sts; repeat from * around, join with sl st in fourth ch of ch-7. *(5 ch-3 sps)*

Rnd 4: Sl st in first ch sp, ch 4, (3 tr, ch 4, 4 tr) in same sp, ch 4, sc in next ch-4 sp, ch 3, sc in next ch-4 sp, ch 4, *(4 tr, ch 4, 4 tr) in next ch-3 sp, ch 4, sc in next ch-4 sp, ch 3, sc in next ch-4 sp, ch 4; repeat from * around, join with sl st in top of first ch-4.

Rnd 5: Ch 1, sc in first st, *ch 4, (5 tr, ch 5, 5 tr) in next ch sp, ch 4, skip next 3 sts, sc in next st, ch 5, skip next ch sp, sc in next ch sp, ch 5, skip next ch sp, sc in next st; repeat from * around, join with sl st in first sc.

Rnd 6: Sl st in next 4 chs, next 5 sts and next ch sp, (ch 4, 5 tr, ch 6, 6 tr) in same sp, ch 4, skip next 4 sts, sc in next st, ch 4, skip next ch sp, sc in next ch sp, ch 4, sc in next ch sp, ch 4, skip next ch sp, sc in next st, ch 4, skip next 4 sts, *(6 tr, ch 6, 6 tr) in next ch sp, ch 4, skip next 4 sts, sc in next st, ch 4, skip next ch sp, sc in next ch sp, ch 4, sc in next ch sp, ch 4, skip next ch sp, sc in next st, ch 4; repeat from * around, join with sl st in top of first ch-4.

Rnd 7: Sl st in next 5 sts, sl st in next ch sp, (ch 4, 6 tr, ch 3, 7 tr) in same sp, ch 4, skip next 5 sts, sc in next st, ch 4, skip next ch sp, (sc in next ch sp, ch 4) 3 times, skip next ch sp, sc in next st, ch 4, skip next 5 sts, *(7 tr, ch 3, 7 tr) in next ch sp, ch 4, skip next 5 sts, sc in next st, ch 4, skip next ch sp, (sc in next ch sp, ch 4) 3 times, skip next ch sp, sc in next st, ch 4, skip next 5 sts; repeat from * around, join. Fasten off.

Finish according to General Instructions on page 143.

Ornament No. 4

FINISHED SIZE: Cover fits 3" metallic ball.

MATERIALS:
- ❏ 15 yds. white size 30 crochet cotton thread
- ❏ No. 11 steel hook

BASIC STITCHES: Ch, sl st, sc, dc.

ORNAMENT COVER

Rnd 1: Ch 12, sl st in first ch to form ring, (ch 3—*counts as first dc,* dc) in first st, 2 dc in each ch around, join with sl st in top of ch-3. *(24 dc made)*

Rnds 2–4: Working in **back lps** *(see Stitch Guide),* (ch 3, dc) in first st, dc in next st, (2 dc in next st, dc in next st) around, join with sl st in top of ch-3. *(36 dc, 54 dc, 81 dc)*

Rnd 5: Working in **back lps,** ch 1, sc in each st around, join with sl st in first sc. *(81 sc)*

Rnd 6: Working in **back lps,** ch 1, sc in first st, ch 3, skip next 2 sts, (sc in next sc, ch 3, skip next 2 sts) around, join. *(27 ch sps)*

Rnd 7: Sl st in first ch sp, ch 1, sc in same sp, ch 4, (sc in next ch sp, ch 4) around, join with sl st in first sc.

Rnd 8: Sl st in first ch sp, ch 1, sc in same sp, ch

continued on page 151

5, (sc in next ch sp, ch 5) around, join with sl st in first sc.

Rnd 9: Sl st in first 3 chs, ch 1, sc in same ch as last sl st, (ch 3, sc in same ch, ch 3, sc in third ch of next ch sp) around, join with sl st in first sc.

Rnd 10: Sl st in first ch sp, ch 11, skip next 5 ch sps, (sc in next ch sp, ch 11, skip next 5 ch sps) around, join with sl st in first ch of first ch-11.

Rnd 11: Working in **back lps**, ch 1, sc in first st, ch 6, (sc in sixth ch of next ch sp, ch 6, sc in next sc, ch 6) around, join with sl st in first sc.

Rnd 12: Ch 1, sc in first sp, ch 3, (sc in next ch sp, ch 5, sc in next ch sp, ch 3, sc in next sc, ch 3) around, join with sl st in first sc.

Rnd 13: Ch 1, *3 sc in next ch sp, (5 dc, ch 5, 5 dc) in next ch sp, 3 sc in next ch sp; repeat from * around, join with sl st in first sc.

Rnd 14: Ch 1, sc in first 3 sts, skip next 5 sts, *(7 dc, ch 7, 7 dc) in next ch sp, skip next 5 sts, sc in next 6 sts; repeat from * around, join. Fasten off.

Finish according to General Instructions on page 143.

Ornament No. 5

FINISHED SIZE: Cover fits 3" metallic ball.

MATERIALS:
- ❏ 15 yds. white size 30 crochet cotton thread
- ❏ No. 11 steel hook

BASIC STITCHES: Ch, sl st, sc, dc, tr.

ORNAMENT COVER

Rnd 1: Ch 20, sl st in first ch to form ring, ch 3 *(counts as first dc)*, dc in same st as joining, 2 dc in each ch around, join with sl st in top of ch-3. *(40 dc made)*

Rnd 2: Working in **back lps** *(see Stitch Guide)*, (ch 3, dc) in first st, dc in next st, (2 dc in next st, dc in next st) around, join. *(60 dc)*

Rnd 3: Working in **back lps**, ch 1, sc in first st, ch 5, skip next 2 sts, (sc in next st, ch 5, skip next 2 sts) around, join with sl st in first sc. *(20 ch sps)*

Rnd 4: Working in **back lps**, sl st in next ch sp, ch 1, sc in same sp as sl st, ch 6, (sc in center ch of next ch sp, ch 6) around, join.

Rnd 5: Sl st in first ch sp, ch 1, (sc, hdc, dc, tr, dc, hdc, sc) in same sp as sl st, (3 dc, ch 3, 3 dc) in next ch sp, *(sc, hdc, dc, tr, dc, hdc, sc) in next ch sp, (3 dc, ch 3, 3 dc) in next ch sp; repeat from * around, join.

Rnd 6: Ch 1, sc in first st, ch 5, skip next 6 sts, sc in next dc, ch 3, (4 dc, ch 4, 4 dc) in next ch sp, ch 3, skip next 2 sts, *sc in next dc, ch 5, skip next 7 sts, sc in next dc, ch 3, (4 dc, ch 4, 4 dc) in next ch sp, ch 3, skip next 2 sts; repeat from * around, join.

Rnd 7: Sl st in next ch sp, ch 1, 5 sc in same sp as sl st, sc in next ch sp, ch 3, (5 dc, ch 5, 5 dc) in next ch sp, ch 3, sc in next ch sp, *5 sc in next ch sp, sc in next ch sp, ch 3, (5 dc, ch 5, 5 dc) in next ch sp, ch 3, sc in next ch sp; repeat from * around, join.

Rnd 8: Ch 1, sc in first st, sc in next 4 sts, ch 5, skip next st, next ch sp and next 5 sts, *(6 dc, ch 6, 6 dc) in next ch sp, ch 5, skip next 5 sts, next ch sp and next st◊, sc in next 5 sts, ch 5, skip next st, next ch sp and next 5 sts; repeat from * around ending last repeat at ◊, join.

Rnd 9: Sl st in next 2 sts, ch 1, sc in same st as last sl st, ch 11, skip next 2 sts, next ch sp, and next 6 sts, *(7 dc, ch 3, 7 dc) in next ch sp, ch 11◊, sc in center st of next 5-sc group, ch 11, skip next 2 sts, next ch sp, and next 6 sts; repeat from * around ending last repeat at ◊, join. Fasten off.

Finish according to General Instructions on page 143. ❄

The Man Behind the Magic

The real St. Nicholas was born in 280 A.D. in Patara, a city in Asia Minor. He was a Christian priest, who later became a bishop. He came from a wealthy family and traveled the country helping people, giving gifts of money and other presents. His gifts were given late at night, because he did not like to be seen when he gave them away.

A famous story about St. Nicholas involves a poor man who had no money to give to his three daughters on their wedding day. St. Nicholas dropped bags of gold into the stockings which the girls had left to dry by the fire. The sisters found the gold and ever since, children have hung up stockings on Christmas Eve, hoping they will be filled with presents by Chirstmas morning. Children were also told to go to sleep quickly or he would not come!

Not much has changed and Santa Claus (or St. Nicholas) will not arrive this Christmas unless the children go to sleep early!

Winter Treasures

Designed by Carol Tessier

General Information

Each pattern contains written instructions for the crochet piece only. Use the following instructions for finishing.

To **stiffen,** apply undiluted fabric stiffener to the item, shape using wadded up pieces of plastic wrap or place on cardboard covered with plastic wrap; use rustproof straight pins to secure pieces as needed. Let dry completely; remove plastic wrap, cardboard and straight pins.

Decorate each ornament as desired using craft glue to attach ribbon roses, leaves, dried flowers, ribbons, strung beads, potpourri sachets, etc. Use glitter glue pens to add sparkle.

Piano

FINISHED SIZE: Approximately 3½" × 3½" × 3¼" high without Hanger.

MATERIALS:
- ❑ 50 yds. cream size 10 crochet cotton thread
- ❑ 15 yds. gold No. 8 metallic braid
- ❑ 2 yds. of gold No. 16 metallic braid
- ❑ 12" of ¼" gold metallic ribbon
- ❑ 2" piece and 6" piece of ⅛" wooden dowel
- ❑ Three gold 10mm round fluted beads
- ❑ Three gold 12mm × 14mm pyramid beads
- ❑ Gold paint
- ❑ Small paintbrush
- ❑ 4" × 8" piece of cardboard *(from writing tablet back)*
- ❑ 4½" square off-white light-weight fabric
- ❑ Plastic wrap
- ❑ Fabric stiffener
- ❑ Spray adhesive
- ❑ Craft glue
- ❑ Rust-proof straight pins
- ❑ Utility knife
- ❑ Embroidery needle
- ❑ No. 7 steel crochet hook or hook needed to obtain gauge

GAUGE: 9 sts or ch = 1"; 7 dc rows = 2".

BASIC STITCHES: Ch, sl st, sc, dc, tr

LID
Row 1: With crochet cotton, ch 33, dc in ninth ch from hook, (ch 2, skip next 2 chs, dc in next ch) across, turn. *(First 3 chs at beginning of row count as first dc—10 dc made.)*

Row 2: Ch 5, skip next 2 chs, dc in next dc, (ch 2, skip next 2 chs, dc in next dc) across, turn.

Row 3: Ch 4 *(counts as tr)*, skip next 2 chs, dc in next dc, (ch 2, skip next 2 chs, dc in next dc) across, turn. *(9 dc, 1 tr)*

Row 4: Ch 5, skip next 2 chs, dc in next dc, (ch 2, skip next 2 chs, dc in next dc) 6 times, skip next 2 chs, tr in next dc leaving ch-4 unworked, turn. *(8 dc, 1 tr)*

Row 5: Ch 3, dc in next dc, (ch 2, skip next 2 chs, dc in next dc) across, turn. *(9 dc)*

Row 6: Ch 4, skip next 2 chs, dc in next dc, (ch 2, skip next 2 chs, dc in next dc) 5 times, tr in next dc leaving ch-3 unworked, turn. *(6 dc, 2 tr)*

Row 7: Ch 4, skip next dc and next 2 chs, dc in next dc, (ch 2, skip next 2 chs, dc in next dc) 3 times, tr in next dc leaving ch-4 unworked, turn. *(4 dc, 2 tr)*

Row 8: Ch 4, skip next 2 chs, dc in next dc, ch 2, skip next 2 chs, dc in next dc, skip next 2 chs and next dc, tr in last ch-4, turn. *(2 dc, 2 tr)*

Rnd 9: Working around outer edge, ch 1, 2 sc in each ch sp and sc in each st around with 3 sc in end of each row, join with sl st in first sc. Fasten off.

Rnd 10: Working in **front lps** *(see Stitch Guide),* join No. 8 metallic braid with sc in first st, ch 3, (sc in next st, ch 3) around, join. Fasten off.

BOTTOM
Rows 1–8: Repeat rows 1–8 of Lid.

Rnd 9: Working around outer edge, ch 1, 2 sc in each ch sp and sc in each st around with 3 sc in end of each row, join with sl st in first sc. Fasten off.

Rnd 10: For **Sides,** with crochet cotton, ch 81, sl st in first ch to form ring, ch 3, dc in each ch around, join with sl st in top of ch-3. *(81 dc)*

Rnd 11: Ch 3, dc in each st around, join.

Row 12: For **Keyboard,** working in **front lps,** ch 3, dc in next 27 sts leaving remaining sts unworked. Fasten off.

To assemble Bottom, using embroidery needle and crochet cotton, sew **back lps** of rnd 11 to **both lps** of rnd 9 *(see illustration 1 on page 154).*

Trace outline of assembled Bottom on one end of cardboard, trace outline of Lid on other end of cardboard; for **Patterns,** mark a second line ⅛" inside each traced outline. Cut the two pieces from cardboard using inside Pattern lines as guides. Lay aside.

Rnd 13: Working in **front lps,** join No. 8 metallic braid with sc in first unworked st on rnd 11, ch 3, (sc in next st, ch 3) around to row 12, (sc in

continued on page 154

Winter Treasures

continued from page 153

end of row 12, ch 3) 2 times; working in **both lps,** sc in each st across row 12, (sc in end of row 12, ch 3) 2 times, join with sl st in first sc. Fasten off.

Rnd 14: Working on opposite side of ch on rnd 10, join No. 8 metallic braid with sc in any st, sc in each st around, join. Fasten off.

ASSEMBLY

1: Paint 2" piece of dowel with gold paint and allow to dry.

2: Using embroidery needle and No. 16 metallic braid, embroider straight stitches *(see Stitch Guide)* on Keyboard according to illustration 2.

3: Stiffen crochet pieces *(see General Information on page 153),* placing Lid cardboard piece wrapped with plastic wrap inside Bottom to shape. Remove and discard cardboard when dry.

4: For **Outer Bottom,** spray bottom side of Bottom cardboard piece with spray adhesive *(see illustration 3);* lay fabric wrong side up on flat surface, press sprayed side of cardboard centered on wrong side of fabric; spread glue around edges on other side of cardboard, fold fabric over edges and press in place on glue; trim excess fabric. Let dry.

5: To assemble Legs, glue beads on 6" piece of dowel *(see illustration 4—round fluted beads are tops of Legs).* Let dry. With utility knife, cut off exposed dowel sections.

6: To assemble Piano, glue Lid and Side together *(see illustration 5),* glue painted dowel to inside corner of Side and to corner of Lid; glue wrong side of Outer Bottom to outside of Bottom; glue tops of Legs to Outer Bottom according to circles on illustration 3.

7: For **Hanger** *(optional),* cut a 12" strand of No. 8 metallic braid, run through center of Lid, tie ends together.

8: Decorate as desired.

Gazebo

FINISHED SIZE: 3¼" high without Hanger.

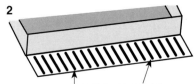

1

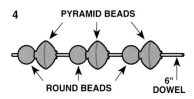

2

STRAIGHT STITCHES

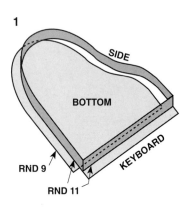

4

PYRAMID BEADS

ROUND BEADS

6" DOWEL

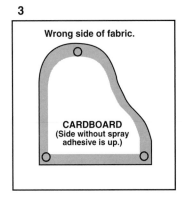

3

Wrong side of fabric.

CARDBOARD
(Side without spray adhesive is up.)

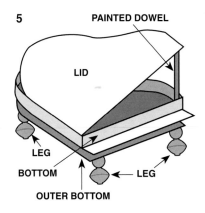

5

PAINTED DOWEL

LID

LEG

BOTTOM

LEG

OUTER BOTTOM

MATERIALS:
- ❏ 40 yds. cream size 10 crochet cotton thread
- ❏ 15 yds. gold No. 8 metallic braid
- ❏ 10" of ⅛" gold metallic ribbon
- ❏ One bamboo skewer
- ❏ Two 2¾" cardboard circles *(cut from writing tablet back)*
- ❏ 4" circle cream lightweight fabric
- ❏ Fabric stiffener
- ❏ Plastic wrap
- ❏ Craft glue
- ❏ Rust-proof straight pins
- ❏ Bobby pins for markers
- ❏ No. 7 steel crochet hook or hook needed to obtain gauge

GAUGE: Bottom rnds 1–3 = 1¾" across.

BASIC STITCHES: Ch, sl st, sc, dc, dtr *(see Stitch Guide)*.

BOTTOM
Rnd 1: With crochet cotton, ch 5, sl st in first ch to form ring, ch 3 *(counts as first dc)*, 11 dc in ring, join with sl st in top of ch-3. *(12 dc made)*

Rnd 2: (Ch 3, dc) in first st, 2 dc in each st around, join. *(24)*

Rnd 3: (Ch 3, dc) in first st, dc in next st, (2 dc in next st, dc in next st) around, join. *(36)*

Rnd 4: (Ch 3, dc) in first st, dc in next 2 sts, (2 dc in next st, dc in next 2 sts) around, join. *(48)*

Rnd 5: (Ch 3, dc) in first st, dc in next 3 sts, (2 dc in next st, dc in next 3 sts) around, join, **turn.** *(60)*

Row 6: Working this row in **front lps** *(see Stitch Guide)*; for **Fence,** ch 6 *(counts as first dtr and ch-1)*, skip next st, dtr in next st, (ch 1, skip next st, dtr in next st) 23 times leaving last 11 sts unworked at center front, turn. Fasten off. *(49 sts and ch)*

Row 7: Join metallic braid with sc in first st, sc in each st and in each ch across with last sc in fifth ch of ch-6. Fasten off.

Front of row 6 is right side of work.

Rnd 8: Working in **back lps** of rnd 5, join metallic braid with sc in any st, ch 3, (sc in next st, ch 3) around, join with sl st in first sc. Fasten off.

ROOF
Rnd 1: With crochet cotton, ch 5, sl st in first ch to form ring, ch 3 *(counts as first dc)*, 11 dc in ring, join with sl st in top of ch-3. *(12 dc made)*

Rnd 2: Working this rnd in **back lps,** ch 4, skip next st, (dc in next st, ch 1, skip next st) around, join with sl st in third ch of ch-4. *(12 sts and chs)*

Rnd 3: Working this rnd in **back lps,** (ch 3, dc) in first st, 2 dc in each ch and in each st around, join. *(24 dc)*

Rnd 4: (Ch 3, dc) in first st, dc in next st, (2 dc in next st, dc in next st) around, join. *(36)*

Rnd 5: (Ch 3, dc) in first st, dc in next 2 sts, (2 dc in next st, dc in next 2 sts) around, join. *(48)*

Rnd 6: (Ch 3, dc) in first st, dc in next 3 sts, (2 dc in next st, dc in next 3 sts) around, join. *(60)*

Rnd 7: Ch 3, dc in each st around, join.

Rnd 8: Working this rnd in **back lps,** ch 3, dc in each st around, join. Fasten off.

Rnd 9: Join metallic braid with sc in first st, sc in each st around, join. Fasten off.

Rnd 10: Working in **front lps** of rnd 1, join metallic braid with sc in any st, sc in each st around, join with sl st in first sc. Fasten off.

Rnd 11: Working in **front lps** of rnd 2, join metallic braid with sc in any st, ch 4, (sc in next st, ch 4) around, join. Fasten off.

Rnd 12: Working in **front lps** of rnd 7, join metallic braid with sc in any st, ch 4, (sc in next st, ch 4) around, join. Fasten off.

ASSEMBLY
1: Stiffen crochet pieces *(see General Information on page 153)* placing one cardboard circle covered with plastic wrap inside Roof piece with edge at top of rnd 8; let dry. Remove cardboard circle after thoroughly dry.

2: For **Inner Roof,** lay fabric circle wrong side up on flat surface with one cardboard circle centered on top; spread glue around edges of cardboard circle, fold fabric over edges and glue in place. Let dry.

3: Mark first, 7th, 13th, 19th and 25th dtr sts of row 6 on Bottom.

4: For **Pillars,** cut five 1¾" pieces of metallic ribbon, glue end of one piece over each marked stitch covering stitch completely from bottom to top.

5: Cut five 1¾" pieces from bamboo skewer; glue one piece behind each metallic ribbon Pillar and to back of stitch behind metallic ribbon.

6: With fabric side out, glue Inner Roof to inside of Roof with edge at top of rnd 8.

7: Glue tops of Pillars to inside of rnd 8 on Roof.

8: For **Hanger** *(optional)*, cut a 12" strand of metallic braid, run through ring on rnd 1 of Roof, tie ends together.

9: Decorate as desired.

Swan
FINISHED SIZE: 3¼" high without Hanger.

MATERIALS:
- ❏ 80 yds. cream size 10 crochet cotton thread
- ❏ 5 yds. gold No. 8 metallic braid
- ❏ 2 white 2mm pearl beads
- ❏ 10" piece of white 3mm chenille stem
- ❏ Cream sewing thread
- ❏ 2" × 2½" Styrofoam® egg
- ❏ Gold glitter glue
- ❏ Fabric stiffener
- ❏ Plastic wrap
- ❏ Rust-proof straight pins
- ❏ Beading needle
- ❏ Embroidery needle
- ❏ No. 7 steel crochet hook or hook needed to obtain gauge

GAUGE: 9 dc = 1"; 7 dc rows = 2".

BASIC STITCHES: Ch, sl st, sc, hdc, dc, tr, dtr *(see Stitch Guide)*.

continued on page 156

Winter Treasures

continued from page 155

BODY, NECK & HEAD

Rnd 1: For **Body,** beginning at tail, with crochet cotton, ch 3 *(counts as first dc)*, 11 dc in third ch from hook, join with sl st in top of ch-3. *(12 dc made)*

Rnd 2: (Ch 3, dc) in first st, 2 dc in each st around, join. *(24)*

Rnd 3: (Ch 3, dc) in first st, dc in next st, (2 dc in next st, dc in next st) around, join. *(36)*

Rnd 4: (Ch 3, dc) in first st, dc in next 3 sts, (2 dc in next st, dc in next 3 sts) around, join. *(45)*

Rnds 5–7: Ch 3, dc in each st around, join.

Cut away a small portion of the Styrofoam egg to form a 1½" × 2" flat side for bottom *(see illustration)*.

Insert Styrofoam egg into Body with large end at tail; continue working around egg.

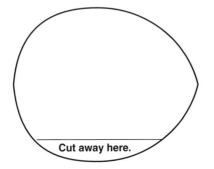

Cut away here.

Rnd 8: Ch 3, dc in next 2 sts, dc next 2 sts tog, (dc in next 3 sts, dc next 2 sts tog) around, join. *(36)*

Rnd 9: Ch 3, dc in next 2 sts, dc next 2 sts tog, (dc in next 3 sts, dc next 2 sts tog) around with dc in last st, join. *(29)*

Rnd 10: Ch 3, (dc next 2 sts tog) around, join. *(15)*

Rnd 11: Ch 3, dc in each st around, join.

Rnds 12–13: For **Neck,** ch 1, sc in each st around, join with sl st in first sc. *(15 sc)*

Rnd 14: Ch 3, dc in next 2 sts, dc next 2 sts tog, (dc in next 3 sts, dc next 2 sts tog) around, join. *(12)*

Rnd 15: Ch 1, sc first 2 sts tog, sc in next 4 sts, sc next 2 sts tog, sc in last 4 sts, join. *(10)*

Rnds 16–17: Ch 1, sc in each st around, join.

Rnd 18: Ch 1, sc in first st, sc next 2 sts tog, (sc in next st, sc next 2 sts tog) around, join. *(8)*

Rnds 19–25: Ch 1, sc in each st around, join.

Rnd 26: Ch 1, sc first 2 sts tog, sc in each st around, join. *(7)*

Rnds 27–38: Ch 1, sc in each st around, join.

Rnd 39: Ch 1; for top of **Head,** 2 sc in each of first 3 sts; sc in last 4 sts, join. *(10)*

Rnds 40–41: Ch 1, sc in each st around, join.

Rnd 42: Ch 1, sc in first st, (sc next 2 sts tog, sc in next st) 3 times, join. *(7)*

Rnd 43: Ch 1, sc in each st around, join. Leaving 8" strand, fasten off.

TAIL

With crochet cotton, ch 5 loosely, sl st in first ch to form ring, ch 1, 5 sc in ring, sl st in ring, (ch 21, sl st in ring, ch 15, sl st in ring) 5 times, join with sl st in first sc. Fasten off.

WING (make 2)

Row 1: With crochet cotton, ch 27 loosely; beginning at tip of Wing, sc in second ch from hook, sc in next 5 chs, hdc in next 3 chs, dc in next 3 chs, tr in next 3 chs, dtr *(see Stitch Guide)* in next 3 chs, tr in next 2 chs, dc in next 2 chs, hdc in next 2 chs, sc in last 2 chs, turn. *Row 1 ends at center Front. (26 sts made)*

Row 2: Ch 1, sc in first 24 sts leaving last 2 sts unworked, turn. *(24)*

Row 3: Skip first st, sl st in next 2 sts, sc in next st, (ch 3, skip next st, sc in next st) 10 times, turn. *(10 ch sps)*

Rows 4–11: Ch 1, (sl st, ch 1, sc) in first ch sp, (ch 3, sc in next ch sp) across, turn. *(2 ch sps at end of last row)*

Row 12: Ch 1, (sl st, ch 1, sc) in first ch sp, ch 3, sc in next ch sp, turn. Fasten off. *(1 ch sp)*

Sew ends of rows 1–3 on both Wings together with embroidery needle and crochet cotton.

Row 13: Working across both Wings on opposite side of starting ch on row 1, join metallic braid with sc in first ch at tip of one Wing, sc in each ch across both Wings. Fasten off.

Front of row 13 is right side of work.

ASSEMBLY

1: Fold chenille stem in half, insert ends into Head and Neck through center of rnd 43 leaving ¼" at folded end of chenille stem extended past rnd 43 for **Beak.** Thread embroidery needle with 8" strand at end of rnd 43, weave through tops of stitches on rnd 43, pull tight around chenille stem, secure.

2: Fold Neck back across top of Body *(opposite flat side of egg)*; using embroidery needle and crochet cotton for all sewing, sew rnd 21 to top of rnd 9, sew rnds 16–20 to rnds 10–11. Curve chenille stem to shape Neck.

3: Tack center of row 12 on Wings together; with Wing tips at top, place Wings around Body matching row 12 to center of rnd 1 on Body and center of row 13 on Wings to row 11 on Body just below Neck; sew ends of rows 4–12 of Wings to edges of flat area at bottom of Body.

4: Sew Tail to rnd 1 on Body with loops at top.

5: Using glitter glue, apply glitter at random to loops on Tail; cover Beak completely with glitter.

6: With beading needle and sewing thread, sew one pearl bead on each side of Head for eyes.

7: For **Hanger** *(optional)*, cut a 10" piece of metallic braid, run through top of stitch on rnd 9 at center top of Body, tie ends together.

8: Stiffen tips of Wings *(see General Information on page 153)*.

9: Decorate as desired.

Bassinet

FINISHED SIZE: 3" high without Hanger.

MATERIALS:
- ❏ 55 yds. cream size 10 crochet cotton thread
- ❏ 10 yds. gold No. 16 metallic braid
- ❏ 3" × 4" lightweight cream fabric
- ❏ 3" × 4" thick quilt batting
- ❏ 2" × 3" cardboard *(from writing tablet back)*
- ❏ Plastic wrap
- ❏ Fabric glue
- ❏ Fabric stiffener
- ❏ Rust-proof straight pins
- ❏ Bobby pin for marker
- ❏ No. 7 steel crochet hook or hook needed to obtain gauge

GAUGE: 8 dc = 1"; 2 dc rows = ½".

BASIC STITCHES: Ch, sl st, sc, dc.

BASSINET
Rnd 1: For **Bottom,** with crochet cotton, ch 11, 2 dc in fourth ch from hook, dc in next 6 chs, 6 dc in end ch; continuing on opposite side of ch, dc in next 6 chs, 3 dc in next ch, join with sl st in top of ch-3. *(Ch-3 at beginning of rnd counts as first dc—24 dc made.)*

Rnd 2: (Ch 3, dc) in first st, 2 dc in each of next 2 sts, dc in next 6 sts, 2 dc in each of next 6 sts, dc in next 6 sts, 2 dc in each of last 3 sts, join. *(36)*

Rnd 3: (Ch 3, dc) in first st, 2 dc in each of next 5 sts, dc in next 6 sts, 2 dc in each of next 12 sts, dc in next 6 sts, 2 dc in each of last 6 sts, join. *(60)*

NOTE: *Mark the **front lp** (see Stitch Guide) of the 12th dc on rnd 3.*

Rnd 4: For **Skirt,** working this rnd in **back lps,** ch 1, sc in first st, ch 3, (sc in next st, ch 3) around, join with sl st in first sc. *(60 ch sps)*

Rnd 5: (Sl st, ch 3, dc, ch 2, 2 dc) in first ch sp *(first shell formed);* skip next ch sp, dc in next ch sp, skip next ch sp; *for **shell,** **(2 dc, ch 2, 2 dc)** in next ch sp **or** in next dc; skip next ch sp, dc in next ch sp, skip next ch sp; repeat from * around, join with sl st in top of ch-3. *(15 shells, 15 dc)*

NOTES: *Work shell in ch sp of shell on last rnd unless otherwise stated.*

*Work **dc front post** (**fp**—see Stitch Guide) and **dc back post** (**bp**) around next st.*

Rnds 6–9: For **beginning shell (beg shell),** sl st in next st, (sl st, ch 3, dc, ch 2, 2 dc) in next ch sp; fp, (shell, fp) around, join. At end of rnd 9, fasten off.

Rnd 10: Join metallic braid with sc in first st, sc in each st and 3 sc in each ch sp around, join with sl st in first sc. Fasten off.

Rnd 11: For **Sides,** with right side of work facing you and Skirt hanging down, working in unworked **front lps** of rnd 3, join crochet cotton with sl st in marked st on rnd 3, ch 3, dc in each st around, join with sl st in top of ch-3. *(60 dc)*

Rnd 12: Ch 3, dc in each st around, join.

Row 13: For **Canopy,** ch 3, (skip next dc, shell in next dc, skip next dc, dc in next dc) 6 times leaving remaining sts unworked, turn. *(6 shells, 7 dc)*

Row 14: Ch 3, *shell, dc back post (**bp**—see Notes above);* repeat from *, (2 dc in next shell, bp) 2 times, shell, bp, shell, dc in last st, turn. *(4 shells, 5 bp, 6 dc)*

Row 15: Ch 3, shell, fp, 2 dc in next shell, fp, (skip next 2 dc, fp) 2 times, 2 dc in next shell, fp, shell, dc in last st, turn. *(2 shells, 5 fp, 6 dc)*

Row 16: Ch 3, 2 dc in next shell, bp, skip next 2 dc, bp 3 times, skip next 2 dc, bp, 2 dc in next shell, dc in last st, turn. *(5 bp, 6 dc)*

Row 17: Ch 3, skip next 2 dc, fp, (skip next st, fp) 2 times, skip next 2 dc, dc in last st, turn. *(3 fp, 2 dc)*

Row 18: Ch 3, skip next 3 sts, sl st in last st. Fasten off. *(1 ch sp)*

Rnd 19: With right side of rnd 12 facing you, join metallic braid with sc in first unworked st on rnd 12, sc in each st around to Canopy, 3 sc in end of each row across Canopy with 3 sc in ch sp of row 18, join with sl st in first sc. Fasten off.

FINISHING
1: Cut one piece from cardboard according to full-size pattern piece. Cover cardboard with plastic wrap.

2: Stiffen Bassinet *(see General Information on page 153)* placing covered cardboard on inside to shape Bottom. Remove cardboard when thoroughly dry; discard plastic wrap.

3: For **Mattress,** cut quilt batting according to pattern piece; glue to one side of cardboard piece. Cover batting with fabric and glue edges of fabric to other side of cardboard piece. Trim away excess fabric. Place Mattress inside Bassinet.

4: For **Hanger** *(optional),* run metallic braid through row 18 of Canopy, tie ends together.

5: Decorate as desired.

FULL-SIZE PATTERN

Wishing Well
FINISHED SIZE: 3¼" high without Hanger.

MATERIALS:
- ❏ 30 yds. cream size 10 crochet cotton thread
- ❏ 10 yds. gold No. 8 metallic braid

continued on page 158

Winter Treasures

continued from page 157

- ⅛" wooden dowel:
  - Two 3" pieces
  - One 1½" piece
- Plastic wrap
- Rust-proof straight pins
- Gold paint
- Small paintbrush
- Fabric stiffener
- Craft glue
- No. 7 steel crochet hook or hook needed to obtain gauge

GAUGE: Rnds 1-3 = 1¾" across.

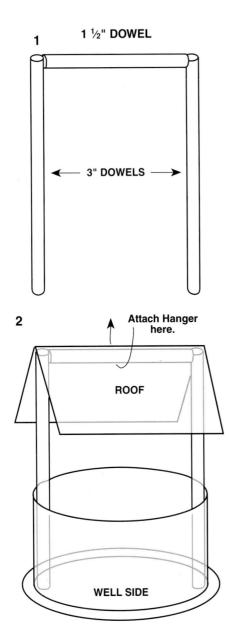

1

1 ½" DOWEL

← 3" DOWELS →

2

Attach Hanger here.

ROOF

WELL SIDE

BASIC STITCHES: Ch, sl st, sc, dc.

WELL

Rnd 1: For **Bottom,** with crochet cotton, ch 3 *(counts as first dc),* 11 dc in third ch from hook, join with sl st in top of ch-3. *(12 dc made)*

Rnd 2: (Ch 3, dc) in first st, 2 dc in each st around, join. *(24)*

Rnd 3: (Ch 3, dc) in first st, dc in next st, (2 dc in next st, dc in next st) around, join. *(36)*

Rnd 4: For **Side,** working this rnd in **back lps** *(see Stitch Guide),* ch 3, dc in each st around, join.

Rnds 5–7: Ch 3, dc in each st around, join.

Rnd 8: Ch 1, sc in each st around, join with sl st in first sc. Fasten off.

Rnd 9: Join metallic braid with sc in first st, sc in each st around, join. Fasten off.

Rnd 10: Working in remaining **front lps** of rnd 3, join metallic braid with sc in first st, ch 3, (sc in next st, ch 3) around, join. Fasten off.

ROOF

Row 1: With crochet cotton, ch 13, dc in fourth ch from hook, dc in each ch across, turn. *(11 dc made)*

Rows 2–6: Ch 3, dc in each st across, turn.

Rnd 7: Working around outer edges, ch 1, 3 sc in end of each row and sc in each st around, join with sl st in first sc. Fasten off.

Rnd 8: Join metallic braid with sc in first st, ch 3, (sc in next st, ch 3) around, join. Fasten off.

ASSEMBLY

1: Paint dowels with gold paint and allow to dry.

2: Stiffen crochet pieces *(see General Information on page 153)* shaping Roof by placing rows 3 and 4 over square edge of box or book covered with plastic wrap and let dry.

3: Glue dowels together according to illustration; glue to inside of Well Sides *(see illustration),* glue Roof over top of assembled Dowels.

4: For **Hanger** *(optional),* cut a 12" strand of metallic braid, run through Roof and around 1½" dowel, tie ends together at top.

5: Decorate as desired.

Victorian School Girl

FINISHED SIZE: 2¾" high.

MATERIALS:
- 50 yds. cream size 10 crochet cotton thread
- 2 pieces of ⅛" satin ribbon each 6"
- 10" of ⅛" satin ribbon for Hanger *(optional)*
- Polyester fiberfill
- Fabric stiffener
- Rust-proof straight pins
- Embroidery needle
- No. 7 steel crochet hook or hook needed to obtain gauge

GAUGE: Rnds 1–7 of Head = 1½" high.

BASIC STITCHES: Ch, sl st, sc, hdc, dc.

GIRL

Rnd 1: For **Head,** beginning at top, with crochet cotton, ch 5, sl st in first ch to form ring, ch 2 *(counts as first hdc)*, 11 hdc in ring, join with sl st in top of ch-2. *(12 hdc made)*

Rnd 2: (Ch 2, hdc) in first st, hdc in next st, (2 hdc in next st, hdc in next st) around, join. *(18)*

Rnd 3: Ch 2, hdc in next st, 2 hdc in next st, (hdc in next 2 sts, 2 hdc in next st) around, join. *(24)*

Rnds 4–6: Ch 2, hdc in each st around, join.

Rnd 7: Ch 1, hdc in next st, (yo, insert hook in next st, yo, pull through st, insert hook in next st, yo, pull through st, yo, pull through all 4 loops on hook) around, skip ch-1, join with sl st in next hdc. *(12 sts)*

Rnds 8–9: Ch 1, sc in each st around, join with sl st in first sc.

Rnd 10: For **Bodice,** (ch 3, dc) in first st, 2 dc in each st around, join with sl st in top of ch-3. *(First ch 3 counts as first dc—24 dc)*

Rnd 11: Working this rnd in **back lps** *(see Stitch Guide),* (ch 3, dc) in first st, dc in next st, (2 dc in next st, dc in next st) around, join. *(36 dc)*

Rnd 12: (Ch 3, dc) in first st, dc in next st, (2 dc in next st, dc in next st) around, join. *(54 dc)*

Rnd 13: Working this rnd in **front lps,** ch 1, sc in first st, ch 3, (sc in next st, ch 3) around, join with sl st in first sc. Fasten off.

Rnd 14: Working in **front lps** of rnd 10, join with sc in first st, sc in each st around, join. Fasten off.

HAT

Rnd 1: With crochet cotton, ch 5, sl st in first ch to form ring, ch 3, 11 dc in ring, join with sl st in top of ch-3. *(12 dc made)*

Rnd 2: (Ch 3, dc) in first st, 2 dc in each st around, join. *(24)*

Rnd 3: Working this rnd in **back lps,** ch 3, dc in each st around, join.

Rnd 4: Working this rnd in **front lps,** (ch 3, dc) in first st, dc in next st, (2 dc in next st, dc in next st) around, join. *(36)*

Rnd 5: (Ch 3, dc) in first st, dc in next st, (2 dc in next st, dc in next st) around, join. *(54)*

Rnd 6: Ch 1, sc in each st around, join with sl st in first sc.

Rnd 7: Sl st in each st around, join with sl st in first sl st. Fasten off.

Rnd 8: Working in **front lps** of rnd 2, join with sl st in first st, sl st in each st around, join. Fasten off.

ASSEMBLY

1: Stuff Head with polyester fiberfill. Stiffen crocheted pieces *(see General Information on page 153).*

2: For **Braids,** cut 36 strands crochet cotton each 12" long. Using embroidery needle, sew center of strands evenly spaced across first st of rnds 3–7 at back of Head *(see illustration 1).*

3: On each side of Head, separate strands into three equal sections and braid for 2¼"; tie a 6" piece of ribbon in a ¾" bow around end of braid. Trim ribbon ends to ¾"; trim braid ends ½" below bow.

4: For **Hair,** cut 24 strands crochet cotton each 10"

long. Hold all strands together and tie with separate strand at center *(see illustration 2),* glue knot to center top of Head.

5: On each side, wrap Hair around Head, going under Braids, crossing at back and bringing ends up over forehead for bangs *(see illustration 3);* place a little glue under Hair as needed to hold in place. Trim bangs.

6: For **Hanger** *(optional),* run ends of 10" piece of ribbon through center of rnd 1 to inside of Hat, tie knot in ends and glue to inside of Hat.

7: Glue Hat on Head.

8: Decorate as desired. ❅

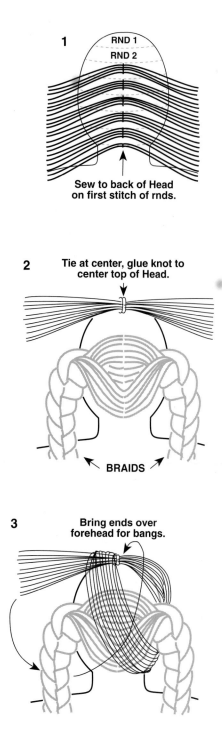

1 RND 1 / RND 2

Sew to back of Head on first stitch of rnds.

2 Tie at center, glue knot to center top of Head.

BRAIDS

3 Bring ends over forehead for bangs.

Stitch Guide

Chain—ch: Yo, pull through lp on hook.

Slip stitch—sl st: Insert hook in st, yo, pull through both lps on hook.

Single crochet—sc: Insert hook in st, yo, pull through st, yo, pull through both lps on hook.

Front loop—front lp: Back loop—back lp:

FRONT LOOP   BACK LOOP

Half double crochet—hdc: Yo, insert hook in st, yo, pull through st, yo, pull through all 3 lps on hook.

Double crochet—dc: Yo, insert hook in st, yo, pull through st, (yo, pull through 2 lps) 2 times.

Change colors: Drop first color; with 2nd color, pull through last 2 lps of st.

Treble crochet—tr: Yo 2 times, insert hook in st, yo, pull through st, (yo, pull through 2 lps) 3 times.

Double treble crochet—dtr: Yo 3 times, insert hook in st, yo, pull through st, (yo, pull through 2 lps) 4 times.

Front post stitch—fp: Back post stitch—bp: When working post st, insert hook from right to left around post of st on previous row.

Back   Front

Post
← of
Stitch

Reverse sc: Working from left to right, insert hook in next st to the right, complete as sc.

1.   2.

Back bar of sc:

Satin Stitch: **French Knot:**   **Straight Stitch:**   **Outline Stitch:**

MEASUREMENTS AND HOOK SIZES

OUNCES TO GRAMS	GRAMS TO OUNCES
1 = 28.4	25 = 7/8
2 = 56.7	40 = 1 2/5
3 = 85.0	50 = 1 3/4
4 = 113.4	100 = 3 1/2

HOOK AND NEEDLE SIZES

U.S.		METRIC	U.K.
	14	.60 mm.	
	12	.75 mm.	
	10	1.00 mm.	
	6	1.50 mm.	
0	5	1.75 mm.	
1	B	2.00 mm.	14
2	C	2.50 mm.	12
3	D	3.00 mm.	10
4	E	3.50 mm.	9
5	F	4.00 mm.	8
6	G	4.50 mm.	7
		4.75 mm.	
8	H	5.00 mm.	6
9	I	5.50 mm.	5
10	J	6.00 mm.	4
		6.50 mm.	3
10½	K	7.00 mm.	2
		8.00 mm.	
		9.00 mm.	
	P	10.00 mm.	
	Q	16.00 mm.	

STANDARD ABBREVIATIONS

beg	beginning
ch, chs	chain, chains
dc	double crochet
dec	decrease
hdc	half double crochet
inc	increase
lp, lps	loop, loops
rnd, rnds	round, rounds
sc	single crochet

sc next 2 sts tog ....(insert hook in next st, yo, pull through st) 2 times, yo, pull through all 3 lps on hook

hdc next 2 sts tog .....(yo, insert hook in next st, yo, pull through st) 2 times, yo, pull through all 5 lps on hook.

dc next 2 sts tog ......(yo, insert hook in next st, yo, pull through st, yo, pull through 2 lps on hook) 2 times, yo, pull through all 3 lps on hook.

sl st	slip stitch
sp, sp	space, spaces
st, sts	stitch, stitches
tog	together
tr	treble crochet
yo	yarn over

The patterns in this book are written using American crochet stitch terminology. For our International customers, hook sizes, stitches and yarn definitions should be converted as follows:

THREAD/YARNS

Bedspread Weight	=	No. 10 Cotton or Virtuoso
Sport Weight	=	4 Ply or thin DK
Worsted Weight	=	Thick DK or Aran

US	= UK
sl st (slip stitch)	= sc (single crochet)
sc (single crochet)	= dc (double crochet)
hdc (half double crochet)	= htr (half treble crochet)
dc (double crochet)	= tr (treble crochet)
tr (treble crochet)	= dtr (double treble crochet)
dtr (double treble crochet)	= ttr (triple treble crochet)
skip	= miss

CROCHET HOOKS

Metric	US	Metric	US
.60mm	14	3.00mm	D/4
.75mm	12	3.50mm	E/4
1.00mm	10	4.00mm	F/5
1.50mm	6	4.50mm	G/6
1.75mm	5	5.00mm	H/8
2.00mm	B/1	5.50mm	I/9
2.50mm	C/2	6.00mm	J/10

But, as with all patterns, test your gauge (tension) to be sure.

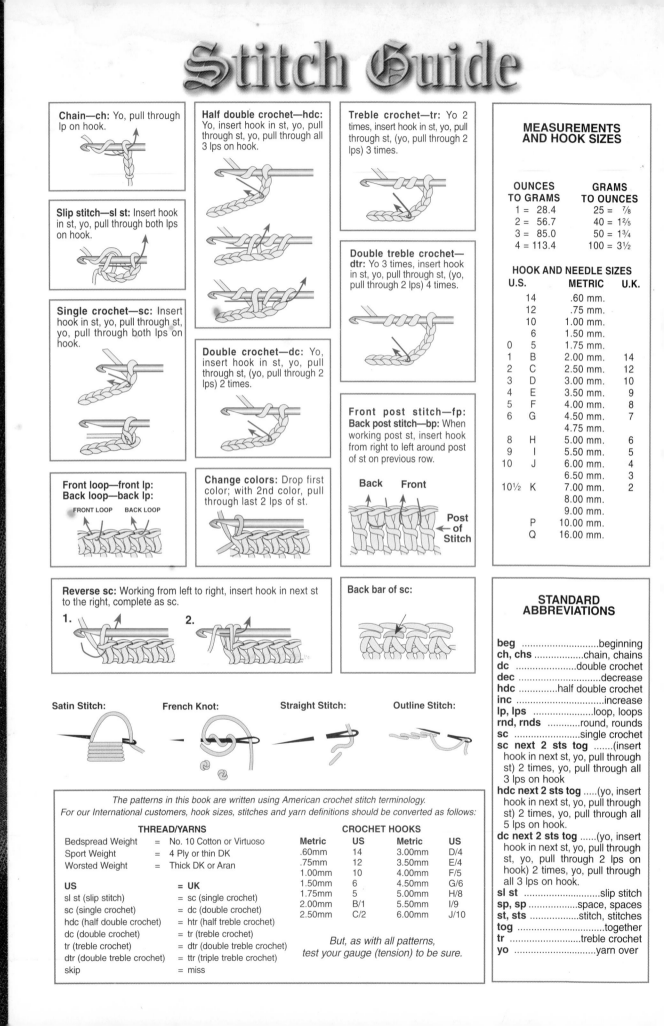